History Judged Them, But Did History Get It right?

By

Joan B Pritchard

ISBN: 9781916820890

INDEX:-

About the Author

The author has now retired and spends much of her time researching people and events from the past; she then mingles established fact with a little fiction and even fantasy, so as to enhance the reader's involvement and understanding of her chosen characters from history. She has already produced several similar novels, which are also intended to inform, as well as to feed the reader's imagination. She hopes you will seek out others of her books, and above all, enjoy them.

WHO STARTED THE GREAT FIRE OF LONDON?

A young girl sat on the stone doorstep, and between her fingers, she held a piece of burnt bread, which she crumbled into even smaller pieces. She made the bread crumbs last as long as possible, chewing them thoroughly, before tackling the worst burnt bits of the crust. She'd found the bread in the corner under where the rope ladder once was, the ladder that reached upwards, into the bakery's two bedrooms. She picked it up gingerly at first, ate some, but it tasted horrible.

I'll save the rest for late, when I'm really hungry. She knew, if she chewed slowly, her hunger would be held at bay, and this was important, if she wanted to survive; she could see there was no food in the bakery now. Everything had been burnt to a crisp. The rope ladder had gone completely of course, and nothing remained but a few tufts of burnt rope. *How will I get upstairs now?* she wondered. She looked upwards, and realised she was being silly - there was no ceiling, and therefore no bedroom floor above, so the ladder would have been of no use anyway. Overnight, the bakery building had become nothing but a shell. Unusually, it had been built using some stone, so the supporting walls were still intact – but only just. The wooden parts were all gone.

She looked down at her front. and was surprised to see everything was black and grey; her dress, her hair, her feet, all were covered in ash; scattered around her bare feet, were piles of dust and debris. In fact, debris was everywhere, and she could see that the house across the lane, had actually fallen into the lane. There were jagged, wooden staves lying on the ground, and any house lucky enough to have glazed windows, unfortunately had them no longer – their support had also been made of wood, and hadn't stood a chance against the intense heat of the fire. Rubbish was strewn both inside and outside the bakehouse; the whole place was a shamble.

The girl had wisely hidden in the outside yard, whilst the fire raged, and gobbled up her home. *What else could I do? Nowhere was safe – and my father had disappeared. I was alone right in the eye of a firestorm.*

She stared down at the burnt clumps of thatch that had once been part of the bedroom floors above, but were now nothing but smoldering tufts. The timber planks that had once supported the plaster walls, now lay mingled with peeling strips of whitewash, and the supports of the wooden shutters were no longer there. The part of London where the bakery was, housed nearly all the very poor, and the lower-middle classes; there were many shops, small factories, and of course, the meat market, from which the smells were mouth-watering on that fateful night. The fire had worked its magic on all of them, and overnight, they'd become mere hovels. Some buildings had been lucky enough to have glazed windows, but only very few – now there were none at all. The fire acted indiscriminately in its destruction.

In the air, there was still an acrid smell of smoke, that had found its way into every nook and cranny in the bakery. The girl's nose and eyes, even her chest felt as though they were going to burst, and she found it hard to breathe. When she managed to gulp down some air, everything hurt even more. So, she cried! What else could she do? She was scared and alone, with no-one to share her misery. She was all alone in a derelict hovel with no food or water, or even a bed to lay her tired head upon. Even worse, in the confusion of the previous night, she had lost her father, Thomas. He'd gone, disappearing just after the fire had begun.

The morning light was beginning to appear now, and maybe she'd find someone outside. The lane certainly looked empty, but everyone couldn't all have run away, could they? She would soon find however, that most had indeed run away, desperate to escape the intense heat and flames. Some people obviously thought they could out-run the fire, and although she hoped they 'd been successful, she doubted it. Dawn was lightening the horizon, and the faint light gave her the first proper view of the greatest disaster the city of London would ever know. The first she'd known there was danger, was when she'd seen her father, grab his shoes, and scramble out of the small window in his bedroom. The fire had started just after midnight, and by the next morning, it's hold on the poorest part of the city was swallowing everything in its path. It, was moving very fast because of a strong East wind, that blew the flames towards the West of the city, and then even further afield. It had soon become a wildfire, in everyone's eyes.

Back outside, sitting on the front doorstep of the bakehouse, she looked down the lane she'd once known so well; it had become a blackened hell-hole, almost unrecognizable. Broken timbers, and people's possessions were scattered everywhere. Suddenly two strangers appeared out of the thick smoke. Thy were carrying buckets of water, and a stirrup-pump, but the water soon ran out, and they had to beat a hasty retreat. Their fire-fighting equipment was totally ineffectual, but at least the men were trying. The fire was slowly disappearing out of Pudding Lane, having done all the damage it could there.

Rosie Farynor had lived in the lane's bakery, along with her father Thomas. It was the only home she'd ever known, and she enjoyed helping in the bakehouse. Just then, she was worried as well as scared. *Where has my father gone? What a time to run off and leave his family – right in the middle of a disaster? Was he safe? Had the fire gobbled him up, or had he been struck by falling masonry, and lying in some street, nameless and unconscious? He'll come back soon, I just know it.*

Soma time ago, Rosie's mother had died from a sudden fever. One day, and quite out of the blue, she'd sickened, and within a few hours, was dead. The Great Plague had taken her away, as it had so many others in the country; somehow it managed to miss the rest of the Farynors, all of whom it completely by-passed. It seemed catching the Plague was a matter of chance.

The Farynors just had to carry on with the work in hand, as baking was their only source of income, and they knew they were lucky to have it. The young girl immediately took on all the chores her mother had once done. Thomas was lucky to have a daughter, ready and willing to do her share of the work. She worked so hard, the smaller family seemed no less efficient, and the loaves continued to come out of the oven.

But it was now after the Great Fire, and the girl was alone. She wondered, '*Am I an orphan?*' She certainly felt like one. Of course, she would continue to search for her father, but at that moment, she had no idea where to start. It was still too dangerous to wander the streets, as they were full of rubble and quite impassable in places; chunks of building materials were still precarious, hanging by a thread, and ready to fall, on some surprised casual passer-by. She thought of her father continually, but persuaded herself his absence would soon be noticed, after all he was the king's baker, making special loaves for both the palace and the court. Oh yes, he would soon be missed; lack of something as basic as bread would soon lead to a hunt for the missing baker. At least, she hoped so.

The fire continued to spread and burn over the next four days, and after that time, the bakery in Pudding Lane was declared to have been the initial source of the fire, a theory that has never been questioned to this day; the question as to who started it however, is still being asked. The irony was the fire was encased between two landmarks in the city, and both were 'food' related. It had started in Pudding Lane, where there was a large meat warehouse, as well as several other commercial enterprises; the fire's final stopping place was at Pie Corner. Pudding Lane could have been called Offal Lane, as the word pudding was used in lieu of the word offal – offal being animals' innards, organs, and guts. I think you'll agree Offal Lane just wouldn't have sounded right, especially to the better-off amongst the city gentry.

Whatever the name, the words Pudding Lane were on everyone's lips, and it was at this time when Sir Christopher Wren, and Robert Hooke his colleague, were commissioned to design the Monument, a memorial which still stands on the same spot today. The Monument was intended to be an eternal reminder of the atrocities inflicted on the medieval part of London, and its people.

The huge Monument was erected there, for all to see, and to remember Farynor's Bakery itself, was only a short distance away. It actually stood in a small enclave just off the lane, called Fish Yard, but again, Pudding Lane sounded so much better than Fish Yard. Medieval England liked to call a spade a spade, but even to plain speakers, Pudding Lane sounded better than Fish Yard.

The young girl's name in this tale, was Rosie - Rosie Farynor (English spelling Farriner), and she was about twelve years old. at least that's what she thought she was. She knew she'd always worked in her father's bakery, since she'd first been able to walk; she'd never had any form of schooling, but then, her being a girl, it would have been a waste. What would a girl have done with an education – nothing but a waste of money?

It was late on the night of 1st September, a Saturday, and as midnight moved into the early hours of 2nd September, Rosie was awakened by an acrid smell of smoke. She could hear loud shouting from the street outside; it sounded like everyone was going mad. She could hear someone inside the house crying, screaming in fact. It was a girl's voice – but it soon stopped, and Rosie, forgot all about it. She had much more to worry about. It was then she saw her father's back, as he scrambled through the small window in his bedroom; he seemed to be talking to someone, who'd gone through the window ahead of him – but she couldn't be sure and she could see no-one. *He must be going for help. Yes, that's what he's doing. He should have checked on me first though, just to make sure I was all right. I mustn't judge him though, as he must know what he's doing; he'd never leave me to the horrible fate of a fire, would he?*

For the present however, Thomas Farynor's whereabouts were unknown, so Rosie was left to fend for herself. Her first thought was to leave the bakery, and go into the yard at the back, where the baking was always done. The building was open to the elements, so the heat from the oven, could evaporate. Because of the fire, there was still a lot of thick, suffocating smoke, that made Rosie retch. It wasn't ideal, but where else could she go? She huddled down into a corner, and did what she thought was best - she prayed. *Should I run away like my father? Is he doing the right thing, and I'm not? Oh God, help me please.* What she didn't know, nor did anyone else at the time, was that there was no right or wrong thing to do. None of the run-aways could have known, but the fire was preceding their escape route, and those who'd gone, were simply running ahead of the worst of the fire.

And this was the reason young Rosie found herself sheltering in a corner of the yard, wishing the horror would stop. Her theory about Thomas's escape might not be right, but she preferred to believe it, rather than that he'd deserted her. He'd been known as a respectable man, being both the king's baker, and a warden of the local church. Surely, not the kind of man, who'd run off, and leave his daughter in danger.

He had run away however, but it might have been in an attempt to protect his reputation, after all, he wasn't stupid, and he realised he could be blamed for causing the fire. There was no question about it, even early on, that it had started in his bakery. He hadn't been thinking straight, but one thing he wanted to avoid at all costs, was to have a brush with the law. He'd already had a few run-ins with it when he was young, and didn't want a repeat performance.

He'd remembered it was his daughter's turn on the night the fire started, to dampen down the embers that still glowed in the oven after the baking was done, then he remembered too, he'd been the one supposed to re-check she'd done it properly - that was the safety routine they'd both agreed. *Did I double-check last night? I'm sure I must have.* He asked himself the question, and answered it himself. *Of course, I did, and so did my daughter. We both couldn't have got it wrong.* There was still some doubt in his mind however, and he desperately wished there wasn't, therefore a speedy disappearance was the safest solution. Anyway, no-one would ever blame a young girl, but they might be happy to blame an old man. Better to be safe than sorry, he told himself, 'running off was the best bet in the circumstances.'

Some of his neighbors had known Thomas when he was younger, and would have had a different explanation to the one the girl held. He'd never told his family about his skirmishes with the law, but then it had all happened long ago. The truth was, he'd had several visits from the law in the past, when as a child, he'd been found wandering the streets, after running away from his master. He'd been detained in a juvenile correction facility several times, but each time, he'd somehow managed to escape. In the end, the authorities gave up on him, and turned their back on the wayward youth. The next mention of his movements was in 1629, when it was noted he was working as a baker's apprentice in the city. Farynor was of Dutch origin, and liked to brag about his baking skills; he liked to say he'd been born to bake - after all, his surname was almost the same as the French word for flour – farine. Of course, these early misdemeanors might not have been the reason he ran from the fire, although running away had always been his chosen option in the past. Avoiding the authorities at all costs had obviously always been his first priority, and as he'd told himself, anyone left behind would be quite safe.

Inside the bakehouse, Rosie was very afraid; there were burning tufts of the brushwood used to light the oven still smoldering on the floor, and burnt thatch was dropping from those bits of ceiling still in situ. Everywhere the thatch landed, a fresh fire would begin. She had to stamp them out quickly, and thanked God she was wearing her stout, black boots. The floor too, was fast heating up, and she feared it would soon be ablaze as well. No roof, no ceiling, and soon no floor – not a home at all.

When she ran out into the lane, she couldn't believe her eyes. Nearby properties were now ablaze, as well as the bakery and its immediate neighbors on either side. Farynor's Bakery sat between two businesses, one a Blacksmith, the other a Glazier; their occupants were fast emptying their premises of anything that was movable it was a desperate attempt to escape the flames, and to save as much as they could. Rosie peered through the smoke, but could see very little.

It had been a long, hot summer that year, which helped the fire get a hold; it was perfect conditions for the spreading flames, with everything dry as a bone. Unbidden, the thought came into her head, '*What if it was our oven that started the fire? I know it was my turn that night to dampen down the embers, but Father always checked I'd done it thoroughly. I know that was his routine, but what if he'd forgotten that one night, a night when I was careless? A stray spark could have jumped from the smoldering embers, and landed on the dry straw – and then whoosh, it was well away. The long, hot Summer months had helped make this a possibility. It didn't bear thinking about, so she stopped doing it. She didn't have that power however, and kept right on wondering if her family had been the guilty party. Father was always so careful with the oven, after the day's baking was finished. Their routine was the same every night; first Rosie would dampen it down, then Thomas would check it.*

She tried to put these thought out of her min, but it was difficult. Her throat felt raw, and she realised how parched she was. She needed a drink, but would she be able to swallow it anyway? It was an academic question, as there was no water to be found. For a moment, she imagined she was holding a beaker of cold water, which she would sip slowly – even dabbling her burnt fingers into its soothing coolness. She had no water however, in fact, she had nothing at all. She quickly snapped out of her day-dream, and moved from her cramped position.

Gingerly pushing open the door, she peered into the smoke-filled lane. The floor of the bakery was so hot now, it was burning her feet, and she could smell the leathery soles of her boots burning in the heat. She looked up, and saw there was now no ceiling; all the thatch used for padding, had dropped below, and was lying in small, smoldering piles around the room. She could see the sky now – through gaps in the roof, and there was just enough light showing, for her to spot some broken bits of bread in the corner; broken bits of black and burnt bread, which now seemed so welcome. Thank God, maybe she wouldn't starve after all. She still craved that cool drink however, but of course, the bakery pump was gnarled and twisted out of shape – the intense heat had seen to that. She went back outside into the lane, and stopped a passer-by, asking if he knew where she could get some water, but he just pushed past her, shouting "Get about your business girl." He was obviously scared, and running for his life to God-only-knew where. There were no friendly faces that night, in fact there weren't many faces of any description. She thought how odd it was, that fear made some people truculent, even cruel, but that's how it was.

What a welcome sight! *I wonder if the river has burst its banks again, and the water has found its way into Holborn. Would the Thames be too far away for that? I'm not sure, but either way, some welcome water has found its way to Pudding Lane. The gutters were running with water, and she thanked God for it, as she* scooped some into her hands, and gulped it down, before dipping her sore, burnt fingers into its coolness. She was glad she couldn't see her face, as she knew it had been burnt as well. In fact, if it looked anything like her hands did, she doubted she'd ever want to see it again. She retraced her steps then, as it seemed safer to go back, rather than forward; she bumped into things in the thick smoke, but soon, found herself back at the hovel of a bakery that had once been her home.

In Pudding Lane, the fire may have become less intense than before, but it had already done its worst, and the lane was unrecognizable. The fire was moving fast, spreading quicker and much further than anyone could have foreseen. It was helped by the strong East wind of course, a wind that was pushing the flames ever-onwards into the West of the city. Rosie went back into the yard, where she curled up again in the same corner as before. The cool water had helped of course, helping her to fall into a sleep of utter exhaustion. She was safely away from the hottest parts of the bakery, so she was able to feel reasonably safe. To sleep was a merciful release, and she succumbed to it.

As she slept, she wasn't to know the long-established medieval city of London was undergoing huge changes, due to a sudden and unexpected wildfire. So thorough was that destruction, that details would eventually emerge, recording almost 70,000 homes had been lost in the fire, with 80,000 people being made homeless within just four short days. It seemed the old, walled part of London hadn't stood a chance, as all the odds were stacked against it. After two days of the spreading flames, the king's military were called in to help. When news reached him at the start of the disaster, Charles had immediately offered his men's services, to the Lord Mayor of London, and his councilors, but his first offer was rejected, most likely because the city authorities still didn't wholly trust King Charles. It seemed old memories and hatreds were slow to die, the reason being, when Oliver Cromwell had been in control of the country, and had executed Charles 1st, the city of London was completely on the side of the Parliamentarian Cromwell, and to-a-man, mistrusted the royal family, especially the 'closet' Catholic King. Charles 1st, father of the present monarch. So, the son's offer was not welcomed at first, but as the firestorm ate up even more of the city, mistrust had to be put to one side, and his offer of help was at last accepted.

The bells were ringing all over London, crying out to the people. Outside their usual religious routines (or on the birth of a royal baby), church bells were used only to warn the people of an impending change coming their way – therefore woe betide the person who ignored these warning. When bells were heard at unusual times, it inevitably meant something big was about to happen, and they should sit up and take notice. It may not have been a perfect means of spreading the news, but it was all that was available at the time.

In the end, Charles was forced to assert his authority over the Lord Mayor's ineptitude and dithering ways, after all, it was his people who were suffering. It had been known for some time that the Lord Mayor was a buffoon of the first order, so, Charles over-ruled the man's authority, and immediately ordered the delivery of hundreds of tents to an open piece of ground in the city centre. The ground lay in an area called Holborn, quite near Chancery Lane, and was known as Lincoln's Inn Fields. Until this time, it had been a lovely, open piece of parkland, which suddenly had to become a hive of industry, with people buzzing around like worker-bees. The military set up the temporary tents for the homeless; it may not have been ideal, but it was better than the 'nothing' they'd been left with. The open green covered an enormous area, which was soon full of people from all corners of old London those whose homes had been burned to the ground, were in such a derelict condition, that they were unsafe for habitation, and could only qualify as hovels. The tents were a Godsend to London's homeless however, and the people were grateful to their king.

After a few terrible nights in the bakehouse, Rosie was lucky enough to be offered a place in one of the tents. Although she didn't want to share with some stranger, she knew beggars couldn't be choosers, and accepted the place gratefully. As things turned out however, she was to share with a family of four, who were not very easy to get along with, and who completely ignored the young girl. Five people in such a limited space, meant they had to take turns in lying down to sleep. The rule was that all single people had to share with families, as it was the practical thing to do. Rosie however, drew the short straw with her family, and was told she'd have to be the one to sleep sitting up, with her back propped against the tent wall. It wasn't good, as when it rained, she would be cold, wet and stiff, caused by the wet canvas.

She chose to visit the bakehouse every day, just to get away from the cramped tent. Anyway, it made her feel she still had a home of her own. The building was still standing, although nothing like what it had once been. She knew it was now a burnt-out shell of a building, but it was where her memories were still, memories of lovely, sweet-smelling bread, and delicious, buttery buns and rolls. *My God, my mouth is actually watering at the thought. I must stop it, or I'll go mad.* The tempting reminder of how the bakery used to smell, reminded her how hungry she was, and so, she tried (but not too hard) to put such thoughts out of her mind, and get on with just surviving.

On the third day, she felt stronger (and braver) - brave enough to search through the burnt rubble lying around the bakery, and to her delight, she found a large pot with only one crack near the brim, and no dents. It looked like it could be useful, if only she had some food to cook in it. It was black with soot and ash, but when she'd scraped that off, she was pleased to find it still contained some sort of honey - something sticky anyway, but with a lovely, sweet smell. The contents had obviously been boiled in the heat of the fire, and what had once been sugar, was now a tasty, caramel sauce – just as nice as honey really, and like manna from Heaven to a girl whose stomach was growling with hunger. It looked a bit like candle wax, but she knew it wasn't that, so she tentatively scooped a finger-full of the 'sweet wax', and held it to her lips. As it worked its way between her lips, and into her mouth, she found it tasted wonderful. A very distinctive taste, so welcoming, warming and sweet, that it actually hurt her empty stomach, and she had to tell herself not to gobble it all down in one greedy meal. She'd been hungry for so long now, she knew her body wouldn't be able to cope with the sudden richness – welcome though it was.

She covered the pot with a make-shift lid of broken crockery, and went on searching through the debris. A box of very burnt oats emerged from behind the oven. It had been lying half-inside the bakery, and half-outside, so it was only partially burnt. At the time, ovens were attached to the outside of a house wall – for safety reasons. A rather ironic precaution, considering what had just happened to the city. She placed the oats beside the pot, and continued her search, but was forced to stop, as she suddenly found herself inexplicably tired, and with all her strength gone. She didn't know it, but lack of food was having a serious effect on her, and she also hadn't slept much the night before, as sleeping upright wasn't conducive to a good night's rest. She gave in, and rested on her laurels for a few minutes.(and on a couple of empty sacks)

Whether it was the effects of the sugary syrup she'd just tasted, or the fact she was plain- exhausted, she soon fell into a deep sleep. She began to dream, and in the dream, she was mixing the caramel syrup with the oats, and mixing them both with a little water – water from the outside gutter, of course. But water was water! She could almost taste the sweetness even in her sleep, and found it all amazing; somehow the water had miraculously appeared, and she couldn't remember going outside to fetch it. In her dream, she also found a twisted bucket, but it had a hole in the bottom; not that that mattered in her dream, as she just simply plugged it with a pebble, a clean, shiny pebble which had also mysteriously appeared. She licked her lips in appreciation of her imagined creation - what a wonderful dream it was. Unfortunately, when she eventually woke up, she found she was still in the derelict bakery, and just as hungry as before.

The dream however, had inspired her, and when fully awake, she set to with a plan. She mixed the oats, which she'd first soaked in gutter water, together with the sweet-tasting syrup and spread the mixture across a tray, she'd found on the floor. A few pieces of thatch were enough to make a small fire inside the semi-broken oven, making Rosie the first person ever, to create a health-food bar. It tasted very nice, but she ate too much, and ended up with a stomach cramp. Her healthy bars however, encouraged her to search throughout the bakery for more things, until 'Eureka!', she found a bulging sack behind the outhouse in the yard, and it was full to the top with un-burned oats. "Thank-you God," she murmured, "Thank-you for looking after me." Considering what she'd just been through, and what was still ahead, she certainly earned the word 'forgiving.'

In one of her neighbor's destroyed homes, she found an even bigger bag of caramelised sugar, which was an excellent substitute for the burnt sugar she'd used before. It was in a solid lump of course, but she knew how to deal with that. Taking it from some poor unfortunate's derelict house was, of course, looting. but if you didn't know where your next meal was coming from, she felt the theft hurt no-one. Anyway, who would ever know?

She made the decision to take a tray of the sweet concoction to Lincoln's Inn, where she planned to give away her goodies, or preferably to sell them to the tent dwellers; luckily, many were delighted with her sweet, crunchy biscuits, and willingly passed over their pennies. So delighted were they, that they began to look out for her, with their pennies already in their hands. Being a kindly soul, she only sold to those who had the money, giving free to those who had nothing. She didn't know it then, but she was showing signs of being quite an entrepreneur.

It took four full days, before the authorities were confident that all fires had finally been extinguished. The infamous, and incompetent Lord Mayor, Sir Thomas Bloodworth, was finally accused of unnecessary dithering, and his servants even spread the word that, when he was awoken early on the morning of the first day, and was told about the fire, he turned over onto his side, went back to sleep, and told the messenger to come back later at a more reasonable hour. When he finally arose from his slumbers, he wandered down to Pudding Lane, to see for himself what all the fuss was about, and even when he saw some of the destroyed buildings were now nothing more than hovels, his words were, " Pish! A woman might have pissed it out." Then, he apparently returned home to his bed once again.(In one of the wealthier, and safer parts of the city) A very caring man indeed, and one who enjoyed the accolades of the crowd, when they finally discovered what he'd done, except the words they shouted were, 'Boo, and Shame on you', and not ' Hurray, and Well done', which he'd expected. (In fact, he only heard the former words, so wrapped up was he, in his own delusions.) He was just the kind of person to be in charge, when disaster struck! 'Thank God for King Charles,' was the opinion of the people!

By Sunday night of the fire, and after 24 hours, the decision was at last taken - firebreaks were the only solution, and this was immediately tackled by the king's military. The Tower of London was in the direct line of the fast-approaching fire, and the building had an arsenal full to the brim with gunpowder, and other flammable materials – it would make the biggest bonfire ever known to man. If the fire was allowed to reach there. For various reasons therefore, saving the Tower of London was of paramount importance, and the king's navy was given the task of overseeing the firebreaks needed to stop the spread of the fire, and do it as quickly as possible. After four days and nights of the firestorm however, it was too late to stop the destruction of those homes within the medieval city; and so, old London perished. The fire had succeeded in wiping out an enormous area, which included the famous, and much-loved, St Paul's Cathedral. Many people took this as a sign that London was finished, but the king's military had other ideas, and didn't give up.

In the meantime, the East wind had done its worst, and had fanned the flames all the way from Pudding Lane across to the West of the city – and beyond. Without the wind that first and second night, the fire wouldn't have done nearly so much damage, but man couldn't control the weather, and that was that. Parts of the Roman walls that had stood solid and upright for centuries, were also victims of the fire, and most parts still standing, were demolished for safety reasons.

Although Rosie didn't understand all the conversations she heard between the soldiers at Lincoln's Inn, she understood enough. She kept quiet, so they'd forget she was listening, and they'd be free to speak their minds. One man was saying, "Picture the warren of streets making up the medieval part of the city; picture the homes, mostly built of wood and thatch, and all standing cheek by jowl to each other; then, there's the upper floors, the jetties, that projected outwards, over the streets below; picture all this, and you have a disaster waiting to happen." He was obviously enjoying having everyone's attention, so he went on, "Those wooden jetties, protruding into the street, were used to cram even more people into the houses; they were built upwards and outwards until they were naught but a few inches apart. Narrow warrens of alleys, overhanging windows and jetties, overcrowding in each house - and you have the perfect scenario for disaster." He was warming to his subject now, "And what about all those warehouses where barrels of tar were stored? What do you think happened when fire found its way into those places – or even before the fire actually arrived, the intense heat could have set them ablaze all on their own? Storing flammable barrels of tar should never have been allowed so close to people's homes – and yet, they were – and why was that? I'll tell you why, 'Because no-one cared about the poorest people of London.' Since Good Queen Bess's day, it's been known that wattle and daub buildings were unsafe, especially in built-up areas. Yes, daub can help keep the heat in, and the cold out, but wattle is nothing but dried-out wood, waiting for a spark to ignite it."

With regard to his criticism of the barrels of tar, his argument could have been even stronger, had he known about the concept of 'spontaneous combustion', and how the tar could set itself alight just from intense heat, let alone actual flames." This was a knowledge man had yet to acquire!

However, this man was obviously one of Nature's thinkers, and he had done his homework, and continued with his lecture, "The type of buildings in London's poorest parts had actually been declared illegal many years ago, and our King Charles himself, had issued a proclamation as recently as last year, declaring any builders found to be either erecting, or maintaining those houses already condemned as unsafe, and not fit to live in, were to be arrested by the Sherris's office. But surprise-surprise, the practice went right on. The building of upper stories and jetties in city tenements was to be prohibited from then on, but of course it wasn't – there was too much money to be made in patching up old properties, and piling more and more people into the houses." He was truly angry and paused suddenly, as though he'd seen a face in the crowd he recognised, but didn't want to see there, but he couldn't help finally adding, "No, strike that, it was the authorities themselves who allowed the dangerous practice to continue. The king issued a second proclamation, warning the people living in the houses, of the fire hazards created by the narrowness of the streets, which were so narrow in some cases, that two people couldn't pass each other, without one standing back first. What could the poor do – they needed someplace to live! The man who chose to turn a blind eye to this corruption was the Lord Mayor of London, Sir Thomas Bloodworth – a bloody waster if ever there was one."

The man's outburst had drawn quite a crowd, and some started asking him questions, '*Are you saying it was our own fault then? Or was it the fault of the Lord Mayor and the Aldermen – is that what you're telling us?*'

The man, who was one of the soldiers, suddenly realised he was still in uniform, and that he should tread carefully; he spotted another 'suspicious' face join the crowd, and he knew it was time to beat a hasty retreat. So, he did just that!

The medieval city centre had been originally created by the Roman invaders in the first century AD, and its subsequent upkeep and maintenance were not something the invaders took seriously. Later invaders followed the Romans, such as the Saxons, the Vikings, or whoever else chose to invade the green and pleasant land of England. In his turn, each invader chose to neglect the poorest and earliest parts of London; there was no bricks or stone for the Pudding Lanes of the city, unlike the areas chosen by the wealthy and important people in each generation. Such on-going neglect was the main reason the fire of 1666 spread so quickly. Since the Romans' arrival, the buildings had grown in a higgledy-piggledy way, hence the final and worst disaster anyone had ever known. Rosie eagerly absorbed all the new information, realising she was learning more as a homeless victim of the fire, than she'd ever learned working for her father.

Then, the inevitable happened, and human nature being what it was, and still is, the scared, miserable people, who now had nothing, needed to find someone to blame, and so, they turned on each other. This became another job for the soldiers, having to keep the peace. It wasn't easy as many people felt they'd been neglected and abandoned to their fate. As was usual, foreigners in the city were an easy target, and so, the rumors began, and spread around Lincoln's Inn as fast as the wildfire itself. Any wandering French or Dutch men found in the city were immediately accused of setting fires, and therefore must have been responsible for the Great Fire. The ongoing Anglo-Dutch-French War did nothing to help the many foreigner in the city, and it became unsafe for them to wander around the streets. For a while, street violence was alive and kicking and unjust attacks were commonplace.

One evening a few weeks later, Rosie was listening to a conversation between two men, as all three stood at the emergency water pump, recently erected at the end of Pudding Lane. She'd just asked if either of them had seen her father, a question she'd asked many times over the past few weeks. But, it was to no avail! No-one had seen him! She'd even checked with the local hospitals and mortuaries, but no Thomas Farynor had been reported in any. The men were discussing the son of a French watch maker. He was from Rouen in France, and called Robert Hubert, Lucky for short, although one day (soon) the nickname would turn out to be ironic. His name, like the fire, was fast spreading throughout London, and he was soon tracked down and arrested. He was indicted at the Middlesex sessions on 16 September 1666, and imprisoned at the White Lyon prison in Southward. Things were moving fast. The fire had only happened a few weeks before, but things were about to move even faster, and in just one month's time, Lucky Hubert would be dead.

In his confession, the Frenchman claimed he'd had an accomplice, one Stephen Peidloe, and that between them, they had created a crude fire grenade by placing gunpowder, brimstone, and other flammable materials, onto the end of a pole. They pushed he pole through the open window of Farynor's bakery. It had been Peidloe's responsibility to 'stop up' all the water cocks in the Pudding Lane area, where they'd been placed to protect the people from the many businesses in the area. His work was important, as he was a significant part of the sabotage i.e. to abort any efforts that might be made to extinguish the fire.

Lucky didn't help his defence however, as he described exactly where in Pudding Lane the bakery was, and the Prosecution jumped on this clear evidence of his planned involvement in the crime. It was almost as though the Frenchman was trying to condemn himself, or as has been suggested, torture may have been used on him, in order to get the desired answers. The authorities knew they had insufficient proof of the man's guilt, there was no clear evidence after all, but to calm the people, a scapegoat had to be found, and quickly; and when all was said and done, the man had already confessed to the crime. At his trial however, one inconsistency that was neatly overlooked, was that his claim to have thrown the grenade through the ground floor window of the bakery, couldn't possible have been true, a fact easily confirmed by the Sheriff when he visited Pudding Lane. He found there was no window on the ground floor of the bakery. So, what was the truth? The Prosecution jumped on Hubert's many contradictions in the evidence he gave, and easily managed to sway the jury, and the judge to find against the defendant.

It all happened quick as a flash then, and the confusion evidence served its purpose, as Robert Hubert was immediately condemned to death. The result of his trial had of course, been a foregone conclusion, but to be fair to the authorities at the time, he had already confessed his guilt, leaving the jury little option. Lucky, who turned out not to be so lucky, was therefore executed immediately.

Yes, the Frenchman had confessed to starting the fire in Pudding Lane, but some believed at the time, that he may have been either mentally unstable, or that he'd been forced to undergo extreme torture. There were others who believed the Frenchman to be innocent, one of them being the authorities themselves, but he served as a suitable scapegoat, and that appeased the people. The strange thing was, that when Hubert heard the fire hadn't reached Westminster, he added new details to his confession. These showed an obvious disappointment that his crime hadn't achieved its desired result; it now seemed possible, that he'd been politically, and/or, religiously motivated? Based on this new fact, it became possible that the old demon of religious fanaticism, was raising its 'ugly' head again; had he been an agent of the Holy Father in Rome, and did he admit to the crime, because he believed he was fighting for the one, true faith? Who knows? His changed confessions added more confusion to the case, as another claim was that he was a French spy, working under the orders of the Catholic Jesuits. To make matters even more complicated, Hubert was a Protestant, and not a Catholic. Confused? You must be! Read on however for even further confusion.

Apparently, Lucky had been visiting Sweden, for what reason, no-one knew, but he'd not long returned to England from that country when he was arrested. Ironically, and to put yet another spanner in the works, the captain of the ship on which he'd travelled, came forward and gave a sworn statement to the court, saying that when the fire started on 2 September, Hubert was on board his ship, a ship which didn't land in England until two days after the start of the fire. This new evidence obviously meant Hubert had to be innocent, despite his confession, so was he mad after all, or did he just want his five minutes of fame? At his trial, his state of mind was commented upon by the Lord Chancellor Clarendon, who stated that, in his opinion, Hubert 'was a poor, distracted wretch, weary of his life, who chose to part with it in this way.' Whatever the truth, Robert (Lucky) Hubert was hanged at Tyburn on 27th October 1666.

His stories were so far-fetched, that the interrogators finally gave up on him, whilst at the same time, they chose to accept his confession as gospel. As said above, a scapegoat was needed, particularly after all four fifths of London had been destroyed. The people were baying for blood, and anyone's blood would do. The decision to overlook the sea captain's evidence had been taken, and that was that. Hubert's motives for confessing remain as mysterious today, as they were to the authorities conducting his trial in 1666. (Note the three sixes – the sign of the Devil – another point raised by the Prosecution at the trial) ***After*** his body was cut free of the hangman's noose, the cheering mob tore his body into bits, before it could be passed to the surgeons for dissection. The authorities had fed the people's hunger for blood – or so they believed.

Back at the water pump in Pudding Lane, the two men were still laughing fit to burst at Lucky's story, although Rosie thought it all rather sad. One of them wiped away his tears of laughter with the back of his hand, "The funniest thing of all, is the stupid Frenchie hadn't even been in England the night the fire started, but was travelling by sea from Sweden at the time. The crazy French bastard died for nothing." And the two drunken cronies wandered off down the lane, picking their way through the fallen debris. It was quite amazing, Rosie thought, but even in the direst of circumstances, people could still find something to laugh about, even if it was the death of an innocent, but rather stupid Frenchman.

Another odd, but similar story, came from the county of Wiltshire, quite some distance from London. In a small village called Kellaways, 3 miles from the town of Chippenham, a man was heard to speak out against the government, and imply the destruction of London by fire. The threat was real, and was subsequently reported to a member of Parliament, who arranged for an arrest warrant to be issued. The unwise braggart's name was John Woodman, and the warrant had been issued by way of an official Parliamentary enquiry into the matter; details of this still remain today, well-noted in the House's archives. When an attempt to issue the warrant was made, it was found that the said John Woodman had suddenly, and surprisingly, 'gone out of the county'.

He may have realised he'd shot his mouth off rather stupidly, and either made a quick escape to a safe place, or he'd travelled post-haste to London, to carry out the dastardly deed he'd bragged about. Woodman had spoken out in a Chippenham public house called The Lyon, and had apparently declared his intention publicly and loudly, with the words that, 'He (talking to his companion) would shortly see London alight.' A strange prediction indeed!

On their way home from the town's market, John Woodman and his companion Henry Baker, were having a dispute about the buying of a yoke of fat bullocks. Their conversation was overheard by William Ducket Esq. who was the afore-mentioned member of Parliament; his position in politics deemed that his word could be relied upon. John Woodman was the seller of the animals, and Baker the buyer, but Woodman wasn't ready yet to part with the animals in question. Baker however, wanted them immediately, and an argument ensued, drawing their argument to the attention of others in the tavern, Duckett in particular. Woodman decided to take the bull by the horns (if you'll pardon the pun), and said he couldn't sell them just yet, as he had to leave the county for a few days, and he would deal with the matter when he returned. Although asked by Baker, Woodman refused to say where he was going, or why.

The discussion continued, and as disagreements sometimes do, it became personal. Woodman said, ***"You are brave blades at Chippenham, you made bonfires lately for heating the***

Dutch, but since you delight in bonfires, ye shall have your bellies full of them ere it be long." He added that if Baker were to live one week longer, he should see London as sad a London, as ever it was since the world began. He finished by saying that, ***'in a short time after, you will see as bloody a time as ever was, since England was England.*** His words remain for posterity to this day.

This conversation was clearly overheard by others, but nothing more was thought of it at the time, until the news of London's Great Fire reached the West Country', whereupon Henry Baker approached his Member of Parliament, Ducket, and a warrant for Woodman's arrest was then issued. At the point of serving the warrant, it was found that ***the accused had indeed left the county, and his whereabouts were unknown.*** On the whole, a pretty damning discovery for Woodman, which prompted the question, 'Where did he go when he left Chippenham, and what did he do? There never was a satisfactory reply to that question, and the man was never charged with the crime! Basically, because he couldn't be found.

Of course, there were many such reports made to the investigating Sheriff's office, but were they genuine, or merely those who wished to be seen carrying out their civic duties? Of course, they could have been just searching for that illusive five minutes of fame! Who can tell – but here are some reports noted at the time, to give you a taste of the difficulties faced by the county Sheriff?

1. An Irish Catholic in the Greyhound Inn in London, warned others 'there would be sad desolation in September'.
2. John Packer, a doctor, said he'd seen a man near the Old Bailey throw something flammable into an apothecary's window.
3. In Bridewell, John Stewart reported he'd seen an old man set a pile of papers ablaze, and when he grabbed hold of him, the man's cloak and wig fell off, to show a monk's garb underneath.
4. A French manservant, whose advances were rejected by an English maidservant, was reported as saying, "You English maids will like the Frenchmen,

when there is not a house standing between Temple-Bar and London Bridge.

5. In Enfield, an old Catholic woman told others a whole week before the fire that there was a plot to burn the Capital to ashes.'

These are just some examples of people's tales, but they all add to the conclusion that no-one really knew who'd started the fire. Their tales probably caused the city's Sheriff and his team, more headaches than anything else, but it seemed even in 1666, that some people just wanted that elusive five minutes of fame, and would say anything to achieve it.

A few more weeks had passed since the worst night of 2nd September, and people were beginning to re-establish a routine, a strange routine perhaps, but a routine nonetheless. Even Rosie was getting on with her life! Some nights she'd sleep in the tent with the unfriendly family, who'd suddenly become friendlier, since they'd tasted her sweet biscuits; other nights she'd stay in the derelict bakery she'd once called home. In a strange way, it gave her a reassuring feeling of belonging. Her fame was beginning to spread, and she continued to search through the rubble that lay scattered around Holborn; she needed to find make-shift utensils for her sweetmeats, pies, puddings and bread. Very few utensils had survived the bakery fire, as they were swallowed up in the intense heat around the bakery oven.

Extinguishing the fire hadn't been an easy task for the men involved, especially as their only equipment were small, leather buckets, axes, and water squirts. Items suitable for small fires, but not for 'The Great Fire of London.' They used the water cocks that were dotted around the streets of course, but many of those were distorted out of shape, and their struggle to control the over-powering fire must have been a David and Goliath ordeal! The Navy were called in to deal with the worst of the fires, and it was they, who used the gunpowder, stored in the Tower of London, to blow up the buildings ahead of the fire's path; this was to create the firebreaks, and stop the fire in its tracks. Word quickly going around the city, was that in just four days, the fire had covered one and a half miles across the city - it must have been a humungous effort to stop its spread.

Rosie continued to take samples of her work to the tents at Lincoln's Inn, and people actually began to queue up waiting for her to arrive. One day, she arrived a little later than usual, and saw a circle of strangers sitting around a make-shift camp-fire. They seemed amiable enough, and were laughing at each other's jokes, so she approached them with her tray of goodies. There were townsfolk in the circle, some soldiers, and one very tall man with long, black hair, who seemed to be holding court amongst the group. It was a very apt observation by Rosie, especially when she eventually discovered who the man was. There was something about him that spoke of authority, but he was laughing and talking with the men in a friendly enough manner, so she approached the circle with her tray of sweet treats, first holding out her hand for their pennies.

Lots of people bought the biscuits, telling Rosie she was a wonder. One man explained to the tall stranger, "This young girl lost her home and her family in the fire, but she's managed to turn her misfortune around, and has taken care of herself since the disaster, and taking care of us as well – see the excellent biscuits she produces from almost nothing." The tall man immediately held out his hand for a biscuit, but Rosie pulled the tray away, and said "No, no Sir, I need a penny from you first, before I let you taste my wares."

The man looked puzzled, as if he didn't understand what she'd said. It was the word 'penny' that seemed to throw him – also he was obviously unused to people denying him anything he wanted. The soldiers laughed at their friend's confusion, whilst he spoke to the girl, "Well little maid, I'm afraid I don't have a penny", to which Rosie cheekily replied, "Then Sir, that's a pity, as it means you can have none of my biscuits." She smiled as she spoke though, after all the man was well-dressed, and looked as if he could easily have afforded a penny. Surely, he must have been pulling her leg.

"Rosie, bow your head when you are addressing your king; King Charles the second of this great country of ours, and a man who has been helping us with the clearing of the city's debris. He even took part in a chain of men, to carry buckets of water from the water cocks. He has been a most useful king!" The soldiers laughed at the girl's confused expression.

Determined not to be put down, Rosie answered, " If you have no money Sir, but you've been helping the fire fighters, you may indeed have one of my biscuits," and she held out the tray to the king, who quickly took one before she changed her mind. He thanked her, adding, "I really am the king, you know."

"You don't have to tell me you're the king Sir, as I'd have given you a biscuit anyway, just for the help you've given these brave men. "She felt quite indignant, as she realized he might have been laughing at her over the 'penny'

"I am happy to work alongside my people, just as you are doing. Thank you for the biscuit, it was most tasty." For a moment, he looked rather crestfallen, as if he realised he'd just been rebuked by the little maid. Then, when he looked again at the torn and tattered dress she was wearing, he realised how much she must have lost, and he felt an immediate need to get back into her good books, " I really am the king, Rosie, and I deem it an honour to help these brave men. I'm sure you would do the same in my shoes; in fact, you are doing the same it seems." He was licking his lips as he spoke, "By the way, that biscuit was so nice, and of course, if I had the money, I'd buy a second one."

At his praise of the young girl, whom the others regarded as an angel, several of the men cheered heartily, and offered him a penny for the biscuit. The King was amongst friends, of that, there seemed little doubt, and so, he didn't hesitate in accepting their penny.

Like the phoenix rising from the ashes, the medieval city of London was slowly coming alive again. Alive, but not yet thriving – not yet anyway. Nothing would ever be the same again of course, but people being people, the Londoners knew it was no good crying over spilled milk, and they had to get off their backsides, and begin to rebuild their city. One good thing that had come out of the disaster, was the formation of a fire fighting brigade, who would be trained to deal with such catastrophes in the future. This developed at the insistence of the city's insurance companies, who feared a future disaster might re-occur, and on that occasion the costs would be even higher than at present. It was such companies, that also forced the creation of the city's very first fire brigade, and following that, the beginning of such fire brigades across the entire country.

Within the area consumed by the Great Fire, it was later confirmed that 70,000 inhabitants lost their homes, leaving only 10,000 homes untouched; four fifths of the city had gone; 13,200 houses and 87 churches were burned to the ground, and despite the authorities claiming at the time, that only 6 lives were lost in the blaze; later investigations showed this just wasn't true, and the number of deaths was much higher. Many, many injuries were sustained during the four days, and for many days and weeks thereafter, people continued to die from complications of those injuries; some hit by falling debris or intense heat and burns – all consequences of the fire but not included in the statistics recorded at the time. It wouldn't have been good for propaganda, and not something the man in the street had to know. No accurate details of any deaths were collected, and so, the report of six deaths was nothing more than a myth, most likely spread by London's better-off, wealthy people, who hadn't suffered much at all, from the fire; their brick, solid stone buildings, plus good foundations, had saved them very well. The low number of deaths may also have helped ease their consciences, and it suited those in authority to allow this belief to stand. Subsequent investigations revealed, that the intense heat of the fire had reached 1,700 degrees in places, therefore challenging the myth o so few fatalities. The majority of the fire had been in the poorest parts of the city, so the accurate collection of data wasn't considered 'too' important.

Records from the time, also showed that, since the beginning of the year 1666, London had experienced an extreme drought, which turned the whole city into a tinder-box, just waiting for a spark. The timber-framed buildings had completely dried out, and those wooden jetties almost touching each other across narrow streets, became an absolute death trap. Couple this with the storing of flammables, such as oil and turpentine, in the warehouse basements, which was the normal practice; also, with the countless stables full of dry hay - and you have perfect conditions for the biggest bon-fire ever known to man.

There were also eye-witness reports at the time, which made a lie of the reported number of deaths. Some descriptions offered pictures of such horror and devastation, that the true loss of life must have been high indeed. The sad fact that must be repeated is the majority of those who were actually killed, or died of subsequent injuries, were the city's poor, and working classes. Accurate statistics therefore, would have been difficult to assess, and as there was a complete city to rebuild, so little attention was probably given to this.

The young entrepreneur, Rosie Farynor was however unaware of such things; she was not a defeatist however, and continued to scour the streets, but now looking for peddlers who were scraping a living, by selling bits and pieces to those who had the money. Rosie's pennies were invaluable, and she was careful to use them sparingly. She bought some dried plums, some sugar and more honey and oats. The ability of being able to buy things, was new to her, and made her feel quite like a lady of leisure; a lady of leisure however, who then took her purchases back to the burnt-out hovel she'd once called home, and where she hid them in a secret place, so no-one could steal them. Thieves were all around at such a confusing time, and in the burnt-out areas of the city, there were vagabonds, thieves, and murderers, forcing the people to watch each other with an eagle eye.

After experimenting with her newly-acquired ingredients, Rosie returned to Lincoln's Inn two days later. This time, she had a choice of biscuits and cakes, which were immediately snapped up by the tent dwellers and soldiers alike. She was well pleased with herself! As she sold her last biscuit, a uniformed messenger arrived from the palace. He had a letter for the 'Biscuit Lady.'

A flustered Rosie took the letter, but looked desperately around. *What am I supposed to do with this? What is it?* She couldn't read, and for the first time in her life, felt an annoyance with her lack of education. One of the soldiers stepped forward, and gallantly offered to read it to her. He cleared his throat, and read aloud:

Dear Madam

I recently had from you some biscuits you had baked. I am writing to ask if you would care to come to the palace and cook in the kitchens there? You are providing a service for my unfortunate people, and the offer of the palace facilities, is my humble way of saying thank you. Please say you will come.'

Your Servant

Charles 11 Rex

"My God Rosie Farynor, it's from the king, and he's signed it your servant, and used the word humble. I shouldn't think he does that very often. What are you going to do?"

"What do you think I'm going to do? I'm going to the palace. It's not far from here, so it's no trouble." The man laughed; she actually made it sound as if she would be doing the king a favour. What a girl!

Soon, she'd moved her meagre bits and pieces to the enormous kitchens in Whitehall Palace, where the chefs looked at her utensils with disdain, and immediately provided palace alternatives. She'd arrived through an entrance at the back of the building, and had to show her letter from the king, before she was allowed into the building. At first, she was kept standing alone in the doorway of one of the biggest kitchens she'd ever seen, or would probably ever see. There were so many pots and pans hanging around the walls, that she actually had to shield her eyes from the glare of their brightness. Three huge fireplaces stood around the walls, and one in particular was kept alight all the time! Rotating on an iron spit, was what looked like a haunch of deer; there were several oven doors built along one wall, and great, wooden tables stood around the room. The tables were covered with dishes of all kinds; casseroles, pie dishes, soup tureens, and tall stacks of plates and bowls. To Rosie, who'd been used to her father's small bakery, the sight was unbelievable. Not paying her any attention were four cooks, who were all running around the room, shouting orders as they went. They wore white chef's hats, and long aprons tied around their ample waists. The four clearly stood out from the rest of the staff. It was a place of great activity, with young maids and pages darting to and fro, whilst carrying out orders from everyone. Various sized knives were attached to one wall, and many pottery pots stood, one on top of the other. What they contained was written on their labels, but as Rosie couldn't read, their contents would have to remain a mystery.

At first, the kitchen occupants ignored the young girl, and stepped around her whenever she was in their way. She was questioned by an elderly woman dressed all in black, with a lace mantilla flowing from her head. The woman had suddenly appeared, and to Rosie, looked very daunting, but she quickly explained the king had sent for her, and showed her his letter. The woman, who turned out to be the housekeeper, seemed to know all about the 'Lass of Lincoln's Inn', and told her to put her things over by the door, and come sit in her office, next door to the kitchen. Rosie did as she was told, and watched as the housekeeper whispered in the ears of all four chefs, explaining the girl was a protégé of the king. *Am I a protégé, whatever that is? I hope it's something nice.* The chefs weren't too happy at having to share their kitchen with such a lowly person, but had to accept the situation, when the housekeeper insisted the king's orders had to be obeyed; Rosie Farynor was to be made welcome at his palace!

The housekeeper explained further to the chefs, "The maid won't be here every day; she'll come only two or three days each week, but the king has made it clear she's to be given free access to any ingredients and facilities she wishes. He believes she's especially talented at baking, and has instructed that some of her baking is made available for afternoon tea in the day-salon. She is to be encouraged to try out new recipes, using only the best ingredients available. She did add however, "He doesn't want any wastage though, as the people in the street are starving, so any spoiled dishes (hers as well as ours), are to be kept, and distributed amongst the people."

She showed Rosie around the huge kitchen then, explaining who did what, but stressed she must always be courteous to the chefs, the ones in the white hats, and she must always obey their orders. The girl wasn't surprised at this, as she'd always had to obey someone's orders. She experimented with ingredients, thought up new recipes, and even struggled with a recipe book, which one of the chefs had loaned her. Of course, she couldn't read it, but she did have a good memory, and after he'd read something just once to her, she found it easy to remember. She made sure she kept well out of the way of the other kitchen workers as well, although some of the more junior staff were friendly, and didn't seem to mind showing her a trick or two. The good ingredients made her delicacies taste even better, although at first, she actually missed the old biscuits, where tiny bits of burnt thatch would often trap themselves between her teeth.

The money she earned from the sales of her food at Lincoln's Inn, she used to buy honey and oats, sugar if possible, and soon she became a regular user of the kitchens at Whitehall Palace. Of course, she used many of the palace's ingredients as well, but she liked also to use what she'd earned herself. Luckily, the palace workers followed the king's orders, and helped the girl whenever they could, and so the few pennies she earned, were put to the good use of buying her 'very-much-much-reduced' ingredients from the palace chefs.

Back at Pudding Lane, she continued to work at patching up the oven at the bakery; there certainly was enough fuel lying around, to build a small fire. On the odd occasion, when it wasn't in use, she was allowed to use an oven at the palace; unfortunately, most ovens were in constant use, so she found her old oven handy, if not efficient. Whatever she produced however, was much appreciated by the people of Lincoln's Inn.

Now she wasn't so afraid of the written word, she asked one of the soldiers at Lincoln's Inn if he would help her answer the king's letter. In the letter, she asked him to thank the king, to thank him profusely, but to explain that, were she to accept his kind offer of the palace kitchen, she couldn't possibly stop going to Lincoln's Inn with her goodies. The people there had come to expect and rely on her, after all she'd been the first welcome sight, who'd turned up with something positive, only a very few days after the horrendous fire. They'd named her 'The Lass', and would call out, "Oh good, the Lass is back? Where have you been, we've not seen you for days." With the better palace ingredients, her goodies were of course tastier than ever, and her fame began to spread even further by word of mouth. She soon became used to her new name, and 'The Lass of Lincoln's Inn' felt an inexplicable pride in their choice of her name. It made her feel important, and that she still had a place in the community.

Nowadays, she had the use of a little cart, courtesy of a stable lad at the palace, and it made moving her delicacies to the people much easier. Her menu had grown as well, and she now included honey loaves of bread, just like the ones her father used to bake. In reality, her ingredients came almost free from the palace kitchen, although she did try to pass over some of her pennies to the housekeeper, who looked quite shocked at the suggestion. "His Majesty sees and appreciates what you do, and recognizes it as a way of helping his people. Even the king calls you 'Lass ', and often enquires how you are getting on." King Charles had been impressed to learn that she often baked well into the small hours of the morning, before going straight to Lincoln's Inn to see the people. *Where does she get her energy from, he wondered - it's amazing?* He knew then, that his judgement of Rosie had been right. She'd even begun to help in the kitchen, and quickly found it was the best way to make friends. On one occasion when she visited the 'Inn ', some of the people quizzed her about what it was like in the palace. They found it amazing, that she lived in two worlds - Lincoln's Inn and Whitehall Palace. Not many people could make that claim.

"It's incredible," she told them, "and I've only been in the kitchens! The rest of the palace must be amazing. Everyone's been kind to me, and I really believe the king is my friend." At her words, the folk whispered to each other, "It sounds like our Lass is getting a bit above herself', but they just laughed, and continued to encourage her to bring them more of her special goodies.

London was beginning to come alive again; not much perhaps, because it still had a very dazed and confused population, but there was some movement, and that was what mattered. As said before, it really was like the phoenix, and was literally rising from the ashes; there was much to be done however, and it would take many years, as well as a great deal of money, not just to make things good, but to make them better than ever before.

The famous architect. Sir Christopher Wren, had been appointed to oversee and plan the resurrection (and betterment) of not only St Paul's Cathedral, but of the many buildings lost in the fire. To plan a better and safer layout of the streets –

preferably not so fire-friendly. London was being pulled up by its boot-straps, perhaps slowly at first, but very surely. The first task was the biggest of all - the clearance of the wrecked streets, courts, yards and enclaves, and also the immediate replacement of water cocks, pumps, and pipes. Sanitation would be all important in the new city, even if it hadn't been in the old! People in the street were already talking about a 'new London', a better London, and a safer one for all, and not just for the well-off! In the air, there was a sense of anticipation, and an awareness that better-built homes were on their way. They believed London would never see slums again! (Oh. how wrong they were!)

There was still no sign of Rosie's father however, although a long time had now passed. She'd almost given up hope of ever seeing him again. *I really must be an orphan, with absolutely no family.* She continued with her regular trips to Lincoln's Inn Fields, although it seemed the number of tents there was getting smaller each visit. Although still so young, she saw the tent people as her mission in life, and believed it was the reason she'd been allowed to live through the horrors of the fire. She was meant to help those others, who'd lost everything, just as she had done. A year later, Christopher Wren was also busy overseeing the erection of a specially-designed, stone pillar, created in memory of what had started in Pudding Lane (or in Fish Yard!) At the top of the very tall pillar, a viewing platform had been added, so that anyone could look around, and see the new city as it emerged from the wreckage. It was intended the pillar should stand there forever, as a reminder that nothing should be taken for granted, and that London had a responsibility to look after its own people. And of course, the pillar still stands there to-day on Monument Hill.

Rosie had just finished selling her goods at Lincoln's Inn, and was returning to the bakehouse when she saw her again. She must have been about five years old, but not much older. Very thin, with straggly brown hair, swollen bare feet, on which Rosie could see red and painful chilblains on the toes. There was something familiar about the child, and Rosie knew she'd seen her before. Now, where could that have been? It had to be amongst the tent dwellers at Lincoln's Inn; she must be one of their children, although most of the youngsters weren't allowed to stray away from the camp. Still, what was it to her? She had to hurry home now, as darkness wasn't far off, and although London was beginning to look better, it wasn't safe for a young girl to be on the streets so late. However, she couldn't shake off the feeling the girl was following her. *She's watching me, I know she is. What can I have that she wants?* Then, it dawned on her, if she was as hungry as she looked, she was probably hoping Rosie would have something left on her tray, some goodie that no-one had bought.

She stopped, and waited for the child to catch up with her, before saying, "Hello, can I help you?" The little girl dropped her gaze, and just continued to stare downwards with the round, bulging eyes of a hungry person. Rosie noticed she had ugly sores at each corner of her mouth, a sure sign of malnutrition; she had seen that look before - the child was starving. This took Rosie back to the first two or three days of the fire, when she too, had nothing to eat or drink; but this child looked much worse than she ever had. There were still two small buns left on the tray, so she leaned forward, and held the tray towards the girl.

"Go on dear, you can have one, but I'm saving the other for my own supper." She wasn't really, but it allowed her to break the ice with the girl. Darting forward, the girl snatched the bun from the tray. She didn't smile, nor say thank you, but her desperate eyes stared straight into Rosie's own, and she knew she was grateful. Unable to just walk away, and leave the child there alone, she held out her hand, and asked if she could take her back to her mummy and daddy. "What's your name? Come on, you can surely tell me your name, after all you're eating my supper."

Through chapped, blistered lips, the child said, "Aiooh. My name's Aihoo." Rosie was just about to say that was a funny name, then realised that might sound offensive, so instead ,she asked where she lived. Aihoo told her she lived down by the big river, under the arches there, and that she didn't have a mummy or a daddy.

Oh my God, how sad is that? At least I had a family, especially a mother who loved me. How on earth had this little girl managed through the fire? It was a miracle she was still alive."

Rosie invited her to the bakehouse saying, "It's not much I'm afraid, but at least it's warm, and I have a candle for light." The girl stepped forward quickly, in case the nice lady changed her mind. She took hold of the outstretched hand, and meekly walked alongside her new friend. She showed no fear, and Rosie hoped that didn't mean she'd trusted just anyone in the past. So, she did what she believed any good Christian would do, and she took the child along with her, knowing already she'd give her the other bun as soon as they got home.

The two girls fell into a pattern from then on, and wherever Rosie was, Aihoo wasn't far behind. For someone in such strange circumstances, the child was quite ready to talk, and over the next few days, she chatted with her good Samaritan, telling her all she could remember. She did have a mother at one time, but not a father; her mother hadn't been particularly nice, and when she met a sailor, who was willing to support her, she left Aihoo by the Thames, telling her to stay there, and talk only to people who could give her something. She handed her daughter threepence, and told her to make it last!

That was it, what else could Rosie do? An orphan herself, and still only thirteen (she believed), she unofficially adopted Aihoo, who was more than happy to stay with the nice lady, who fed her. To the child, Rosie seemed very grown up; she didn't seem to understand, that her benefactress was still a child herself. Child or not, Rosie **was** a person of independent means, and was discovering how to make her way in the world. She'd just have to take Aihoo along with her. Amazingly, Aihoo was very helpful to have around, so helpful in fact, that Rosie even took her along when she visited the palace kitchen.

The king's housekeeper gave Rosie some special cream for the child's sores, and between this, and the little snacks the kitchen staff were always slipping her way, Aihoo soon looked like a regular girl, and not a neglected waif. The housekeeper even found some spare maid's clothes, which were far too small for any of the current staff, and gave them to Rosie for both herself and the child. As she watched the little one chatting to the palace servants, she was glad she'd 'adopted' her that first night. She was company, and stopped Rosie feeling like an orphan herself – she had a family again. Aihoo was chatty, kind in her own way, and obviously adored her new friend. As time passed, and new houses were slowly beginning to appear, it was good to see how much more solid and safe they were, compared to what had been there before. To begin with, they had sound foundations, and very little wattle and daub – jetties were also not encouraged.

Rosie, with Aihoo in tow, went right on with her baking and cooking, and soon, the tents were disappearing slowly and surely, as the people found some better accommodation. Very slowly, the homeless were being housed, mostly in new-builds, but also in houses repaired by the builders.

On the day the Monument to the Great Fire of London was due for its official commemoration, Rosie and Aihoo were still busy fulfilling the need for fresh bread and cakes for the people. Now, the pennies were rolling in, and to keep her money safe, Rosie had to hide her small money-box in a concealed recess behind the old oven. Better to be safe, than sorry!

On this very special day, the two girls were preparing to leave the bakery, when Rosie suddenly had a thought. Aihoo was growing up, and looked totally unlike the girl found wandering the London streets. She must have been about seven or eight now, and Rosie could see the pretty girl she would become one day. She and Aihoo hadn't talked for some time about the child's mother, or about her life before they'd become friends. Secure in her friendship with Rosie, Aiooh wasn't particularly interested in discussing that horrible time in her life, but for Rosie's sake, she would.

"About your name? I know you're happy to use my name of Farynor, but what about your first name? Are you sure Aihoo is what your mother called you?"

"Oh yes Rosie, I'm sure. Wherever I was, or whatever I was doing, if she needed anything, she'd shout, "Aihoo, come 'ere, Damn you. I don't know why she always said Damn you, but she did. The child was quite unperturbed by her mother's cruel attitude. Rosie however, was staring hard at the child, "Aihoo – Aihoo – she always called you that, and added Damn you – is that right?"

The child nodded, showing little interest, and that's when the penny dropped with Rosie. "Your name isn't really Aihoo; I always thought that was too unusual. She didn't even bother to give you a proper name, did she? When she called you to get you to do something for her, she was really saying, 'Hey you come here, Damn you'. You were so young, you picked it up as Aihoo, and it stuck."

She reached out, and wrapped the girl in her arms. She felt sad for the little girl; what an uncaring mother she must have had. But she knew the child was happy now, so she just smiled and said, "I love you Aihoo Farynor, I really do." As she looked into the little face, she realised God himself must have sent the little guardian angel to support her in her mission at Lincoln's Inn; why else would she have appeared the way she had – as if from nowhere? She'd been sent for a purpose, Rosie now had no doubt.

The two young entrepreneurs had come equipped for the opening of the Monument, and they carried a trayful of goodies to sell to the crowd. The designers of the Monument were already there, both Sir Christopher and his colleague Robert Hooke were surrounded by a growing number of people. There had been much discussion about who should officially declare the Monument open to the public. Should it be Sir Christopher Wren the renowned architect, Samuel Pepys the writer-cum- civil servant and friend of the king, or should it be the king himself? Pepys had taken on the official role of recording the events of the Great Fire, and laid down for generations to come, a very detailed description of the horror that had swallowed up the city on those few, fateful days. When the fire broke out, he was stationed at the Navy Office on Seething Lane, where his home was attached to his office, and where it soon became known, much to the people's amusement, that he'd buried his special wines and a block of Parmesan cheese in his garden. The irony was that the Great Fire never actually reached Seething Lane, so Pepys' efforts were unnecessary. It was never known if he got back his cheese, in fact, it might still be buried there to this day.

King Charles never saw himself as a contender for the honour of opening the Monument, but in the end, the final decision was left to him, and he already had a suggestion in mind. On the day of the commemoration however, it was Wren who made the opening speech, and who welcomed everyone who'd come, first reminding them the reason they had all gathered that morning. He began by explaining the Monument had been erected on Fish Street Hill exactly 202 feet from the spot where the Great Fire had begun - in the bakery of Thomas Farynor of Pudding Lane.

Explaining about the Monument, he said, "It is a fluted Doric column made of Portland stone, and is the same 202 feet in height, as its distance is from the bakery. It took 6 years to design and construct, and has inscriptions in Latin on three sides. It gives the history of both the Great Fire, and how it is believed it began. The design is in allegorical form, describing the enormity of the fire, and how King Charles, with the help of his brother James, directed many of the reconstructive works." (He said this, although the work of the royal brothers was probably minimal, compared to that undertaken by others). He continued, "Several carved figures adorn the pillar, ending with figures of Plenty and Peace, to imply a new London, and whilst it was considered at one point to place a phoenix rising from the ashes at the pinnacle of the Monument, it was finally agreed a viewing platform would be best. The platform is reached by a narrow winding staircase of 345 steps, and those who feel able to climb them, will see spread before them, the glorious, and spectacular city of London itself – as it slowly, but surely, rises from the ashes." Wren may have been primarily an architect. but he seemed also to be a talented orator.

The weather was fine, the dignitaries, including King Charles, all stood around, and the solemnity of the occasion was not lost on anyone present. The Great Fire of London would be remembered for all time to come. Never again would the structure of the greatest capital in the known world be neglected, and left to suffer through neglect. (It may have been a vain hope, but at the time, it was sincerely meant.)

Looking at the Monument more closely, it can be seen how the final inscriptions and carvings on the pillar, presented yet another possible source of blame as to how the fire actually started. It must be remembered that although the country was established as a Protestant one in the 17th century, with the monarch as the Head of the Church of England, there remained many Catholic and disgruntled dissenters, who remained faithful to the old religion. Within the country therefore. there still existed significant unrest in parts of the population, particularly amongst the higher echelons of society. The real dissention may even have included certain of the monarchy itself, especially where James, the king's brother, was concerned. He obviously remained a declared Catholic on the inside, whilst pretending an allegiance to the Church of England on the outside. Both his daughters, Mary and Anne, had been raised as Protestants, something which would later open the door to their gaining a throne. Openly, Charles appeared to be Protestant (for the sake of the throne – after all 'Paris is worth a Mass', as the famous French king once said), but he gave signs that he could be easily swayed in the other direction. It must have been like walking a tightrope for him, as he was regularly pulled in more than one direction. He was not stupid however, and knew on which side his bread was buttered. Henry V111 had made England Protestant, and the monarch The Head of the Church of England – therefore Charles had little option but to follow suit,

The Monument's design, and all its illustrations, were attributed to Wren, but historical drawings show it was actually designed by his colleague, Robert Hooke; Wren's initials, giving his approval, always showed clearly against each design, and the drawings are still available to view today. The graphic allegorical designs were attributed to the acclaimed artist Caius Gabriel Cibber. Whichever designer was actually responsible for its design, Wren was given the final credit, which had to include the implication that the Catholic Order of Jesuits should be blamed for starting the Great Fire.

The Jesuits believed there existed significant corruption amongst those who ran the country, in particular within the Protestants, and would have welcomed a return to the old faith with open arms. Hence the inscriptive story (the accusation!) on the Monument; on the north side of the pillar there was a clear description of how the fire began, and of how it was finally extinguished. The Latin words, 'Sed Furor Papisticus Qui Tamdiu Patravit Nondum Restingvitur' were clearly depicted for all to see; the translation of this is, 'but Popish frenzy, which wrought such horrors, is not yet quenched.' When the design was finally approved, this inscription was added, on the orders of the Court and of the city's Aldermen. At this time the country feared a new Popish plot might be imminent were Charles to die, and his brother James take the throne. Such suspicions were ever present in the 17th century, and was known to affect the country as a whole. The original text inscribed on the east side of the pillar, blatantly blamed Roman Catholics for the fire, with the unchallenged words, 'burning of this protestant city, begun, and was carried on by the treachery and malice of the popish faction.'

A bold and damning accusation if ever there was one, but it was clear, it was directed towards the Catholic Jesuits and the Vatican in Rome, rather than the Catholic faithful in general. The Jesuits had an intense dislike of the fast spreading Protestantism sweeping Europe, and saw it as an overwhelming threat against the true faith, which was their own, of course. This hatred began from the moment the priest, Martin Luther, first nailed his defamatory condemnation of the Catholic church to the wooden door of a House of Religion. His accusations dramatic? Certainly! Accurate? Assuredly!

It was true that over time, the Catholic church had become corrupt in many ways, and was by far the richest institution anywhere in the world. The need to suppress Protestantism was a cause the Catholic Jesuits in particular, took to their hearts, strengthening popular belief at the time, that the destruction of London was deliberate, and brought about by the Popish hatred of Protestantism.

The Lord Mayor's office obviously believed this, as it was their Aldermen who authorised the inscription on the Monument, and in so doing, confirmed their belief that a 'Popish Plot' was the cause of the fire. Jesuit hatred of all but their own faith, has been made abundantly clear, and to explain the Mayoral office's claim, perhaps the excerpt below, from the Jesuit Oath of Induction of its members, may explain why such a damning accusation was made, and believed.

' I do further promise and declare that I will, when opportunity presents, **make and wage relentless war,** secretly and openly, against all heretics, **Protestants** and masons, as I am directed to do, to extirpate them from the face of the whole earth: and that I will spare neither age, sex nor condition, and that I will hang, **burn**, waste, boil, flay, strangle, and bury alive these infamous heretics: rip up the stomachs and wombs of their women, and crush their infants' heads against the walls in order to annihilate their execrable race. '

Known for their prophetic powers, and how they often declared what was about to happen, does beggar the question, Why?' Couple this skill with the utter hatred a novice to the brotherhood has to swear, and the question 'why' comes again to mind. I doubt you will ever have heard words so full of loathing and hatred for fellow man, than the oath you've just read. Was such damage part of their plan to abolish all Protestants? It could of course be an explanation as to why the people at the time pointed a finger straight at their Order, accusing them of involvement in London's disaster. Who can ever know, but by the end of the 18th century, the machinations and the intrigues of the Jesuit order, had become so well-known to the world in general, that they were even banished from Catholic countries, such as Portugal, Naples, Malta and Parma. The Jesuit order is the one and only single Catholic order ever to have been dissolved. Pope Clement X111 was about to suppress the Jesuit Order in 1769, when he suddenly fell ill on the night before, and died. His successor, Pope Clement XV1 signed a Brief of Dissolution in 1774, obviously following his predecessor's beliefs. As he signed it, he said to those around him, "This suppression will kill me." Strange posters immediately appeared on the palace walls of the Vatican with the letters 'L.S.S.S.V. The letters stood for 'Sara Sede Vacante, which translated meant, 'In September the See of Rome will be vacant.' Pope Clement XV1 was subsequently poisoned on 22nd September 1774. Another example of Jesuits' ability to foresee the future, after all those posters didn't hang themselves on the walls.

The name Ignatius Loyoland was a name well known to the Catholic Jesuits. (He took his name Ignis from the Latin word for 'fire' – fire as a means of destruction, and obviously portraying the Jesuit choice of weapon. Ignatius made many inflammatory speeches against Protestants, and the preferred means of getting rid of them. His speech was called 'The Pyrotechix Loyolana Ignatian Fire Works', and spoke of, 'The fiery Jesuits temper being an historical compendium of their rise, their increase, their doctrines, and their deeds of the Jesuits. (Soken in 167) The work was produced for 'the faithful' to highlight IN CAPITAL LETTERS, variations on incendiaries, gunpowder, fire-brands, fire, flames, and burning.' Everything was described in detail as an exposition of Jesuit mastery of the art of making and directing fireballs.

For the sake of fairness and impartiality however, it's only right to quote for your information words also claimed by the Order. Compare the statement below with the words in their sworn Oath of Allegiance. That statement reads: -

'We are the Society of Jesus, a Roman Catholic order of priests and brothers, founded half a millennium ago by the soldier-turned-mystic Ignatius Loyola. We seek to find God 'in all things,' and to dedicate ourselves to the 'greater glory of God, and the good of all humanity. We believe in collaboration with laypersons, who are part of our extended family We are the largest male religious order – pastors, teachers, chaplains, doctors, lawyers and astronomers. We care for the whole person, body, mind and soul. We have Retreat centres, Campuses, Ministries – to discuss and practice God's presence in our lives. We work on behalf of global justice, peace, and dialogue.

We take 3 vows – poverty, chastity, and obedience. **We accept that we must be ready to accept whatever mission the Pope requires,** and to work towards the greater good of all people from all faiths and cultures.'

Here, you have both sides of the coin: how the people in 1666 saw the Jesuit Order, and how the Jesuits now portray themselves to the world. The decision is yours now: could the Jesuits have been involved in London's disaster in 1666 – or is that pure supposition? Having said all of this, it should also be noted that the words of blame inscribed on the Monument were subsequently chiseled out at the time of the Catholic Emancipation in 1830. Later generations therefore, made up their own minds, but then, they hadn't been around when the catastrophic fire ravaged the city.

Despite – or because of all this, the Monument's opening ceremony was still in progress, and at King Charles' absolute insistence, it was none of the 'big-wigs', who were chosen to cut the official ribbon, and declare the magnificent pillar open to the public. The king had seen at first hand, the incredible work one young person had put into helping the homeless, the maimed, and the desperately poor folk of London. His choice was clear, and undisputed by anyone around him.

So, the Lass of Lincoln's Inn's tray of goodies was taken away from her temporarily, and she was given a large pair of scissors to cut the pretty, blue ribbon, which hung around the pillar. The scissors were rather big for her small hands, but she refused to accept anyone's help. There! It was done! Following Sir Christopher Wren's few words of welcome, the opening ceremony was finally over, and Rosie's empty tray was returned to her. Of course, the tray was now completely empty of goodies, but full of shiny pennies

It was after this ceremony, when Rosie and Aihoo were last seen walking towards Holborn. People remarked how alike the pair were, just like sisters. That was the last time anyone ever saw Rosie Farynor, the Lass of Lincoln's Inn. Aihoo was 'found' two days later, when she made her way to the Whitehall Palace kitchens; she was hungry, thirsty and very disheveled. She told the anxious housekeeper that she didn't know where Rosie was, and that after she'd been tucked up in her straw bed in the bakery loft, she never saw her friend again. She waited inside the bakery for Rosie to return, even putting herself to bed at the right time, on the second night, but by morning, Rosie was still missing. Where had she gone? It wasn't like her to go off without telling Aihoo where she was going, or when she'd be back.

On the second day, the young girl was sitting by the warm oven, when she saw a man standing on the doorstep, and peering inside. She didn't know him, and was scared. He was a tall, well-built man, perhaps in his fifties, and he looked as if he'd been living rough. Aihoo took an instant dislike to him, before spotting two other people standing just behind him. The girl and the boy looked alike, and also had a look of the man, who said loudly,

"I am Thomas Farynor, the king's baker, and this is my bakery. I have been away for some time, but have returned now to take what is mine." He indicated his companions then, "and this is my daughter Hannah, and my son Thomas. Because of the fire, we've been living in the country with my cousin. The fire drove us from the city, or we'd have died right here in this building." He peered closely at the young girl, "May I ask who you are please?"

The names he gave only added to Aihoo's confusion, and she wished again Rosie would come home. She'd know what to do; she'd never heard her friend mention these names, in fact, Rosie had told her she'd lost her father in the fire. So, who were these people, and why were they laying claim to the bakery? She said nothing however, mainly because she didn't know what to say.

The man took a step inside the bakery, and asked, "What about our maid? Where is she – was she hurt in the fire? She refused to come with us on the night it all started, but insisted on hiding in the attic – she thought she'd be safer there. The stupid girl!" He stopped talking, realising he was offering an explanation to a mere child, and a child he'd never seen before. She was probably some toe-rag who'd lost her family in the fire, and was taking advantage of the empty bakery; at that thought, he looked around the room. 'My God, it was a mess, but at least the roof was still intact.

The girl Hannah suddenly spoke up, "Chase her off Father – she means nothing to us, and this is our home after all." She didn't sound like a kind person, and her next words backed this up, "Fetch the Sheriff Father, and he'll soon get rid of her – what do you say Thomas?" She turned to her brother, and waited for him to speak. She was disappointed however, as he just stared at his feet, and ignored the question. He had no interest in the little girl.

"Where is Rosie? I'm waiting for my Rosie to come home." Aihoo's eyes filled with tears, as she said quietly, "Her name is Farynor, same as yours."

Rosie! Rosie! Who the hell is Rosie – and she's certainly not a Farynor." The man was quite indignant at the thought of some 'fictitious tramp' claiming to be his relative.

Aihoo knew it was time to go. The family were angry people, and she'd become the point of that anger. She may only be young, but she wasn't stupid. She made up her mind to go find Rosie. She pushed past the man, and ran along Pudding Lane as fast as she could.

Where can I go? Not back to the Thames; please God, not that! She was perhaps eight or nine years old - perhaps ten - and for the second time in her young life, she was all alone in the city. *Rosie – Rosie, where are you? I need you, and I don't like that man, Thomas – or his angry family. Please come back, I need you.* She had a sudden thought, '*I know, I'll go to the palace; that's where she'll be. Why didn't I think of that before? She'll soon chase those people away!*' She ran the whole way from Pudding Lane to Whitehall. Of course, the palace kitchen was already bustling with activity, but a couple of maids called out to her, "Where's Rosie today? We've not seen her for a couple of days?"

And so, Aihoo now knew the Lass of Lincoln's Inn wasn't at the palace either. *Where could* she *be?* The housekeeper came over to enquire why the child was alone. "That doesn't sound like the Rosie I've come to know," was all she said, before disappearing to seek an audience with the king. And that was how the monarch himself became involved in the disappearance of the Lass of Lincoln's Inn.

Rosie seemed to have disappeared from the face of the earth, and ironically it was on the very day when the last few tents were finally removed from the Holborn field. They'd been there far longer than was first anticipated, and their final removal returned the pretty parkland to a natural habitat. (except of course, for the inevitable rubbish that remained behind, but which would soon be cleared away.) King Charles instructed his housekeeper to take little Aihoo to the royal nursery, and settle her there with his other children. He thought she'd be good for his spoiled offspring, and she was about to find out she'd just well and truly landed on her feet!

He told himself, 'Rosie was fond of the child, and I was fond of Rosie. It's the least I can do to protect her protégé." And he was as good as his word. Aihoo stayed in the palace, after all there was nothing left for her in Pudding Lane, except a family who didn't want her. Rosie's absence from the streets of London continued, and the king ordered posters to be put up across the city, providing a very accurate drawing of the missing girl. He also offered a reward for any information as to the Lass's whereabouts, but despite this, no-one came forward with any news. There was also a fine imposed on anyone caught adding beards and moustaches to Rosie's pretty face; after which rude words appeared as well, suggesting all sorts of strange places she might be! How dare anyone desecrate the image of the Lass of Lincoln's Inn? So highly thought of was the girl who'd baked for the homeless, that the desecration of the posters angered the people so much, the fine had to be doubled - on the king's instructions.

The Lass's mysterious disappearance was even the subject of questions raised in Parliament, resulting in King Charles' instruction to his courtiers and ministers to accept a special mission - to go and find Rosie Farynor, the Lass of Lincoln's Inn – or at least, to discover what had happened to her. A massive exercise was undertaken, with all the nooks and crannies of London being searched – and then it was all done again for a second time. Despite everyone's efforts, this proved pointless, and it seemed the Lass of Lincoln's Inn had disappeared for good. Finally, and on the chance she may have returned there, a Sheriff finally visited Farynor's Bakery, and was surprised to find the family had come home. Thomas was questioned of course, but this just added to the confusion. He explained he, and his son and daughter had been staying with relatives in the country-side, and had enjoyed it so much, they'd remained there for a few years. Now however, the Farynor family was back, and ready to set up business in the old bakery, which still belonged to them.

"Rosie – Rosie who? I don't have a daughter called Rosie This is my only daughter, and her name is Hannah. My son Thomas is standing over there. They're the only children I have, and they've been living in the country-side as well. " He seemed genuinely confused, in fact he seemed angry, as the Sheriff seemed to be accusing him of deserting some child, and leaving her to fend for herself. "I wouldn't do such a thing," he said, " So, whoever the girl is, she's a liar, and no kin of mine."

There was of course, the other matter that needed discussing. This was the first opportunity the authorities had to question the man, whose carelessness many believed had been the cause of the disaster.

"He's as slippery as an eel, and I wouldn't trust him as far as I could throw him – and that wouldn't be far 'cause he's a big bloke." The Sheriff was reporting to his superior, and made it obvious he didn't like the baker – royal baker, or not. "He claims he knows nothing about our Rosie, and denies leaving anyone in the bakery on the night the fire started – let alone, a young child. Except of course he knew the young house maid had been left there – at her own wishes he claimed." He produced a signed statement, made under oath, which he'd extracted from the baker, and in it, Farynor had claimed he'd actually seen the Frenchie, Lucky Hubert, throw a grenade through the bakery window on the Sunday night. He said Hubert had another man with him, who was obviously there to help.

"I challenged him at this point, and told him it had recently come to light that Hubert was still at sea on the night in question, and so, he couldn't have been in Pudding Lane on 1st September." Farynor became aggressive on hearing this, and said the sea captain must be telling lies. "I saw him here – well, I saw a man I later learned was Hubert – and that's all I know."

The Sheriff persisted however, asking him to point out the window Hubert had used. Of course, there was no window on the ground floor, which made Farynor become even angrier, "For God's

sake man, I got it wrong, the grenade must have been thrown through the door– it was a long time ago, I'll have you know. .Yes, that's it, he threw it through the door, and not through any damned window." He looked quite pleased with himself, but the Sheriff obviously wasn't. He tried once more, "Are you sure you dowsed the oven properly that night? You weren't careless, and just went to bed, ignoring the possibility of a stray spark? Isn't that what happened? It seems most likely to me."

But Farynor was insistent that hadn't happened, and the fire had nothing to do with him. Unfortunately, carelessness on his part couldn't be proved, and no charge was ever brought against him. The baker soon pulled himself together, and set about re-building his bakery. He'd made quite a bit of money whilst staying with his relatives, and now, he could put it to good use, and rebuild his livelihood. Work was after all, the best way to get over a bereavement, at least, that's what he said. He was obviously referring to his lost maid-servant – the one he'd left alone to die in the attic – because he knew nothing about 'any

Rosie.' Anyway, baking was his in his blood, and something he'd often say was, "Farynor is my name, and Farine is what I deal in." (Farine being the French word for flour.) The Sheriff thought it remarkable how quickly the man 'got back into the saddle again' – what a trooper the man was! He thought with sarcasm.

King Charles however, wasn't interested in Thomas Farynor, and he continued to have his men search for Rosie. However, just as he was beginning to accept he must live with his disappointment, one of his ministers approached him with a strange story. The minister had instructed his 'people' to check all the Church records in the parishes of inner London. Of course, a great number of records had been destroyed in the fire, but some had been kept safe in the dark crypts below the floors of the churches; some records of the most recent deaths would also be safe in the crypts, recent though they were. Safe places for such things proved difficult to find after the fire, and many strange objects would find their way into church crypts. During his search, the minister's man found mention of one Rosemary Farynor (known as Rosie), who'd lived and died in Pudding Lane, in the year 1666.

Amazingly, the youngster had been found dead on the steps of the old bakehouse on the day following the start of the fire. Although the official claim at the time was that not many people had actually died in the fire, this young girl was definitely one who had. Oddly enough, there was a second record of another girl's death in the same bakery, and on the same day. She'd apparently been the Farynor's maid, and had been found in the bakery attic. No details of her were known however, so there were no birth or death dates for her. She'd lived and she'd died, and left no trace of her existence. Rosemary Farynor, on the other hand, was recorded as the daughter of Thomas Farynor, the king's baker. Rosie and her maid were named as being the first victims of the Great Fire of London, and they'd been buried side-by-side in the graveyard of a partially-destroyed church in Holborn, not far from Pudding Lane. When the minister had told the king this, he added the words, "May God have mercy on both their souls." King Charles just nodded his head in agreement.

But after thinking about it, the king wouldn't have it! "Nay Sir, that cannot be her. It must be a coincidence, that's all." He was adamant in his belief, " Rosie Farynor continued to help so many people, and for a long time after the fire. My God, she even helped me when I was hungry, and I invited her to use the palace kitchens, so she could carry on with her baking – baking for the tent people at Lincoln's Inn. Speak to the servants in the kitchen and ask if they remember Rosie; I think you'll find they do." He was sure the church record couldn't be referring to his Rosie Farynor, although the name was not a common one. He chose to ignore the reference to the bakery in Pudding Lane, as he didn't want his minister to be right. It could just be another coincidence! He told himself this, all the time knowing full well the minister was right.

Hoping to be able to please the king, the minister was curious about his master's insistence, and did speak with the palace kitchen staff, the chefs, and the housekeeper, who all agreed they'd known a Rosie who had worked beside them. "She worked here long after the fire had been stopped, long after - and she always took her baking outside the palace, to give to those homeless people in the tents. She did it all with his Majesty's approval of course." Several kitchen staff were nodding their heads in agreement with the chef's words.

No-one could explain the mystery, and no-one could find Rosie. In the end, and despite everyone's disbelief that Rosie hadn't been with them after the fire, there was no option but to accept the girl had died in the fire. There was nothing anyone, including King Charles could do to prove otherwise; it seemed the facts spoke for themselves. Charles was sad, as he'd been fond of the kind girl. and so, he commissioned his craftsmen to make a small stone monument, in memory of her, and place it in a secluded spot at Lincoln's Inn Fields. That stone can still be found today, but only if you know where to look. No-one knows the spot chosen by the king's craftsmen: that was a secret between them and the king. It's still there though, perhaps lost in some thick shrubbery, or concealed beneath the low branches of some old, gnarled tree. If you were to search around, I'm sure you'd find it. It's certainly worth a try!

Rosie's stone reads: -

'In memory of Rosie Farynor, the Lass of Lincoln's Inn
who helped the victims of the Great Fire of London?
by her generosity and kindness to those made homeless
A fairy figure, she might have been, but her help and
support to those in need, came from God and his little angel
We say thank you to him for allowing her a little longer
on earth after her death, in order to help her fellow man.

Rosie was aged twelve and she died in Pudding Lane in
London on 3 September 1666 at the time of the Great Fire. '

God Rest her Soul.

The words, approved by the king, clearly showed everyone's conviction that Rosie had lived and helped after the disaster struck London, but it also alluded to her 'fairy-like', angelic acts after she may have died. Many Londoners had known the girl, and had enjoyed her delicious baking on more than one occasion. She'd been like a light at the end of a long tunnel, and people had thanked God for her. Could the Good Lord really have allowed her to cling on to her life on earth after death, for just a little longer, knowing the important path he'd chosen for her to follow; was she the figure of hope a wrecked society needed? In fact, did Rosie even have a life at all, or was she just one of God's angels on loan from Heaven for a short while?

Had the little ghost been involved in causing a spark to jump from the oven onto the dry hay – not really very likely, and who was it who filled her memory banks with childhood details of a life she'd never had? She certainly did seem to have had memories of being a Farynor daughter, or did the good Lord just make sure she had them? Either way, it doesn't really matter, does it? She'd been placed there at the right time, and in the right place, and with the right memories. And that's all we have to know.

****

Now, we come to the point in my tale, where you take over; the point where you must make a judgement. From the night of 22nd of September 1666, I've given you my thoughts, as well as what I've learned whilst putting the story together. Some of my words may be fictitious, but many of my facts are accurate, and researched. You mustn't be afraid to tackle the issue head on, examine all options, and decide where you place the blame for what happened in the London of 1666. It' not an exam, so don't worry if the question's too difficult; no-one's gong to test you, and any answers you come up with, are private to you, and to you alone. Someone or something started that fire, or did fate arrange for a spark to do its worst that night? If you decide on the latter, then it was an accident, aided and abetted perhaps by a long, hot summer, and a neglected London; neglected by the careless storage of flammables stored close to where people lived cheek by jowl, in those tall, narrow London lanes; or should the blame fall on the long hot summer the city had to suffer from that year? Taking all of this together, was it just an accident waiting to happen? Over to you!

If, on the other hand, your decision is 'Someone must have done it', then it opens up another can of worms. The dubious tales put forward by various up-standing citizens, are all open to question, and there is no actual evidence for their claims. Should you then disregard them? Perhaps some of them, and particularly Robert 'Lucky' Hubert, the foolish Frenchman, but what about John Woodman from Wiltshire, or the Pope's Catholic Order of Jesuits, or indeed the mysterious disappearance of the run-away Thomas Farynor (who could have been working for the Jesuits!), Although he appeared to be an innocent baker of the king's bread, was he just that – and why did he disappear suddenly and for such a long time afterwards? He was also of Dutch origin, and therefore a possible spy for his masters in Holland. All fairly reasonable options! Could John Woodman from Wiltshire have acted as an agent of Holland, or a spy paid by France, or even a minion of the Jesuit Order of Catholics? It's all feasible, although some options are more likely than others.

As a background to the position, England in particular, found itself in 1666, a short, potted history of the 100 years prior to the Great Fire might be of use. In royal circles especially, the period might compare well with Sir Walter Scott's famous quotation, 'Oh, what a tangled web we weave, when first we practice to deceive."

<u>Century Potted History (Apologies for this, but it could help understand the political/religious confusion of the times): -</u>

England's Middle Ages saw the emergence of a religion that differed from the long-established one of Catholicism; England in particular, was reeling from the changes this brought about. It's worth reflecting on such changes, particularly on those issues that caused so much turmoil. Both the introduction of Protestantism, and of the Anglican Church of England affected all people, but particularly amongst those in the higher echelons of society, where power was all important. Of course, Henry V111 was responsible for first throwing the proverbial cat amongst the pigeons, when he broke his country away from the Catholic church in Rome, and usurped the Pope's power over Englishmen; he confiscated all the church's magnificent wealth, and made himself Head of the Church of England. A few changes in such a short time, but ones which had a humungous effect on the people of England.

The decision to make such changes, was aided and abetted, and indeed first suggested, by Henry's first minister, Thomas Cromwell. Although popular history tells us the move was to rid himself of an un-loved wife, Katherine of Aragon, but the new bulging coffers of the royal treasury, brought about by the Dissolution of the Monasteries, was a very welcome addition to the king's treasury – all brought about by separating from the Pope. Religious houses were so wealthy at the time, it was quite obscene, when compared to the poverty that existed amongst folk in England, so in his own eyes, Henry was doing nothing wrong. Cromwell had persuaded the king, that in the written words of a much earlier scribe - one Geoffrey of Monmouth, who had sworn in good faith, and after much historical research, that England was not just a country, but an empire. An empire should have at its head an emperor, and not a king - this change of status meant Henry did not need to bow to the power in Rome, nor seek any concession to divorce Katherine– he was the Holy Father's equal.

Getting rid of Katherine of Aragon was thereafter an easy task, the decision on what to do about Katherine was therefore his to make. Step forward the Greatest Prince in the Christendom, as Henry now saw himself. (Although the Spanish would continue to challenge that title.) The Catholic Church in England had been too wealthy for too long, and when all was said and done, that wealth did not belong to the Pope, but to the English people, to the country, and therefore to the monarch of the people. It wasn't a difficult conception - it was an easy one, especially if you benefitted from it, as Henry did. Geoffrey of Monmouth's probable myth on this matter certainly had a lot to answer for.

Now we begin to see clearly, why religion was such an important part of life in the Middle Ages – for religion, read absolute power: and Henry's new-found powers, attained through a change in religion, also explains why such power was wrested from one faction to the other, in a battle of wills – throughout both the Houses of Tudor and Stuart. As some preferred to believe, it wasn't just about the different beliefs of transubstantiation, something that has often been claimed, but rather about the absolute power religion could wield. With the holy houses having been put firmly in their place in England, the ruling monarchs could do as they pleased. The monks had been chased off and forced to roam the country, starving and penniless; the nuns had been thrown out of their nunneries, with only a tiny pension to sustain them; the magnificent holy cathedrals and abbeys had been blown to pieces, and all their valuables confiscated by the throne i.e. by Cromwell for King Henry. Those now in charge of the country had all the riches, that should have been theirs in the first place. The plump hands of The Pope in Rome no longer had England's wealth, but that was to be a temporary thing, as the Pope might have been the loser on this occasion, but assuredly he'd live to fight again. Protestantism may have started, but it would prove to be a struggle to maintain.

This picture is presented with no apology, but with the intention of showing the importance of religious power in England in the Middle Ages – and why that power **really** changed hands so much.

The (very) potted history: -

King Henry 'feigned' a Protestant faith, (for reasons given above), whilst choosing to die in what he believed to be the one true religion, i.e. Catholicism. His young son Edward V1was more honest about his preferred religion, which was, Protestantism, and worked hard throughout his short life, to suppress and abolish an all Catholic England. The boy even tried to do this from beyond the grave, as in his will, he by-passed his half-sisters – the true heirs to the throne - and bequeathed the crown to his cousin, the Protestant Lady Jane Grey; his plan however, didn't work, and his half-sister Mary, took the throne, with no blood being shed, and had her cousin, the Lady Jane, beheaded after only 4 days as Queen. The Tudor Mary 1st was a staunch Catholic, and immediately executed hundreds of innocent Protestants, purely because they wouldn't swear allegiance to the 'true' faith' – i.e. hers. They were burnt at the stake in great numbers at Smithfield Market, so earning the queen the title 'Bloody Mary.' She had successfully 'got her own back' on her father Henry, for destroying her mother (Katherine of Aragon), and for his decision to break from the Holy Father in Rome. Fire, Fire, and more Fire – it reminds more of the Catholic Jesuit Priesthood's Oath of Allegiance, and of things yet to come.

Mary's sister Elizabeth 1st was however, wiser, ambivalent, and cunning. She would have agreed with the French king's claim that "Paris was worth a Mass': except in this case, substitute France for England, and you have an identical concept. Elizabeth was an autocratic ruler, but she was also pragmatic and cautious, and had no wish to upset her people, in the name of religion. She appeared to turn a blind eye therefore, and although England was still very much a Protestant country, she accepted her subjects' variants in their choices of religion, except that is, where plotters like Catholic Jesuits were concerned; those she would imprison in the Tower of London, and after torture, would have them executed in the same barbarous way that all traitors were treated. On occasion, she might have pretended an impartiality, but she was astutely aware on which side her bread was buttered, and wisely favoured her Protestant subjects more. Whenever she found evidence that her throne was under threat, she could be ruthless. She ruled successfully over both Catholics and Protestants, (but mainly over Protestants) and as long as her coffers were full, she was reasonably content. She died childless however, and the Scottish King James V1 of Scotland became King James 1st of England. He was a staunch Protestant, as staunch as Mary had been a Catholic, and he too, wanted England to follow his lead; unlike Mary however, he was aware he held a much weaker hold on his new country, and his rightful position as king, was often the subject of debate. Every moment of every day, he feared that Catholics were secretly plotting against him, planning to remove the crown from his head – but fortunately not his head from the crown.

Many believed at the time (including King James) that the Gunpowder Plot had been Catholic Jesuit inspired, although attempted on direct orders from the Pope Eventually, James issued a proclamation that demanded all Roman Catholic priests were to be banished, as well as all those who refused take the oath of Supremacy and Allegiance to himself as King, and Head of the Church of England, should be disarmed. This was no idle threat, and was carried out.

James' son was Charles 1st, and who, like his father, was allegedly faithful to the country's Protestantism; in reality however, he remained true to the old faith of Catholicism. (alongside his very Catholic wife) It was because of this duplicity, and his determination to rule as an autocrat, often without Parliament's approval, that he would meet his end, and die on the executioner's block. Following this, the Protestant Lord Protector Oliver Cromwell ruled in lieu of a monarchy, and at the end of his time in charge of the country, Charles 2nd was invited to return from exile in France, to take his rightful place on the British throne. The new Charles had learned his lesson well, and he played the part of a dedicated Protestant monarch quite happily, becoming the merriest and most charming monarch the country had ever known.

He was content to accept that some of his people might be Protestant, whilst some were Catholic. His attitude was much like Elizabeth 1st's had been. Despite having many mistresses, and numerous illegitimate children, he too was to die leaving no legitimate heir. He had successfully played both sides of the game however, but the Anglican church couldn't trust him, and the Catholic church repeatedly criticised him for not keeping his promises to them. That promise had been to ensure the passing of Bills of Indulgence, to protect Catholics in their chosen religion. He failed them in this, and was known (afterwards) to have played yet another duplicitous game, this time with his friend, the King of France. He promised in exchange for France's promise of large sums of money, that he would ensure his country returned to the one, and only religion. (Charles 2nd was always short of money, and the French king had a great deal) To say he was a born sycophant, is probably too kind, as he knew exactly what he was doing, and didn't just want to please all of the people, all of the time, but rather, to agree with the other's point of view **in order** to get his own way.

Following his death, his brother James inherited the throne, and so, religious conflict was once again to raise its ugly head. However, Charles' brother James, made no pretense as to his chosen faith, he was Catholic through and through, and provided blatant and irrefutable proof of this, by declaring his belief in the true meaning of transubstantiation i.e., the bread and wine at Holy Mass, really did change into the flesh and blood of Christ; this was not in line with the Anglican church's doctrine, and so, after much discontent, King James was chased from the country into exile in France, where he remained until he died. (France must have been tired of 'hiding' Britain's monarchs.)

The throne of Britain was now vacant, and James' half-sister Mary and her husband William of Orange, were invited to come from Holland, and take the British throne. History refers to this as 'The Glorious Revolution,' because it was achieved with no blood loss or aggression. Mary and William were both staunch Protestants, unlike James, and so the House of Stuart continued to reign in Britain. King William (Good King Billy) died before his wife, and after some years, a childless Mary joined him. The Stuart line of Protestants continued with Mary's sister Anne, then taking the throne. (She was another dedicated Protestant – so no change needed) However, in spite of 17 pregnancies, Anne also died childless, and it was at this point, the House of Stuart would finally end, forcing Britain to look across the sea to a distant blood relative. The German Georgian, and very Protestant, had arrived.

This then, is the potted history of the Tudors, and the Stuarts – without question, a tumultuous time for Britain. From beginning to end, religion was used to appease those in authority, and allow them to grab whatever was there for the taking.

****

When this tale began, it was about the Great Fire of London, but for a better understanding of what might have caused such a disaster, knowledge of these money-grabbing monarchies, may be of use. Hence, the potted history!

Our island country suffered greatly during the Tudor/Stuart period. Of course, good things happened too, but none had the same huge effect as did the ever-changing religion. Catholic, Protestant, Protestant, Catholic – and all for what? The consequences were significant, as religion alternated between the two faiths; for faith however, you should perhaps read power, as that's what it was all after. Greed obviously fuels man's hatred of man, and religion was the means chosen to feed the rulers' greed or power.

Before this tale ends, we should return to the question, 'Who Started the Great Fire of London?' This story began with this question, so it's only right it ends with the same question.

Could it have been a simple oversight by an innocent? Or was it a well-planned and deliberate act by people claiming to act on God's wishes? I'm afraid the decision must be yours. One thing we do know for certain however, is that Rosie didn't commit the crime. Her living image didn't appear in Pudding Lane until after 1st September 1666; by then, it was too late for her to have carried out the dastardly deed.

She'd awoken on the steps of the bakery, it's true, but was it a real, live girl, or was it a God-sent angel to help bring some normality to a people destroyed by chaos? Was it accidental chaos however, or was it man-made? There was no evidence found at the time, or any found since. The young figure of Rosie Farynor came, she saw what was needed, she helped a king, and served her purpose as a messenger from God. Was she the spirit of a baby once born, but who was never allowed to have a life? Yes, there was a young girl found dead amongst the flames and debris of a fire, but was she Rosie Farynor, still-born daughter of a London baker, or was she the little angel sent by God? Questions, questions and more questions, all for you to answer.

Personally, I believe it was the angel of Rosie Farynor, despite what her father, the baker said to the Sheriff, i.e. 'I don't have a daughter of that name.' Did his dying wife intend to name her first child Rosemary – after her own mother – he may never have known this? - What he'd forgotten about was the baby his wife had lost, still-born before Hannah his daughter, and Thomas his son. She'd so wanted that baby! God obviously had another purpose for the child however, and kept her safe with him, until she was needed to fulfill her mission in life. That mission came about in September 1666, when God released her – temporarily.

The tent people of Lincoln's Inn believed her to be real, especially as they munched their way through her goodies, and little Aihoo believed her to be real – hadn't she rescued her from the cold waters of the River Thames, and placed her in the luxury of the king's nursery? One thing for certain however, is that whoever's fault the Great Fire of London was, it definitely wasn't Rosie's.

You may have a different opinion of course, but that's up to you. One thing you should remember however, is next time you're near Lincoln's Inn Fields in Holborn, you should seek out the memorial stone inscribed by a king; a stone which carries the words you already know, so I won't repeat them here. It may be all that remains of Rosie Farynor, the Lass of Lincoln's Inn – the girl who was actually born twice - but a real girl who was there, when the people needed her most.

One day, you should look for that stone.

HISTORY GAVE HER A CROWN – BUT DID SHE WANT IT?

Before telling you about one of the saddest, and shortest English reigns there has ever been, we should look first at what led up to it. To do that, we have to go much further back in time, to see how the English throne eventually fell into the lap of a slightly-built sixteen-year-old girl - a girl, who was not in direct line to the succession, and probably never thought she ever would be. There were others with a greater claim than hers, but she was of royal blood however, being the great-granddaughter of King Henry V11, the first Tudor king, but no-one would ever have thought of her as a potential monarch. As history was to prove however, they were wrong, and one day, she would sit on her great grandfather Henry's throne. Her name was Lady Jane Grey, and she was small, delicate and pretty, but the greatest thing in her favour with regard to her suitability for the crown, was that she was a Protestant, a staunch Protestant; just as was her cousin-once-removed, King Edward V1, the boy-king. He too, strongly favoured Protestantism over Catholicism, much to the chagrin of his half-sister Mary Tudor. Edward was however, determined to carry on his father Henry V111's legacy, and retain for the people, the new Anglican religion, referred to as Protestantism. As in all other periods in history, religion was a bone of contention between those who held the most power, and in the Middle Ages, this was even more so.

However, in order to find out how Lady Jane Grey took centre stage in the religion-torn sixteenth century, we're going to have to look further back in time, to see how it all came about. The early Middle Ages in England was a time of turmoil and confusion, and in order to appreciate Lady Jane Grey's situation on that fateful afternoon when she was told she would be queen, the events that led up to it are important. Please bear with me whilst together, we look at royal turmoil in those dark Middle Ages in England

****

The Wars of the Roses in England, which would last for thirty years, came at a time when the country was still reeling from its Hundred Years War with France. It was the late 1450s, and sadly for the country, a mentally deficient king sat on the throne. He was the weak and witless King Henry V1, who was subject to repeated bouts of madness, at which times, everyone around him had to shelter from his frenzied outbursts; his catatonic periods of silence, when he could hardly speak, were also daunting or those around him. Lancastrian Henry had usurped the crown from his cousin, Richard 11, and was immediately faced with the enormous challenge of a country divided, and of a people starving and exhausted; all because of the long war with the French. In fact, much of the 14th century was not a good time to be an Englishman; the royal coffers were empty, and the ranks between the nobility had broken down. There were also many unemployed soldiers who'd ventured into the countryside to find paid work, now the war with France was over. The Hundred Years War had undoubtedly left England in dire straits. Society, once reasonably intact, had broken down, and there was little protection offered by the Law; suffering most from this was of course, the common man. All levels of society suffered in one way or another - from the highest to the lowest; from the royal courtiers to the farm labourer. Decency and honest were at their lowest ebb, with each man taking what he could, and giving nothing back. The picture looked bleak indeed for England!

Ironically, Henry V1 was the last King of England, who could lay claim to both the warring countries – England and France, but this claim was the reason why the devastating Hundred Years War had lingered on so long. At the start of Henry's reign, nearly all of France still belonged to England, but by the end of his reign, only Calais was controlled by the English. It was a lot to lose in a relatively short reign, but for the record, Henry's claims on France were sound, as his right to rule came from his French grandfather Charles. Unfortunately, Henry never had the capability to fight for his rights; as a ruler, he lacked all of the qualities needed in a strong monarch, and his country knew it. He was neither physically nor mentally equipped to rule, and for most of his reign, he depended completely on his French wife, Margaret, who was the polar opposite of her husband. She was smart, determined, but also cunning and controlling, and therefore, she was inevitably disliked by the English. During several of Henry's bouts of acute depression, she even ruled in his place, and she did it well, making sure life was as difficult as possible for those damned Yorkists, who had always had their eyes on the crown of England. Richard, Duke of Gloucester especially needed close watching, as he was forever sniffing around the Lancastrian court, trying his best to claim the Crown as his own. In fact, as well as Margaret, he too acted as a regent during some the king's lapses, but Margaret was soon to learn he couldn't be trusted.

Following a particularly bad period of catatonic schizophrenia, when Henry's mind had completely shut down for months, Richard was in control and made all necessary decisions. Margaret hated such times, as she knew what the man was capable of; in time however, her husband was finally declared 'fit to rule' again – even if in name only. The England he'd known before, had changed significantly – and for the worse - whilst it had been under Richard's watch. As Regent, Richard had overseen all internal affairs, as well as foreign matters, hence it could be argued, he was the one who really lost most of France. History however, was to record the loss as Henry's, as it took place during his reign, and at a time when the courageous, but 'French' Margaret of Anjou, was hated by the people, and treated accordingly. Richard of Gloucester took decisions for the country, many of which were not good, but all of which unfairly rebounded on 'the mad king'

Henry and Margaret had one son. Edward of Westminster, the Prince of Wales. Being an only child, he was the apple of his parent's eyes, but life couldn't have been easy for him, with a warring country, a mother hated by the people, and a father who suffered from bouts madness. How confused must he have been? On one occasion, when Henry was having one of his seizures, and the Duke of Gloucester had placed him in the Tower of London, allegedly for his own safety, young Edward attempted to regain his father's throne from Richard, and rule in his father's place. Unfortunately, the young man was killed at the very young age of seventeen, fighting a ferocious battle at Tewksbury in 1475. He died at the hands of a Yorkist's sword, whilst his army fought an enemy, much greater in number, and who were professionally trained – unlike his sparse Lancastrian forces.

Richard then had the audacity to have himself proclaimed king in 1471. It had been easy for this, as there was no opposition, and the imprisoned Henry had no idea what was going on in his country; his only son was dead, and his wife was hated by the country. Both Richard and his wife Anne Neville, had been crowned in Westminster Abbey, at the very time he'd imprisoned Henry, with the most likely intention being to assassinate him later.

Now, Richard turned his attention to Margaret of Anjou, the woman who'd always been a thorn in his flesh. She was immediately banished to live in France, where she was to remain for the rest of her life. In an act of barbarous cruelty, Richard sentenced her to walk through the streets of London in ragged, torn clothing, intended to humiliate her as much as possible. Of course, the local people enjoyed the disliked woman's torture, and pelted the her with the worst of rotting vegetables and fruit. En-masse, the people were a vicious and threatening mob, who attacked the pitiful woman with no pity.

Perhaps our sympathy for the Margaret should be tempered however, by a popular story told at the time, about an earlier occasion when she was still a reigning monarch. The Lancastrians had captured two Yorkist spies, and as Henry was once again suffering from delusions, it was Margaret who was to decide their fate. The woman's love of power was evident, when she turned to her then seven-year old son Edward, and asked what he would have her do with the men. The little boy said immediately, and as many an excitable child might do, "Why mother, you should have their heads cut off." Delighted by his response, she ordered the two men to be taken away, and executed within the hour – and so it was done! Perhaps the English people were right after all, in their opinion of the French queen, but then, people's opinions 'may vary'!

In fairness to Margaret, it's only right to give her credit for concealing her husband's mental illness for so long, and it was also attributed to her, that she'd masterminded many of the Lancastrian alliances, needed to fend off the Yorkists. It was she, who was responsible for raising an army, and for helping to orchestrate the return of her kidnapped husband (kidnapped by the Yorkists) and place him back on the throne. She was apparently as beautiful as she was cunning, and certainly played an important part in the Wars of the Roses. However, her last experience of the English must have left her with a permanently bad taste in her mouth.

Now Richard 111 had England in his grasp, except of course, for his brother Edward 1V's sons, the two young princes, Edward and Richard, who had a much stronger claim to the throne than Richard's own. The other Edward – Edward of Westminster - he with the strongest claim of all - had been neatly tidied away in the mud of Tewksbury.

No, the two young princes were the only fly in the ointment left remaining, and now, Richard turned his attention to them. It was a dangerous, unstable time, and many eyes were on the throne, and also on the two princes who now lived in the Tower of London, where they'd been placed ***'for their own safety.*** Richard must have been nervous, sitting on such a shaky throne!

He had played his cards wisely in enhancing his authority; before becoming king, he'd had himself named as the Constable of England in 1469, as well as the Chief Justice of North Wales, then becoming Chief Steward and Chamberlain of the whole of Wales; and by 1471, he'd also gained the title of Great Chamberlain and Lord High Admiral of England. Obviously power-crazy, and with a keen eye to the future, he was amazingly successful at building his empire, and as there was little left to achieve, he next took the throne, and disposed with the whole royal family of Lancaster. Now, Richard 111 would be the last Plantagenet King of England. Unfortunately for him, he would also be the last English king to die in battle – but that was still in the future, and he had other dastardly deeds to commit before that came to pass.

Now, he could focus on his two young nephews, still in the Tower. At the beginning, the boys were allowed to play in the Tower's private gardens, and their rooms were comfortable with servants on-call;– they could often be seen playing their child-like games, but all this was to change, and eventually, the garden privileges were withdrawn, and their personal servants were made to disappear. The comfortable Tower bedrooms became cold, uncomfortable cells for the children.

There was no doubt that Richard saw the princes as a threat, so he then worked hard on Parliament to declare the boys illegitimate, his claim being, that a question hung over the princes' father, and his first betrothed wife. Richard claimed the children' father had not been free to marry their mother, and this mix-up cast a shadow over the boys' legitimacy. He argued that they should be removed from the line of succession, but Parliament didn't listen, as there was no proof to his claim. So, that avenue was closed.

The existence of the boys continued to torment Richard – and he did what he considered necessary. Both youngsters disappeared from the Tower, and were never seen again! Inevitably, many fingers were pointed straight at the self-appointed king, as the only person who would benefit from their disappearance. Were they murdered and their bodies whisked away out of London? How and when could it have happened? Murder couldn't be proved at the time, nor at any time since, but it seemed a likely, and very pragmatic act, for Richard to take. Whatever the truth about the two boys was, they were never seen again, and it was whispered by many that a weighted cushion over their faces had been the instrument of assassination.

So, Richard 111, cruelly known as Crookback, was sitting squarely on the throne at last. He and Anne Neville had one son, Edward of Middleham , the Duke of York, and no time was lost in declaring the boy as heir to his father's throne. This however, was not meant to be, as the young Edward died at the age of just ten, and no subsequent children were born to the couple. Richard 111 really would be the last Plantagenet King of England.

He had been reigning for two years, when one Henry Tudor sailed into Milford Haven from his exile in France. He had come to claim the English throne for himself. Richard and Henry Tudor both had a legitimate claim to the

English throne, as they were both descended from a previous ruler, King, Edward 111. When he left France, Henry Tudor had gathered together an army to invade the shores of England, and was hell-bent on taking the throne from Richard. (Whom he often referred to as 'The Usurper').

Only two years on the throne, Richard was well aware his grasp was tenuous at best, and he knew he always had to be prepared for a challenge. In the Middle Ages, there were many secretive eyes watching a king's every move, in the hope he would slip up, and the throne would become ready for the taking. Henry Tudor was one of these people!

He challenged Richard formally, and the battle was scheduled for the 22nd August, 1485. The two armies were to meet on open ground, just three miles from Market Bosworth. It would be known as the Battle of Bosworth, and if Henry was successful, it would finally bring to an end the country-destroying Wars of the Roses, which had lasted for so long.

For many years, the Yorkists and Lancastrians had played musical chairs with the throne of England – first one side held the power, and then it was the turn of the other. Although the war actually lasted for over thirty years, there were approximately only twenty significant battles during that time, with the most gruesome taking place in 1461, when King Edward V1 was on the throne. It was fought near the village of Towton, and took place during a blinding snowstorm, with the numbers involved on both sides, reported as being more than 80,000 men. The ferocious battle lasted for an incredible ten hours, and it was reported that the nearby river, actually ran red with blood. At least 40,000 men died in that battle, a greater number than any other battle ever fought in Britain.

However, the next challenge for Richard 111 was the Battle of Bosworth or Bosworth Field – this would be the battle that finally brought an end to the War of the Roses.

Henry Tudor, the Earl of Richmond, had landed his ships at Milford Haven, and as he moved through Wales, his army grew in number. When he finally arrived at Bosworth, it was reckoned he had an army of five thousand men, made up significantly of those tired of the Lancastrian-Yorkist antagonists. His men were not trained soldiers, whereas Richard, had eight thousand fighting men, fresh, trained, and ready to do battle. There could be no question as to who was likely to win.

The location agreed for the battle was actually a large field, just three miles from the village of Bosworth Market. The year was 1485 – a date when the people could either lose its last Plantagenet king , and watch a victorious Henry Tudor don the crown of England – or retain the usurper Richard as their king, and see the butchered Henry Tudor dragged from the field. To the people in the villages and towns, it made little difference.

On the August morning, King Richard 111 rode into battle, dressed in full armour, and with his vizor pulled down over his face; he was determined to lead his men from the front. On top of his steel helmet, he wore the crown of England, so his men could follow his movements on the field. With the greater number of troops, Richard was better placed than his opponent, but it was quickly noted that several groups of his army actually changed sides during the battle, and some (in fact a great many) remained along the field edges, unmoving, but watching. They were actually refusing to join the battle, as it was a commonly-held belief at the time, that the people in the country believed the deaths of the princes in the Tower should undoubtedly be laid at Richard's door; and as many believed the older boy was the rightful heir to the throne, they decided to make a stand against what they saw as an injustice, This then, were the silent, watching horsemen sitting along the edges of the battlefield. Many had feigned a loyalty to Richard, just to see him lose at Bosworth; they believed it a suitable punishment for the Crookback King. They'd turned up at the battle scene, luring him into a false belief they were on his side, before blatantly turning against him. It wasn't a chivalrous thing to do, but it was done nonetheless, and Henry Tudor took full advantage of his 'enemy's 'turncoat' behaviour, and continued to rally his own men forward.

In desperation, King Richard moved to attack Henry in one-to-one combat, but he suddenly found he was surrounded by a circle of enemy soldiers. In a split second, he was hacked down by several swords, and he fell to the ground, where blows continued to flail onto his already-injured body. He was also badly beaten about the head, most likely to ensure the crown would fall to the ground. It rolled under a nearby bush, and lay there in the mud. The last Plantagenet had died in a moment, and when his men saw what had happened, they lost control of the battle, and very quickly, it was all over. Worse was done then, as Henry's men savagely stripped Richard of his clothes, before throwing his naked body over a horse; a laughing soldier whacked the horse's rump, and it galloped off with Richard's bleeding body hanging to one side. Another soldier spotted the fallen crown, and placed it ceremoniously on Henry Tudor's head. A spontaneous cheer went up, and the battle was over; the House of Tudor was established at that moment, and would last for the next 118 years.

Subsequently, history agreed that Richard could have won the battle with his larger, well-trained army, but the belief that he'd murdered the young boys who were the rightful heirs, was just too much for honourable men to bear. His deeds had come back to haunt him, and he suffered the consequences of his actions. The people obviously knew more about the things he'd done just to better himself , and they resented them. Many knew he'd brought about the death of Henry V1, as well as the cruel exile of Margaret of Anjou. Amazingly enough, even in medieval England, Crookback's crimes were too heinous for people to stomach, and it was said that he lost his crown, and the battle, because he'd lost the heart and support of the people. It seems 'Ye reap as ye sow' has always been relevant!

As a point of interest, the name 'Wars of the Roses' actually came about long after the struggle was over – not until the nineteenth century in fact. In reality, neither side used roses as their emblem at the time, although the white rose had long been associated with the Yorkists. The battling sides were of course, the House of York and the House of Lancaster, with both aspiring to wear the crown of England; York had its white rose, whilst Lancaster chose the red rose. After the Battle of Bosworth and Henry Tudor's subsequent marriage to Elizabeth of York, the two roses were combined as one, and became today's easily-recognisable emblem of the House of Tudor – the Tudor Rose, with five outer red petals, and five inner white ones. Perhaps not a very realistic rose, but a rose nonetheless, and it would remain the emblem of England's monarchs for the next 118 years. When Queen Elizabeth 1st died childless, the throne passed to the Scottish house of Stuart – and with no battle! Henry V11 had ensured both houses became as one, when he married Elizabeth, Edward 1V's daughter, and made the declaration that any children from their marriage, would be heirs to a united England. The Tudor line was well and truly established!

The year was now 1537 AD, and England had been ruled for several years by the Tudor king. It had been a reasonably peaceful time for the people of England, with no further turmoil between the Lancastrians and the Yorkists, after all, under Henry V11, they were allegedly one and the same. The Tudor hold on the throne however, was not as secure as Henry V11 would have liked (It was after all, a very new royal House), and a very close eye still had to be kept on the French, who were always claiming that Calais belonged to them. The first Tudor union produced two sons and two daughters, so tenure of the throne was as secure as possible.

England most certainly did benefit from having Henry Tudor as its monarch. He was cautious and canny, and before he died, the royal coffers were healthier than they'd been for a very long time. He was an intelligent, well-educated man, and one whose intention from the start of his reign, was to make England a better place for its people. He changed the ways legal judgments were made; no longer did local sheriffs decide the rights and wrongs of legal cases brought before them, but rather the king created several Justices of the Peace, who had the power to maintain public order in areas under each jurisdiction. The country gradually became a fairer and safer place to live, although this would be a high hill to climb. Nevertheless, he made sure it all changed for the better. He also encouraged, and financially supported the navigator and explorer, John Cabot and his sons, in their voyages of discovery; by doing this, he was also successful in raising England's profile across the world. He had an open mind to new ideas, and welcomed foreign academics to his court, to discuss philosophy and theory. Unfortunately, he could sometimes be rather dour, and didn't exactly ooze personal charm, nor did he have good looks. (He was rather short and spindly). He was however, a decent man and a good Catholic, two attributes he encouraged his people to emulate.

The couple's eldest son was Arthur, the Prince of Wales, and he was set to inherit a much richer treasury than his father had done. The royal coffers were over-flowing, when young Prince Arthur married into one of the most influential families in Europe – he married Katherine of Aragon in Westminster Abbey. They were both just fifteen years old. It wasn't until six months later, that the two innocent youngsters were forced to share a bed - an incident that would in many years' time, evolve into one of the greatest 'bones of contention' in the Court, with the result being, that a brand-new religion would emerge across the whole of England.

Meanwhile however, the two fifteen-year-olds were slowly getting to know each other. They'd only met for the first time two weeks before they married, and life was just beginning for both of them. Katherine was a lovely young girl, with dark eyes and reddish-blond hair. She was a princess in her own right, being the daughter of King Ferdinand of Spain, the man responsible for bringing about the successful amalgamation of several smaller Spanish kingdoms, including Castile, and for uniting them as one great country – Spain itself. Henry V11 had received from Ferdinand a large Dowry when Katherine had come to England, and the sum of 200,000 Ducats had changed hands, making Henry Tudor a very happy man.

Everything seemed set fair for the future of the monarchy, and then the Tudor bubble burst. After only five short months of marriage, Prince Arthur died suddenly, almost certainly from the Sweating Sickness, which was rife across the country at the time. Katherine also caught the fever, as the two had slept in the same bed for those few nights, and caught the sickness from each other. It was known to be a killer, but the stronger Katherine survived the ordeal, and somehow shook off the illness, as though it was nothing more than a head cold. Arthur however, was slightly built, almost frail, and had a weak constitution, so after only a short illness, the heir to the English throne died. Except for the ladies who'd accompanied her from Spain, poor Katherine was left a teenage widow, in a foreign land, and with a language she couldn't speak. Suddenly no-one had time for her, and it seemed she was no longer of any value. She was forced to live in various houses of no particular status, and was passed around from pillar to post. She was treated as little more a nuisance now that Arthur was dead, and a penniless nuisance at that. She was given no new clothes, and her household was often short of food.

Henry V11 and his wife Elizabeth, were too devasted by the loss of their son, to worry about a penniless princess. Even as he'd lain in his sick-bed, no one had expected Arthur to die, as if a child lived to be fifteen, there was no reason to suspect he might die. Fevers were unfortunately the killers of children in the Middle Ages, but reaching fifteen usually meant a few more years at least. Alas, it was not the case with Arthur. The new dynasty's future stability suddenly seemed precarious, and Henry was reminded again of just how young his dynasty was. Of course, there was a second son, who had never dreamed one day he might be king – he was called Henry Tudor, after his father, and suddenly 'the Spare' was thrust into the limelight. Now, there hangs an incredible tale; a tale about the most disruptive, arrogant, self-serving king that ever there was.

He'd been only nine years of age when his brother died, and he had to wait another eight years before he was called to his dying father's bedside. The founder of the House of Tudor had only minutes to live, and desperately needed to speak with his heir. Henry knelt by the bed, and asked if his father was in need of anything. The dying king managed to raise his head slightly, and his words were clear, " My Son, as I leave this world behind, and pass safely into our Lord's arms, I leave the throne of England in your young hands. You must care for the people of this country, and safe-guard their daily life from enemies at home, or from across the seas." The old man was forced to stop talking, and the young man clasped his hand gently, telling him not to try to talk any more, but there was much still to say, "Henry, I know I leave England in a good state, and you must ensure this doesn't change; to do this, I need your promise that you will marry your brother's widow, Katherine. Only this way, will Spain continue to act as our friend, and also allow us to keep the dowry her father paid when she married Arthur. Katherine is a good Catholic, with many important relatives, who will assuredly support you with the Holy Father in Rome." Now he really had to pause for breath before asking again for his son's promise to marry Katherine. Henry made it easy for him, and immediately gave his solemn oath that he would marry the Princess from Aragon. He'd always thought highly of her anyway.

The old king nodded his head very slightly, and typical of a man who'd lived his life parsimoniously, spending wisely, and only when it was absolutely necessary, his last words were, "Remember as well Henry, that if you fail to marry Katherine, you'll have to repay 200,000 Ducats to the Spanish king, Ferdinand. I managed to hold off when Arthur died but he'll come back again with outstretched hands, when he hears of my death." The old man was cautious with money to the very end!

King Henry V11 breathed his last, leaving a kingdom to a seventeen-year-old boy, who lost no time in carrying out his father's dying wish, and on 11 June 1509, he escorted Katherine from the Tower of London, where he'd placed her in palatial quarters. She was twenty-three years old, and he was just seventeen. He didn't look seventeen, as he was a mountain of a man; six feet and two inches tall, and handsome, with curly, blond hair. He was known for loving fun, games, dancing and sports, and the over-flowing royal coffers left him by his father, soon began to disappear at speed, as Henry knew how to enjoy himself.

Like his father had been before him, the new king was extremely well-educated, and spoke several languages, including Spanish. He enjoyed reading, especially poetry, and he played the lute beautifully, and even wrote his own music. The song 'Green Sleeves' was of course, attributed to him, although it has been suggested it was actually written for another, and later Queen.

The marriage was successful and the couple seemed happy. Despite several miscarriages however, Katherine produced only one, live child, Mary - and no living sons. This would prove to be Henry's worst nightmare, and considering the difficulties his father had in establishing the House of Tudor, it wasn't surprising that Henry V111 desperately needed a male heir to secure the future of the dynasty. He needed that heir badly, and with the passing of many years, and one miscarriage after another, he looked for someone to blame, as it certainly couldn't be himself! And so, it was after twenty-three years of a relatively happy marriage, Henry eventually fell out of love with Katherine, and put her aside; Katherine's fate was sealed. Over the years, it's often been said that she was Henry's only true love, and had she been able to produce a living male heir, his later five marriages would never have happened, but then that can only ever be speculation.

First seeking permission from the Pope in order to marry his late brother's wife, he sent Cardinal Wolsey, to ask the Holy Father to for an annulment of the marriage, or to give him a dispensation. The Pope refused Henry's request however, despite the fact he'd previously awarded the English king the honour of being called 'Defender of the Faith' – the Catholic faith that was. It made no difference however, the Pope still refused to do what he wanted. So, Henry instructed his own scribes to seek out certain ancient documents, written by the much-earlier scribe, Geoffrey of Monmouth, who'd originally found manuscripts which declared England not to be a mere country, but rather an Empire. This then meant that, as an Emperor, King Henry V111 of England could claim he was subservient to no earthly man, but only God himself, and certainly not to some far away Pope in Italy. It was a known fact that an Emperor's power was far greater than that of a king, so goaded on by his first minister, Thomas Cromwell, Henry declared a new Church of England, of which he was the head. The Anglican Church of England was born, and he could rid himself of his troublesome wife Katherine, and marry the new love of his life, Lady Anne Boleyn. He immediately instructed the Archbishop of Canterbury, and Thomas Cranmer, to declare his marriage to Katherine null and void - annulled in fact, as though it had never happened in the first place. It was the greatest humiliation he could have heaped upon the woman, for whom he'd once declared to be the love of his life. So, enraptured with Anne Boleyn was he, that he actually married her before the Archbishop had actually had time to annul his first marriage.

And so, his tumultuous reign continued. In two years, he'd tired of the woman for whom he'd broken ties with Rome, and had her executed for treason; she too, had failed to produce a male heir. He then married for a third time, and glory be to God, Jane Seymour gave him the son he craved, but in doing so, died within a few days of the birth. It was clearly seen that the king mourned Jane, and for some time, seemed sad and depressed, but after a further two years, he took a fourth wife – a princess from Germany called Anne of Cleeves. He'd agreed to marry her, without first meeting her, but when they did meet – and marry - he found he disliked her so much, that he divorced her within six months. She didn't mind however, as she thought little of him as well; in fact, she said she found him repulsive, and by agreeing amicably to a divorce, she became the king's most wealthy, most privileged, most cherished ' sister ', and they remained friends until his death. He broke the mould in choosing his next wife, as he chose a sweet, and very young girl, called Catherine Howard, who was a close relative of Anne Boleyn. Despite Catherine's tender years (It's thought she was about sixteen, whilst he was forty-nine) she had lived a very full and promiscuous life before coming to Court; a life which was alleged to continue after her marriage to the king.

"Treason! Treason! How could she do this to me? I'll not bear it. No, I will not." He was speaking or shouting at Archbishop Cranmer, who had been the one to tell him of his wife's adultery. "I'll not stand for it Thomas – it'll be the executioner's block for her – maybe even the axe, rather than the sword, as she deserves nothing better." Saying these words must have broken his heart, as they'd been married for one year only, and he still thought the world of her. Her proven adultery however, allowed him no leeway in the matter, and treason had only one punishment – death. He was at Hampton Court, in the chapel, when he learned what Catherine had done, and he rode away that very day back to Whitehall, leaving her behind. He was never to see his young wife again. She, on the other hand, on learning she was to be arrested, ran screaming down the long gallery , begging for mercy, but Henry was no longer there to hear her cries. (It's said Catherine can still be seen running down the same long gallery at Hampton Court, screaming and crying!)

Henry was now fifty-two years of age. He was obese and ill, and suffered with many health problems. He'd had a jousting accident many years before, and from that day, it was said his character underwent a huge change, and he became a completely different man, much more cruel and unforgiving. When he was injured, he'd been unconscious for two hours, which seemed to damage his brain, but it was his legs that caused him the most pain as he grew older. He'd injured his leg in the accident, and the wound remained an open sore for the rest of his life. With the passing of the years, and the steady weight gain, plus his failing health, he again looked for a wife – a comforting wife, who could nurse him. His choice this time was an older lady of good birth. She had a pleasant, caring personality, someone he believed would take good care of him. His small, beady eyes had fallen on Lady Latimer, Catherine Parr, who was thirty-one years old, and who'd been widowed twice before; and she'd nursed both husbands. Yes, she would do nicely! It didn't matter that she didn't want to marry him, as she loved another (Sir Thomas Seymour, the late Queen Jane Seymour's brother), but as was usual, the king gave her no option, and they were married on 12th July 1543 in the royal chapel at Hampton Court Palace. The marriage would last for almost five years, although it was never consummated because of the king's health. She was one lucky woman therefore, to be needed for her nursing skills only!

When Henry's only son, Prince Edward, was just three years of age, he was betrothed to the young Princess Mary of Scots, in a diplomatic attempt to bring Scotland under England's rule, and also to end once and for all, the on-going years of skirmishes and battles between the two countries. It was not to be however, and the betrothal was subsequently cancelled; the young prince was then betrothed to Henry 11 of France's daughter, the Princess Elizabeth. This too fell through, and the boy was allowed to grow un-betrothed and probably quite happy, to the tender age of nine.

Henry V111 died 28th January 1547, and at the end, he had lost the power of speech – but he had already made it clear that Edward, his only legitimate son, was the undisputed heir to the throne. The nine-year-old boy was intelligent and well-read, and also spoke Latin and Greek fluently. Physically however, he was not robust, and grew frailer the older he became. He was enthusiastic in what he believed, and was an ardent Protestant, believing the Anglican church to be the only true religion.

Throughout what was to be a short life, he quarrelled continuously with his older sister Mary, who was as ardent a Catholic, as he was a Protestant. Her faith in her chosen religion continued, and she celebrated the Catholic Mass in private, something Edward tolerated by turning a blind eye to what she did. Celebrating the Catholic mass had been declared an illegal practice, but if Mary kept a low profile, Edward was content – but not happy. As siblings, they were not close, and never had been, the age difference being so great. His other sister Elizabeth was more of a peacemaker, and was popular with everyone. Like Edward, she was of the Protestant faith, and for a while, she lived in the Seymour household with Catherine Parr and Thomas Seymour. (now married and a very Protestant family) This however, was brought to a quick end, when it was noticed that Thomas Seymour appeared to be flirting and trying to take advantage of the princess, and the Maison-de-trois was speedily brought to an end.

Catherine Parr had one child by Seymour, but sadly the lady died in childbirth, and her daughter just seemed to disappear – mainly through lack of interest in her well-being. What happened to her, is not known, and with the high rate of infant mortality at the time, it's quite likely the baby died.

`The new, still very young, and academically-gifted King Edward V1, was determined to protect the relatively new Protestant religion. He was clever beyond what his years might imply, but so young, he could only rule under a Regency Council, overseen first by his uncle, Edward Seymour, first Duke of Somerset, and then three years later, by John Dudley, first Duke of Warwick. There was much contention, and vying for power, amongst the Regency Council members, but particularly amongst the Seymour family, who would continuously bend their young protégé's ears, in order to gain more favours. It must have been difficult for the young boy, being pulled in different directions, and he was aware that his people were also suffering, because of the Council's mis-guidance of internal affairs, and the effects it had on the common man. This 'to-ing-and-fro-ing' probably affected the young king, and may even have hastened the onset of bad health. He had had measles when he was younger, and it's likely he was left with a lingering deterioration of his immune system. He developed a rapid and fatal case of Tuberculosis, and had no strength to fight it off. The scholarly boy, still managed to keep accurate, detailed, and daily accounts of all that was happening at court, and in the country – accounts still available to this day. Edward V1 died at the age of fifteen on the 6 July 1553, whilst resting at the Palace of Palentia, on the outskirts of London. The country went into deep mourning for the young king, who'd died before it even got to know him.

His sister Mary's absolute devotion to the Catholic faith, had caused him great concern in his last few months, and was the reason that forced him to make a significant change in the line of succession. It wasn't until his health had deteriorated so much that he was advised his days were numbered, that he asked his private secretary to bring him his will. Edward had already decided how the succession would go, and he had removed the names of his two sisters, Mary and Elizabeth from the line. This was despite the fact that his father had named them as the heirs, were his son to die without issue. Young Edward was determined that the devoted Catholic Mary, should not be queen, and he believed too, that the Lady Elizabeth was weak-willed and would undoubtedly allow the country to revert to the old religion. He turned therefore, to his three cousins once removed, who were directly descended from his grandfather, Henry V11.

In the previously prepared will, he had taken his freshly-inked quill, and changed the meaning in the document – a change that would lead to many unnecessary deaths in the near future, and would also cause great confusion in both the court, and the country. The will had originally named the three cousins, Jane, Catherine and Mary in that order, as his successors, but by adding in his own hand, the words 'and then' into the relevant sentence, the will then read, my successors to be 'my cousin Jane and her male heirs, **and**

then Catherine and Mary Grey. That seemingly small correction, changed the meaning completely, and was further proof of the young king's cunning and intelligence. The Lady Jane Grey was to be his immediate successor, with any children she had, coming after her. A clever, and rather devious way, of getting exactly what he wanted, which was that only a Protestant would sit on the English throne. And so, holding the quill in one hand, and his head resting on the other, he had mused over the document for just a moment, before adding those momentous words, **and then.** Lady Jane Grey was to be the next queen, by decree of Edward V1 of England. (The original, changed document can be seen to this day, the words written by the king's own hand.)

Edward must have believed he'd tied the hands of his half-sisters, but he didn't reckon with Princess Mary's determination, as well as her promise to herself that she'd pay back her father for his cruel treatment of her saintly mother, the Catholic Katherine of Aragon. Mary had waited patiently for the day when everything would come full circle, and she would take her rightful place on the English throne, as the legitimate heir, and she wasn't going to allow Edward's devious act to spoil that.

As recorded in King Henry V111's will, he had named his daughter Mary, as his heir, should Edward die without issue, then, should Mary also die childness, Elizabeth would be next in line. He refrained from inferring she too, might die without issue, as it must have seemed unlikely that all of his children would fail to produce an heir. Edward had therefore, completely ignored his father's last wishes.

Edward did die childless of course, as did both Mary and Elizabeth. The next in direct line then, should have been Mary Queen of Scots, but by the time Elizabeth had finished dealing with her, and had her head removed from her shoulders, Mart would have had no interest in the English throne. So, when the Virgin Queen finally passed away, the English throne 'fell' neatly into the lap of King James of Scotland, the Queen of Scot's only son. 'Oh, what a tangled web we weave, when others practice to deceive!'

From all of this, we come at last to the tale of Lady Jane Grey, whose story would never have come about without the events that led up to 'that fateful day at Syon House, when her father told her she was to be Queen of England.' Those events I've already provided for your information.

****

The Wars of the Roses, along with the Hundred Years War with France were both forgotten; the mad Henry V1 was long dead, and after that death, England had lost most of France, except for Calais: the evil Richard 111 had died in the mud of Bosworth Field: the pitiful princes in the Tower of London had disappeared: the astute kingship of Henry V11 and his parsimonious ways stopped at his death; and thereafter, then it was time for Henry V111's larger-than-life reign, during which he ordered the desecration of churches and monasteries, he married six wives, and executed two of them: and finally, we come to the doomed reign of the young, and very Protestant Edward V1, who was doomed from the day he contracted measles as a child. And there you have it, in that very potted of history, we've finally arrived at the sad story of a young girl, who became queen, something I first mentioned at the beginning of this tale – the story of seventeen-year-old Lady Jane Grey.

It took all of the above to happen, before this young girl, the eldest daughter of the 1st Duke of Suffolk and Lady Frances Brandon - could play her part in English history. Her mother Frances, was the daughter of King Henry V11's sister, the Princess Mary. (So many Marys, I hear you say!) Jane Grey therefore belonged to the privileged classes of the country, and was close to the royal family, nowhere close enough however, to be considered as a contender for the throne of England.

Jane had grown up with her two younger sisters, Elizabeth and Mary, and was born either in 1536 or 1537, and probably in the month of October, but as records of her birth were not kept, this can only be an assumption. This lack of records, was an indication that Jane's birth was not considered significant by her parents. What a surprise they must have had on learning their eldest daughter was King Edward's heir. As was expected in such a high-status family, the daughters were reasonably, but not excessively educated, as well as trained in the overseeing of the running of a great house. The Grey family were ambitious for their daughters, and planned their places in society would be as advantageous as possible, but the throne of England was more than they could ever have imagined.

Jane in particular, was academically-inclined; she was known for always having her nose in a book, and from the age of three, she was fluent in Latin and Greek. The famous academic John Aylmer was engaged as her tutor, teaching her general subjects, but particularly Hebrew. She much preferred the sanctity of a quiet schoolroom, as opposed to the fresh air of the outdoors – and as for sports, she was totally disinterested.

The picture we see is of a rather serious young woman, who grew up in the luxurious mansion of Brandgate Park in Leicester – near to Charnwood. The Grey family had lived there for more than 200 years, and Lady Frances was known to be very proud of her royal connections, and it was said she never missed an opportunity to flaunt those connections in front of guests. Both she and her husband were very strict with their daughters, and Jane would often complain about the unfair restrictions placed on her as the eldest. So, we have a serious, studious young woman, with no particular interest in the Crown of England, but who was deeply entrenched in the Anglican Church of Protestantism, as were the rest of her family.

At the age of ten, and in line with the practices of the nobility, Jane was sent to live in the Seymour household, with Thomas and Catherine Parr, his new wife. Henry V111 was dead, and his sixth wife Catherine, had at last been able to marry the man she'd always loved. Jane was happy living in the Seymour's' household, and Catherine was a caring woman, who helped the young girl with her studies. She was also a very religious woman, and of course a Protestant. Those days were pleasant for Jane, but they were to be short-lived, as Catherine sadly died giving birth to her first child.

On the death of King Henry, Catherine had in her possession many of the royal jewels she'd been given as queen. Edward Seymour was Thomas's older brother, as well as being the 1st Duke of Somerset and Lord Protector of England, positions he'd held during the young Edward's minority. Knowing well, that Thomas would keep such valuables, should his wife die, Edward demanded their return to the Crown. Thomas took this as an affront against his late wife, and refused his brother's request at first, but later, was forced to agree. The two brothers had quarrelled many times before, and disliked each other. Thomas believed he had a score to settle with his older brother, and on Catherine's death, he devised a plan to bring down his brother. In fact, for some time he had been gathering together the necessary finance, needed to pull off a coup against the brother he hated.

To add to the fund, he had actually been blackmailing one Sir William Sharington, the Vice-treasurer of the Bristol Mint. Thomas had discovered that Sharington had been using his office to feather his own nest, and fiddling the books at the Mint. Everything went pear-shaped however, and the State Privy Council learned of Thomas's plans, and ordered him to appear before the Council to explain himself. That put an end to his devious plan to destroy his brother, but he couldn't stop there, as he'd become so frustrated by Edward's successes at Court, that he sometimes thought he was losing his mind. To bring his misery to an end, he raked his brain for a solution to destroy Edward, and regain his peace of mind. Breaking the control his brother had over the young king would be a start. The more he thought about it, the better his plan seemed, and shortly thereafter, Thomas Seymour, 1st Baron of Sudeley, went into action.

One dark and stormy night, when the young king was staying at Hampton Court Palace, Thomas quietly entered the palace. He stealthily crept to where he knew Edward slept, and with a pistol in his hand, he burst into the boy's bedroom. His plan was to kidnap the king, and once under his control, he would then marry the Princess Elizabeth himself, and as she would one day be queen, he would wear the crown by her side. Yes, it was a plan, but perhaps not a great one. Edward's little Spaniel woke up with fright, and began barking at the strange man, who was waving a pistol around pointlessly. Pandemonium broke out, and the sleeping guard in the hall, suddenly burst into the room, and arrested the intruder. The pistol in the man's hand was all the evidence the guard had needed. To produce a weapon in the presence of the king was an act of treason. Thomas Seymour has sealed his own fate, in a very stupid way.

It had always been known that Catherine Parr had been a steadying influence on her husband, and when she died, he seemed to go to pieces. His plan to marry the Princess Elizabeth was to get the power to rid himself of Edward, the hated Lord Protector of England, and the Regent who had control of the king. As Elizabeth's husband, and King of England, he would have had the authority to do exactly that. None of this was even remotely likely, but to Thomas's sick mind, it was a perfect plan. Sibling jealousy had brought him this low!

It was true the princess had a fondness for Seymour, which more than once had made her behave foolishly, but the ever-watchful eye of her nursemaid Cat, thwarted any wicked plans Thomas might have had, when Elizabeth had lived under his roof for a short time.

At his trial, Thomas was found guilty of 33 separate accounts of treason, and a Bill of Attainder was passed against him. He was sentenced to death by his own brother, the hated Edward, because more skulduggery had been discovered at Thomas's feet. He'd apparently been encouraging piracy at sea, the very thing he was supposed to stamp out in his official capacity. He'd also used his position as the young king's uncle, to slip him pocket money, knowing the boy had often complained his allowance from his other uncle, was both niggardly and sometimes withheld all together. He'd tempted the youngster with bribery to show Edward in a bad light. In effect, he was a thorn in his brother's flesh, but in the end, that brother turned the tables on him, and sentenced the Lord High Admiral of the English Navy to death!

Young Edward had recovered from his terrible experience with his late uncle, and realised there was no time to lose, in putting the country's line of succession in order. He had to focus his mind on what was best for England, and who would safeguard the Protestant faith, in fact he actually saw both things as one and the same. He, and his cousin Jane, had been close since they were children, they were genuinely fond of each other, and shared similar academic minds. His choice was an easy one therefore. He had had a troubled childhood, living through his father's numerous matrimonial problems, and spending most of his formative years with only his sister Elizabeth for company. When not with her, he would often visit the Grey family at Bradgate House, and so, his closeness to Jane continued. His concern for England's future was deeply-rooted in his mind however, and he decided to act on his late Uncle Thomas's advice, and draw up a special document, written in his own hand. This document would become known as, 'The Devise of the Succession', and having done it, he felt much better about the country's future.

As his illness grew worse, Edward called for the Succession document to be brought to him, as he wished to make some important alterations. The line of succession had been quite specific in Henry V111's Will; first Edward, then Princess Mary, then Princess Elizabeth – and only then (possibly to ensure Mary Queen of Scots' elimination from the English line). Surprisingly, he considered it wise to add Lady Frances Grey's name, his great grand-niece, and the daughter of his sister Mary. The proposed line of succession on Henry's death was clear, the only changes that could affect the list, was if any of those named had children of their own. As none of them had, and Lady Frances Grey had already completed her three-daughter family, Edward decided to remove the first names, and make Lady Jane Grey his only successor. He was clever, and did this by one stroke of his pen. On his death, it was to be his cousin once-removed, who would sit on the throne, with no questions asked. Jane was a good, staunch Protestant, who would safeguard the future of England. Edward's Will can still be seen today, with his own hand-written amendments.

******* ***********************************

At Bradgate Hall, Lady Jane had returned from the Seymour household, and had just celebrated her fifteenth birthday. She was completely unaware of what was going on at Court. Perhaps at this stage of the young woman's life, it would be good for you to be able to picture her. She wasn't a pompous or pushy young lady, but one whose childhood was on the point of moving from childhood to adulthood. Taken from a painting of her, and written at the time, the words below are interesting:

‘ Jane is very short and thin, but prettily shaped and graceful. She has small features and a well-shaped nose. The mouth is flexible and the lips red. The eyebrows are arched and darker than her hair, which is nearly red. Her eyes are sparkling and reddish-brown in colour.’

She really was a genteel and pleasant girl, who much preferred to fade into the background of any situation – she was liked by all who met her. How things were about to change in her quiet, scholarly life!

A servant had been sent to ask that she attend her parents in the main room downstairs. She didn't often receive such commands, especially in the middle of her studies – this then, must be serious. She wondered if she'd done something wrong, but she could think of nothing. Lady Frances and her husband were sitting in armchairs on either side of the high fireplace. Neither looked up when she came into the room. Yes, she'd been right – something bad was certainly coming!

The Duke didn't beat about the bush, and said straight out, "Jane, it's time you were married, and your mother and I have found the perfect match for you. He is young, handsome, and well positioned at court." Lady Frances was nodding her head approvingly.

Jane said nothing! She didn't know what to say! She'd known this day would come, but perhaps not quite so soon.

"Well, say something Daughter – you heard what I said? Or must I repeat myself?" Jane's parents had always been strict with their children, and had always expected her especially, to do exactly as she was told. She was a good daughter, and had always obeyed their instructions as best she could, now however, she was surprised. This was big, and would change her life forever.

"I hear you well Father, but I would first like to hear the name of my proposed husband. Only then, can I comment on how I feel." She was growing up, and her keen intelligence made her impatient to get to the root of things. Sometimes, this tendency may have made her appear rude, but that was certainly never her intention.

"That is easily remedied daughter, you are to marry Lord Guildford Dudley, youngest son of John Dudley, Duke of Northumberland, who happens to be the most powerful man in the realm, having governed now for more than five years. To marry into such a family, is a great honour, but one well suited to your lineage." He paused, waiting for Jane to appreciate what a good match he'd found for her.

He continued, "Although you are of an age that makes you suitable for marriage, your mother and I have decided you will wait a year before the ceremony. That year will be spent at the royal Court, where you will receive 'the finishing' of a great lady. You are to arrive at Court next week. Is that sufficient information now?"

And it was! Jane was happy to hear she had another year before her marriage, and she wasn't averse to Guildford Dudley as a husband. And so, she went to court, where , as expected, she adopted a low profile, avoiding the many subterfuges and petty-grievances that abounded within the royal household.

In due course, the marriage was arranged. In fact, it was actually to be a triple marriage, and Jane was married to Guildford alongside her sister Catherine with her betrothed, the Earl of Pembroke, and the third couple was the sister of the Duke of Northumberland himself, and her partner. The date was 25th May 1553, and the ceremony took place at Durham Palace. Celebrations went on well into the night, with much merriment amongst the invited guests. Three new marriages demanded such celebrations!

Now a married lady with her own household, Jane settled down to a normal life. She was still only sixteen, and so far, life had treated her well, something that was on the point of changing. She would soon enter a strange and surreal world, after which, she would end up in the Tower of London, but not as a prisoner, rather as a queen in-waiting.

King Edward had, with a stroke of his pen, removed his half-sisters from the direct line of succession. When he died on 6th July 1553, Jane was declared Queen of England only four days later, on 10 July. The Court had suppressed the king's death for three whole days, whilst the line of succession was settled. Despite her initial protest, Jane's father took her immediately to Syon House on the day before the declaration was made public; Syon House was the London residence of her father-in-law, John Dudley, and it was there, she was told for the first time, that she was to be queen. It was recorded at the time, that she recoiled from the suggestion, and said she had no wish for such a thing, also that she was not capable of full-filling such duties. In her surprise and confusion, she apparently, threw herself to the floor and wept bitter tears. Her desperation and fear were quite apparent, but her unwillingness to accept, fell on deaf ears.

She was told by the Royal Council, that it had been her cousin's last wish, and that she had no option, but to accept the honour of wearing the Crown of England. She realised there could be no argument, and her future was a forgone conclusion; and in the end, she succumbed to the pressure. The sixteen-year-old Lady Jane Grey was to be the next queen, and she was to be accompanied in that role, by her new husband, Lord Guildford Dudley.

But where was Mary Tudor at this time? She wasn't the kind to take this insult in her stride; not only an insult, but a huge miscarriage of justice. No, she was ready to fight for her throne, and she immediately set about doing it. She had spent most of her adult life in the South and East of England, where she owned land and several estates, but she'd also spent three years living near the marshes in Wales. She'd mixed with the people, and despite her obsession with Catholicism, she was liked by the common man. Due to friends she still had at court, she learned of her brother's death, and of the Duke of Northumberland's intention to place his daughter-in-law, on the throne. As Edward's death hadn't been made public for three days, it allowed Mary sufficient time to put pen to paper, and send a letter to the Privy Council post-haste. The letter gave specific details, as to why the throne should now pass to her, as her father's legitimate heir. She even went so far as to say she would forgive the Council's involvement with the Duke's plan, if they would listen to reason; but her letter fell was ignored, and the date was set for Lady Jane Grey's coronation.

Not unexpectedly the strong Mary Tudor, immediately gathered together an army of sympathisers in the East, picking up many more as she travelled towards London. As the hours passed, a date was agreed for a battle between Mary's forces, and those of the Duke of Northumberland, John Dudley. As the most powerful man in government, Dudley had wasted no time in arranging his own fighting force, and was ready to face Mary Tudor.

Meanwhile, Lady Jane Grey was awaiting news in the Tower. She turned to her lady-in-waiting, sighed for the tenth time, and said, "Oh Marion, time is dragging so slowly, and I fear for my father-in-law's safety. The Good Lord only knows what the Princess Mary will do when she finds out what is planned. I fear she will fight tooth and nail for the Crown. Do you not agree?"

The girl answered hesitantly, unsure of what to say, "Oh Madam, fear not, Lord Northumberland is even now dealing with the princess, and he will be back soon to declare his success. Sit here Madam, and I'll brush your hair until it shines."

Comforting though the girl was trying to be, she couldn't have been more wrong in what she envisaged. John Dudley was indeed on his way to face Mary Tudor, but before the battle had even begun, a messenger from the Privy Council reached him, to advise that they had overturned the agreement they'd made with him earlier. They were now willing to accept the Princess Mary's claim to the throne.

Dudley raised his arm to strike the unwelcome messenger, "Rubbish! You're talking rubbish man – the Council reassured me they were completely in agreement that the Catholic Princes Mary was not right for the English throne. Get down on your knees and beg my forgiveness for brining such lies to my ears."

The frightened man did fall to his knees, but instead of asking for forgiveness, he repeated what he'd said before, adding, "I wish the message could be different my Lord, but it is what I was told to say." And so, it was in Dudley's absence, the duplicitous Council had indeed changed their mind. Although he wanted to believe the man was wrong, Dudley knew it was not so, and he sent the messenger back to London.

Within a few hours, it was all over, and the young girl waiting in the Tower, was unaware the coup had failed. Her being queen was not now going to happen, and when she finally heard the news, she asked frantically, "What does that mean? What will happen to me? But there was no-one to answer her questions.

As the Princess Mary, or as she was one day to be called, Bloody Mary, was getting closer to London with her entourage, and her army, she was delighted to hear there was no need for a battle. She had received the news from the Privy Council, that a new vote had been taken, and they would now welcome her into the capital as their queen. Also, that the Lady Jane Grey and her husband had been arrested, and were to be charged with treason. Even Mary was surprised by the Council's sudden change of mind, but then perhaps common sense, and a wish to save their own skins, had prevailed. She had a mighty force behind her, and would certainly have even more, before she reached London.

Along with Jane, her husband Guildford, his two brothers, the Archbishop of Canterbury, and Thomas Cranmer were also arrested, and a special Commission Court was quickly set up in London's Guildhall, to be ruled over by the Lord Mayor of London, and the Duke of Norfolk, as well as several members of the Privy Council. There was no surprise when a verdict of guilty was pronounced on all the prisoners, and each one was sentenced to death. Unfortunately, for Jane, she had signed a number of documents with the signature 'Jane the Queen', and in the Council's eyes, that was clear evidence she was willing to assume the Crown of England. Her sentence was different from the others, and she was told she would be ' burned alive on Tower Hill', or beheaded as Queen Mary pleases.' (Burning alive was the traditional English punishment for treason committed by a woman).

Had she signed those documents whilst under duress? Was she guilty of treason as charged? And was the Will of King Edward to be overlooked? Had Jane Grey knowingly accepted the Crown, in the knowledge that the rightful queen was Mary Tudor? Only one person knew the answer to all these questions, and that was Jane herself.

Now her room at the Tower was changed from a suite of chambers, to a bare-walled cell, with just a small bed and a stool. She had blankets however, and one of her ladies-in-waiting was allowed to stay with her, and bring her washing cloths, and food. The mighty had certainly fallen in Jane's case, but the same thing had happened before, to other royal queens imprisoned in the Tower.

The days passed and no date was set for her execution, then a most unfortunate thing happened, as a new rebellion broke out in the north of the country. It was led by one Thomas Wyatt the younger, and it had been started when he'd heard of Queen Mary's plans to marry the Spanish, and

Catholic King Philip. The rebellion may appear disconnected to Jane's position, but alas for her, it was exactly that rebellion that sealed her fate. In protest against what was happening to his daughter, and in an attempt to reverse her situation, Henry Grey Duke of Suffolk, along with his two brothers, joined Wyatt's rebellion. It was an unbelievable and badly-timed act, and was more than enough to make the Privy Council realise that Lady Jane Grey remained a threat, that was never going to go away; and an execution date of 9th February 1554 was immediately planned for both Jane and her husband.

What happened next, was very surprising, as Queen Mary was hesitating over signing her kin's Death Warrant, and she had actually sent her own chaplain, John Feckenham, to visit Jane in her cell; she'd decided if Jane would convert to Catholicism, then she would be allowed to live. The condemned girl was given three days to make her decision, but eventually she told Feckenham that she was unable to comply with the queen's suggestion. As was said at the time, and many times since, although so young, Jane's strength of character and commitment to her own faith, was quite staggering. Whilst facing either the sharp edge of a sword, or the searing flames of a fire, she remained adamant that her choice of faith could only ever be Protestantism – and she was still only seventeen years of age!

Jane refused the Queen's offer, and her amazing strength actually forced the queen's chaplain, Feckenham, to change his opinion of the young woman. Initially he'd been unwilling to visit her at all, but now he admired her, as well as feeling sorry for her. Therefore, the two most unlikely people became close, and he even asked if he could accompany her to the scaffold. Once alone again, she looked around the small cell, and wondered how her husband was bearing up; he too, was very young, at only 21 or 22, also far too young to die, and in his case, for what?

He'd done absolutely nothing, except marry the girl the late king had chosen as his successor. She had pleaded to be allowed to see him, but her request was denied, and the two executions were arranged to take place on the same day - the 12th February. And she was still only seventeen!

And so, the day arrived. Just picture the view Jane must have had from the small window of her cell. It looked out over a well-trodden path, where that day, people would have been walking to-and-fro, going about their business. That business being to get a good view of what was about to happen. It was to be a big day, and many on-lookers were jostling with each other in the crowd. After all, a royal execution didn't happen often, especially now that Henry V111 was gone, and anyway, people were always interested in the macabre.

She was cold, and her maid wrapped a warm shawl around her frail shoulders, "There Madam, you rest in your chair, and soon it'll all be over, no more fear or dread." The maid knew she was stepping beyond her role, to speak to her mistress in that way, but as she watched Jane, sitting there, she saw that she was trembling, and desperately wanted to comfort her. Suddenly, a rumbling sound was heard on the path outside, and before the maid could move to block Jane's view, a cart came into sight, and the manacled figure of Guildford Dudley passed the window. It was still early, but the young man had been taken from his cell, and outside the grounds, on Tower Hill, where public executions were carried out. Of course, a crowd had already gathered – it was after all a spectacle to be enjoyed!

Without fuss, the young man was beheaded, and his remains brought back inside the Tower grounds; the familiar rumble of the cart's wheels, again drew Jane's attention to the small window, and she saw what she'd dreaded. She knew she would never forget that sound – but then, she didn't have long to remember.

All she said was, "Guildford! Guildford!" and turned back to her maid, "These are for you, please make good use of them - for me." She handed the maid a pair of small leather gloves, and a crisp, lace handkerchief, which the girl accepted gratefully, but the tears were already running down her face. "I'll treasure them always Madam."

It was Jane's turn then, to walk towards the dreaded scaffold, specially erected on Tower Green. Thankfully, it was not the same place as Guildford had died. She climbed the very few stairs to the wooden block, each step tentative and measured. She'd stopped trembling by then, for which she was grateful. In fact, she felt surprisingly calm. If anything, her frail form, and sweet face, made her look even younger than her years; more like a young schoolgirl up before the headmaster. The masked executioner was standing to one side, the axe concealed behind his back. He didn't have the expression of a man who relished the task ahead.

Looking up at the sky, and as was the custom, she made her final speech:

' Good people, I am come hither to die, and by a law I am condemned to the same. The fact indeed, against the Queen's highness was unlawful, and the consenting thereunto by me: but touching the procurement and desire thereto by me and or on my behalf. I do wash my hands thereof in innocence. Before God, and the face of you, good Christian people, this day.'

How controlled was that? Even more unbelievable was that she went on to recite Psalm 51 (Have mercy upon me, O God), and the executioner stepped forward quickly. He asked her forgiveness for what he was about to do, which she willingly granted, adding, "I pray you dispatch me quickly. But my head….." and she held either side of her head in her small hands,. Nothing could have looked more pitiful. “Will you take it off before I lay me down?” she asked. The executioner merely answered, “No Madam.” She reached up then, and put on her blindfold, but then she couldn’t find the block, and with her flailing hands in the air, she cried out, “What shall I do? Where is it?” The Deputy Lieutenant of the Tower, Sir Thomas Brydges, touched her arm, but gently, so as not to startle her. Jane’s head now rested on the block, and she spoke her last words,

“Lord, unto thy hands I commend my spirit.” And with one clean sweep of the axe, the executioner did as she had asked, and ‘dispatched her quickly.’ Her poor, slender form lay in a crumpled heap on the ground, alas without that pretty face – and she was still only seventeen years old!

Henry V11’s granddaughter, Mary Tudor, had succeeded in winning her throne, and ridding the country of Henry’s great-granddaughter, Jane Grey, the imposter. The queen had been successful because she had the good-will of the people behind her; many had believing after all, in her absolute right to the throne. Her popularity was high when she was crowned Queen, but by the time she’d ruled England for just five short years, her popularity had waned significantly, and she was to die as one of the most unpopular monarchs England ever had.

She must have been capable of kindness however, as after Jane, her husband, Jane’s father and her two uncles were executed - she magnanimously decided to forgive Lady Frances, Jane’s mother, the Duchess of Suffolk, and her other two daughters. Presumable this was because, like herself, Frances was Henry V11’s granddaughter. Although part of the traitorous Grey family, Mary obviously saw her as no threat, and Frances later married her Master of the Horse, Adrian Stokes, and lived at Court along with Jane’s two sisters, Elizabeth and Mary, until she died.

****

As the reader, you will have formed an opinion about the traitor Lady Jane Grey – subsequently referred to as a Protestant Martyr? She could after all, have saved herself from the executioner's axe, by accepting Queen Mary's suggestion that she convert to Catholicism, but she refused. She may of course, have envisaged a life after such conversion, and decided it wouldn't have been worth living. Would she have been spied on for the rest of her life, every movement watched by prying, Catholic eyes, in case she strayed from the straight and narrow? Did she hate the thought of a future, where she'd most certainly have had to raise any child born to her, in the one and only true faith – Catholicism? And would that just have been too much for her to bear?

Or was she just a young girl, brought up in a Protestant family, and wishing to remain as Henry V111 had decreed for his people – a Protestant? Mary's singular, and generous decision on the fate of her mother and two sisters, does beggar the question, 'were those three members of the Grey family **not as convinced** of the wisdom of their other, more ambitious relatives had been?' After all, they were invited to live within the Queen's Royal Court, so it seems likely the queen believed they had nothing to feel guilty about. If only Jane had sought their guidance in the first place, perhaps things might have turned out differently. But, was she given the chance?

And wasn't there a French king called Henry of Navarre – also a staunch Protestant, but one who wanted to rule as king over the entire country of France, and not just his own kingdom of Navarre? To achieve this however, he was told he had no choice, but to first convert to Catholicism, the preferred religion of the French people. The dilemma was huge but after four years of stalling and prevaricating, he final gave in, with the words, 'Paris is worth a mass!' His decision was a long time coming, but it did ensure the whole of France belonged to him. He went on to live a long and uneventful life as king, and died contentedly in his bed. The young Lady Jane Grey obviously had stronger principles than he. But who was right – and who was wrong? Who was wise – and who was not? That decision is yours to make. One other question for you to consider lies in the title of this story, 'Was the crown of England forced onto the young Jane – or was she very content to wear it?'

Next time when you're faced with a similar dilemma (if ever), remember both Lady Jane, and Henry of Navarre, and make your decision after considering what they'd each gained from their very different decisions. Is it a case of 'Paris vaut bien une messe' or 'My faith is more important than my life.' What if it had been you – what would you have done? I'm ashamed to admit it, but I know what I'd have done.

ARTHUR PENDRAGON – ASLEEP UNTIL HIS COUNTRY NEEDS HIM

(Background information)

This story is either about a man who was a warrior king, or it's about a myth - a legend of a man who never was. He may have been conjured up by a people who needed a leader – or he was a real flesh and blood hero. Whatever the truth, King Arthur Pendragon served his purpose. This is your opportunity to decide! Having read my story, you'll hopefully be in a position to form an opinion one way or another - but before you do, you'll find below some background information about the time, when the hero in question, was alive, and leading and defending the people of Briton, or Britannia, the latter being the preference of the Roman invaders, when they first invaded the country.

The period is often referred to as the Dark Ages, (a mis-noma some historians would claim), and it was particularly so in Briton, the home of the Celts. Many areas believed it was acceptable to invade each other's lands, and take whatever they wanted; killing, maiming, raping and plundering as they went along. Early in the first centuries BC, this was an accepted practice by most of the Germanic nations, whose own lands were not favourable for the growing of crops, or the grazing of animals. Briton had better conditions in spade-fulls! The Norse countries were cold, often frozen-over for long periods of the year: they were therefore prone to regular flooding as well – a disaster for their crops and animals. How much better it would be if they had Briton's lush, green and fertile land. All they had to do of course, was to cross the sea and take it , which was exactly what they attempted to do when the Romans had finally departed. The Norse invaders who first arrived were known as barbarians, but they were actually Saxons, Angles and Jutes. The Romans had considered them to be ignorant, illiterate, uncultured and unchristian – and should be crushed at all costs. They still worshipped their own Gods, such as Thor and Odin, completely ignorant of the one true God worshipped by the world's 'new' Christians. Christianity was fast spreading throughout Europe, and even the Romans who, until recently, had worshipped their own Gods, now accepted Christianity as the one true faith.

When the Romans finally left Briton, it was to deal with growing problems arising across their vast empire, but they did leave behind in Britannia many ex-soldiers, who had slowly integrated with the local people. It's long been accepted that, although the Romans too, had once been the marauding invaders of Briton, they always left the conquered nations in a more advanced state than when they'd first arrived. Having said that however, the local Brits had become used to the protection offered by the Romans, and for a considerable time they were a confused and undisciplined people – hence, the need for a hero such as Arthur Pendragon. A great leader of men!

By the 5th Century AD, the Romans were long gone, and Briton was left wide open to the invading Norsemen, who'd strangely enough, been forewarned of the Roman departure, and lost no time in sailing their long boats across the wild Atlantic Ocean. They believed Celtic Briton was ripe for the plucking!

If ever the Celtic people needed a leader and a hero, it was at this time, and waiting within the walls of Camelot Castle, in the south of the country, was a man destined to be just that hero, destined to become the saviour of his people. That man was Arthur Pendragon, who would go on to be remembered for the rest of time – and who, even at the point of death, had loved his country and its people so much, that he promised to return from his last resting place, if and when, he was needed.

The question to be considered however is, was he one man, or was he several men? Was he the wishful thinking of a people suffering from the invasion of barbarians, or was he many brave leaders who came forward to defend their country – and became amalgamated into one fighter, named Arthur? Was Arthur therefore, just a combination of several heroes, who rose to be above the others? This is certainly worthy of consideration by people with an open mind.

Without the protection and guidance of the Romans, the Celts were at their lowest ebb, and desperately in need of a strong figurehead, on whom to pin their hopes for the future. And so, we have Arthur Pendragon King of Camelot, and his trusty knights.

The various Celtic communities and tribes were left fragmented because of their different cultures and customs. They had of course, adopted many of the Roman ways, and learned much during the four centuries of that occupation. The Romans in their turn, had been committed to integrate with the locals, a common policy of theirs, and after the initial invasion, the two nationalities did eventually mix. The Celts were eventually realistic as to how much they'd benefitted from the presence of their one-time Roman enemies.

At the close of the 4th century however, with most of the Romans gone, and their forts and garrisons abandoned, the Celts were left alone, to face the marauding barbarians, who were crossing the Rhine in their droves. They were also invading many other parts of Europe, hence the need for the Romans to leave. The new Roman emperor Constantine 3rd had been declared the leader by the military forces, and his first decision was that Britannia must now fend for herself. An alarming decision for the Celts, but an understandable one for Rome, as the soldiers were needed to defend several other hot-spots across Europe.

Denmark, Jutland, and the Dutch Netherlands, agreed to pull their battle resources together, and to travel en-masse across the ocean(s), although their ships had to struggle all the way through the menacing and notoriously-high winds, nothing could have stopped them. They were already hardened against rough elements, and their sea-faring skills were second to none, so the challenging sea-crossings were merely an irritation. They'd always had an eye on the rich pickings on offer in Briton, and although the rough seas might be a struggle, the distance between the countries was short. And so, they came in their droves! They wanted Briton, or Britannia, and were determined to take it.

Although not realised at the time, this would be the start of a new nation of Anglo-Saxons, who in time, would over-run much of Briton, and who. in the later 8th and 9th centuries, would be forced to defend their then-homeland from a fresh, fighting horde of new Viking barbarians, who had come from the same Nordic regions, as they, themselves had once done. The new Vikings would cross the same sea, and attack the same country, as their ancestors had done before them. They would however, be fighting with their own kinsmen, and ancestors! Ironic, or what?

The 5th and 6th AD invasion attacks were suspiciously timely, as they first began along the English coastlines at the very time the Romans left. A spying regime probably existed, which reported the Romans' movements to the Nordic countries, which is why the invaders were ready, and waiting to pounce. Their weapons were superior and efficient, as opposed to what the Celts had, and their fighting skills were amazingly honed to perfection. Surprise was their best attack!

Such invasions were a common practice throughout the Dark Ages – it was happening all across Europe. The morality of taking what didn't belong to you, was not an understood concept, whereas the survival of their own country was of paramount importance. Similar invasions were taking place about the same time, and one in particular involved the Scotti from Ireland who invaded Dalriada (Scotland), the land of the Picts. The Scotti had originally come from France before invading the Irish Isles, where they chose to establish themselves before moving on to attack the Picts. Soon the integrated peoples were known as Gaels – a mixture of the original Scotti, the Irish, and the Picts. The Romans had of course been aware this was happening in the North of Briton, but they'd always had trouble with the fierce Picts, as well as mountainous countryside, so they decided the best policy was just to shut them out. (Hadrian's Wall) The Picts, now reinforced by the Scotti and the Irish, proved too hard a nut to crack for the Romans, and their invasion petered out at the border. This is mentioned merely to show how invasion of another country was quite usual in the Dark Ages – indeed, it had been part of many other cultures s well.

It's easy therefore, to appreciate the desperate situation in which the Celts found themselves – they were left vulnerable and unprepared for attack. Briton was in turmoil when the Nordic Angles and Saxons decided to take what didn't belong to them. They had Briton in their sights, and knew of the country's confusion without Rome's protection, and so they came in great numbers, to plunder and attack the unsuspecting people.

From this turmoil, came Arthur Pendragon, and his name was soon known to all. He was an enigmatic and romantic figure who arrived one day from the mists of time. Suddenly he was there, and at the exact moment he was needed. He rode at the head of an army of chivalrous knights, who were equally determined to chase the Norsemen out of Briton.

Eventually, this man would be claimed King of the Britons, and his name would live forever. Even today, his story, and his promise to return to his country if needed, is known to all, and can be even seen inscribed on the walls inside the Houses of Parliament – proof, if ever it was needed, that our country never forgets true heroes! Such a notable distinction however, is awarded to the very few – and in the case of King Arthur, it's even more unusual, as his actual existence has continued to be debated right up until today. This inscription must surely suggest a strong belief in the man by many people, and moves me to ask again, 'myth or reality' – it's your call!

It's not possible to say exactly when King Arthur sat before his Knights of the Round Table, or when he led them into battle, but it seems probable it was around the middle of the 5th Century. The Germanic barbarians (as the Romans liked to call them) had begun their first attacks as early as the beginning of the 5th century AD, and immediately began to settle in various parts of the country. They used the same template the Romans themselves always did, when they'd first arrive in a country to be conquered; this was the use of the iron fist at first, followed by the softer, velvet one of integration. As numbers grew in the different settlements around the country, the names of new kingdoms slowly began to emerge: Wessex is a prime example, as many of the western Saxons settled there: Sussex too grew in size by the arrival of more Saxons into their midst; and perhaps the most impressive of all - the settlement in Northumbria, which grew enormously in size over time.

It has been argued by some scholars that King Arthur was really a Celtic God, coming straight out of mythology, and not a mortal man at all; they believed his name was actually derived from an existing popular, and highly thought-of Celtic chieftain. (Their argument stropped short however at naming this mysterious chieftain) It could be argued that Lord, Chieftain, King or even God, could all be one and the same. We just don't know! King Arthur's reputation was certainly widely-known at the time, although some exaggeration may have been used, when folklore stepped in, claiming he was capable of killing giants, witches, and monsters, and all at the same time. According to the same folklore, he could also defeat several fighting men with just his sword – in fact, nothing was impossible for the man. He was unbeatable, and his sword was ever-ready in the defence of his fellow-Celts, and that's as much as ordinary people needed to know at the time.

Where was Camelot actually located – no-one is sure? Some believe it might even have been as far away as Scotland (Guinevere was reputed to be a Scottish princess after all) – but then, the elusive Camelot is claimed by so many – who can tell? Cornwall is a definite favourite, and shouldn't be dismissed out of hand. (The hill fortress at Cadbury is one good example of the claim.) What we do know however, is that Arthur came from a gentile and peaceful place, where he was mentored by a wise old magician called Merlin. Merlin was Arthur's friend and guide for all of his life. Guinevere and Lancelot too lived by his side; two people however, who would one day let him down.

These are names that come straight from the annals of time; as does Uther Pendragon, Arthur's father, and Ygrain his mother. There was allegedly a total of 150 knights at Camelot, all chivalrous to the core, and ever-ready to fight in the pursuit of justice. Although gentile and peaceful, Camelot was also ready to fight for justice, whenever it was needed.

The problem of having no written records to provide evidence of either Camelot, or of Arthur himself, becomes even more complicated by the fact that his story wasn't actually recorded until the 12th century, when the scholar Geoffrey of Monmouth put pen to paper and told the tale. (With much poetic licence, it is often claimed). Monmouth was an eminent scribe with a good reputation, but he was also famous for his vivid and imaginative tales. As a historical scribe however, he was also equally famous for his alleged findings of ancient manuscripts – manuscripts which provided him with the information in which we're particularly interested. He found they were about a mystical warrior king called Arthur, who'd faced the onslaught of the Angles, the Saxons and the Jutes. Many such manuscripts would inevitably have been based on 'word of mouth' tales and songs, all handed down from one generation to another. This however, doesn't make them any less true. It should be remembered too, that the spoken language of the time, had many variations, even within the Celtic nation, let alone with the added complication of the invaders' foreign tongues. It would have been almost impossible for details to be recorded with accuracy, at a time when the country was fighting off one invasion after the other. The scribes in the monasteries would have found it difficult to maintain any records, but perhaps they tried, and that's what Monmouth had found many centuries later.

Religious houses were regularly sacked and robbed by the invaders, as religious valuables and holy relics were especially attractive – and so very easy to take from the gentle holy men.

I know the reader may think the author tends to sway to-and-fro – first championing Arthur's existence, and then removing it just as quickly. But that's all part of the challenge I set before you, that challenge being whether King Arthur ever really existed at all.

To defend Geoffrey of Monmouth however, it is known he would have had access to resources now lost to us today: his descriptions of the Nordic raids, their consequences for the Celts, and of course the Arthurian Legend itself, cannot be easily dismissed. (As some non-believers are inclined to do very quickly, and without grounds) Monmouth may indeed have had access to old manuscripts, and relics from long before his own time, and used them as the basis of his tales. Who can say with any certainty? Monmouth's Arthurian legend therefore, should not be considered as mere fabrication, but rather as 'possible' bona-fide evidence, available to a researcher such as himself in the twelfth century. Never a truer word is spoken than, 'Once it's gone, it's gone' – and that's what may have happened to Geoffrey's ancient manuscripts discarded, unimportant, destroyed, or just carelessly thrown away in ignorance of their worth.

A second chronicler named Nennius also refers to Arthur in his writings, calling him 'dux bellorum', which translates as military leader, rather than king. He claims for Arthur, twelve separate and successful battles against the Saxons; he also mentions the great battle at Mt. Badon (a factual, established battle), which is believed by many, to have been the turning point in controlling the vast numbers of invaders. He tells in detail, how King Arthur rode at the head of his army at Mt. Badon. Other scribes throughout the centuries, have also attributed many great victories to Arthur, something for careful consideration.

Strangely enough, the church has always been unusually reticent on the subject of King Arthur. He was not known as a favourite of the church, which was quick to claim that our hero was notorious for relieving the holy houses of their wealth, their valuables and their treasures. This does seem quite likely, as valuables would have been needed to finance Arthur's struggles against the Nordic invaders. (Perhaps the church's staunch silence on the subject of Arthur might be taken as evidence of his existence?)

For the purposes of the tale below, you should know I'm going to assume without question, that King Arthur was not a myth, but a real-live hero; a warrior king, who brought together a broken and devastated country, giving the people hope for the future. Once my story below has been considered by you, the reader, we can then return to the age-old question, 'was he, or was he not a real person? As you continue to read Arthur's story below, I am well aware there is no actual historical evidence of his existence, but I would counter that with, 'neither is there any historical evidence that he didn't exist!'

****

Arthur's Story:-

Let's look now at Arthur, the warrior king. He was born in a magical place called Camelot – born under the strangest of circumstances. Where was Camelot located? No-one knows!. It's been claimed the magical place was actually in Somerset, and was known there as Cadbury – a sight that is identifiable to this day, and historical records do confirm a great leader once lived there, along with his army of knights. Camelot has been described as a small kingdom, where Arthur's father was the chieftain in the local area. His name was Lord Uther Pendragon, and his reputation was fierce. The very word Camelot has had a dream-like quality for centuries, often described as beautiful, magical, and where only 'good' people lived – that was of course, decent people like the Pendragon family. Arthur was fortunate enough to belong to this wonderful place, where he grew happily from childhood to adulthood, completely unaware of the strange circumstances surrounding his upbringing. Even his birth came about through the trickery of magic and duplicity. His mother was Ygrain (Loraine), who lived in Tintagel, along with her husband Gorlois, Duke of Cornwall. Ygraine's husband was actually Uther Pendragon's sworn enemy – he hated the man, whom he'd never trusted, and in order to hurt and shame him, he instructed the magician Merlin to alter his appearance, and turn him into a doppelganger of Gorlois. So successful was his altered appearance, that he was able to join Ygraine in her bed as Gorlois - and that's how Arthur was conceived. Duplicitous, or what? From the very moment of conception, the boy was therefore steeped in mystery, subterfuge and magic. An odd beginning for a boy, but not as odd as fate had already determined his future would be.

When Arthur was born, Merlin took the child from the disgraced Ygraine, and brought him to his biological father's home at Camelot. It is not known if this was done by force, or by mutual consent. Uther was happy to allow this, as he could now watch his son grow, with none of the usual problems of a father. The magician set about raising the boy, as he was in loco parentis, and gave him lessons in all the academic subjects, but also including magic of course. In fact, he took care of the boy's ever need. Merlin's apothecary at Camelot became Arthur's main home, and the boy was determined to become as clever as his mentor. He was fascinated by the magician's clever 'tricks', and soon became knowledgeable in the mystic – and sometimes black arts.

He grew into a tall, strongly built youth, who enjoyed all sports, and who regularly took part in every kind of hunting and jousting that was available Jousting was the most popular pastime at Camelot, and was enjoyed by many of the knights, and like his father Uther, Arthur became obsessed by the true meaning of chivalry, and all it implied. He liked to watch the older knights, desperate to learn more as he watched them ride their magnificent horses in competition with each other. The world was exciting, and Arthur longed for the day he would be considered old enough to join the brotherhood of knights. Sometimes in Camelot, he was able to watch more than a hundred of such joustings, and one day, he made an oath to himself that he would become a knight, just like them.

"No Arthur, your time will come, but not just yet." Uther was sitting on a wooden bench by a roaring fire, when his son asked again if he could join the brotherhood, and joust with the others at court.

"But Father, see how strong I am. I'm actually bigger than some of the knights even now." And he flexed his arm muscles right into his father's face.

"Give it time boy, you're still only 16 years old – far too young to be a great knight. To be a great knight – and not just a good one – is what you must strive for. You've enjoyed working with Merlin, haven't you – I'm sure there's much more he has to teach you?" Uther had had this conversation with his son many times before, and was growing impatient with the boy. "Go now, and see what my magician is cooking up. He tells me he is working on the design of a huge table, which must be round and big, so that many of the knights can sit there, and discuss military matters. One day, I promise you will have a seat there too." He turned his back on Arthur, who had no option, but to accept his father's dismissal, and leave behind the warmth of the fire.

The next two years passed uneventfully, except for the subtle, but enormous treachery of Uther murdering his arch-enemy Galois, and marrying Ygraine, his widow. Her daughters by Galois also came to live at Camelot, and would become more involved with Arthur (her half-brother) in later life – sadly, this would be much to his detriment. He was now acting as Page-boy to several of the knights. He was happy with this, as being close to the knights was all he ever wanted. Soon, he too, would be one of them, and sit at the great Round Table.

Unfortunately, Uther's health had begun to deteriorate, and for some time, he'd found breathing difficult. It had begun as a cold, and developed into a chest infection, which affected both his sight and his balance, and he found he could no longer walk any distance. Eventually, an intense fever completely enveloped him, and he had to take to his bed. The courtiers were worried. If Uther were to die – who would take his place as Lord of Camelot? He had no legitimate son, and although he was fond of Arthur, he couldn't, in all conscience, name him as his successor. That would not be a moral thing to do, as the seniors within the brotherhood of Knights had concluded. They were especially worried, as they all sat in the great hall one day, to discussed the matter. If Uther were to die, how would they choose his successor, and did they have the right to do it anyway? There was no obvious heir, and Uther had never declared one, despite having children by two different women. But then, they'd all been girls, and the knights would certainly look to a man as their leader.

One cold Winter morning, Uther eventually breathed his last and the entire court of Camelot went into deep mourning. Arthur turned to Merlin for comfort, but it seemed the magician was as upset at the chieftain's passing, as the boy was.

"What'll happen to us now Merlin? What'll we do now my father has died - we are left without a leader?" Arthur was in Merlin's apothecary, where it always seemed cosy and warm – and where there was usually some interesting experiment being worked on.

"You mustn't worry about that Arthur – there are many wise elders, who will decide on a new leader. I promise you, your life won't change in the slightest -in fact, it might get even better, if my visions are true." Merlin was well known for the accuracies of his visions, so Arthur felt content at his words. A sudden puff of smoke escaped from a phial, and the boy jumped in surprise. He jumped a second time, when a loud knock on the door interrupted the experiment. Merlin waved his hand to clear the smoke, and called out, "Enter."

A messenger stood there, looking ill-at-ease. He explained he'd been sent to ask the magician to join the senior knights in the great hall, and added quietly, all the time watching Arthur's face - "I'm afraid that now the Lord Uther Pendragon has passed into the next world, the knights would seek your counsel, and ask that you follow me."

It had been expected, and Merlin, with his protegee followed the messenger from the room – there were tears in the boy's eyes, as he feared something bad was coming, but he quickly brushed them away – he was almost a man, wasn't he? . Merlin hadn't been asked to bring Arthur, but the wise old man knew the boy's presence was important.

In the great hall, there were at least ten of the senior knights, some standing, and some seated, but all looking at the newcomers with searching and sad expressions.

Merlin immediately told them not to worry, and that the Lord Uther had already discussed the situation with him – many months before. The magician's knowledge of everything was known to the knights, and his next words were awaited with impatience.

"Lord Uther knew this day was coming, and he had already devised a plan for the choosing of a new chieftain and lord. Through the forest, and beyond the last of the trees, there is a Lake of Shining Water. By the side of the lake is a heavy, large stone, and imbedded deep into it is a long and heavy sword. The sword is old, and very special to the ancients that once looked after us, and has a name all of its own – it is called Excalibur. It once belonged to a giant, who lived on the other side of the lake – close to the far mountains. That giant has passed away long ago of course, but when he died, he left Excalibur to the Lord of Camelot, to be used as a means of testing any future leaders. To withdraw the sword from the stone will need special powers, as well as strength. Whoever is able to withdraw the sword from the stone, is destined to become the next Lord of Camelot. It is not a test for the weak-willed, as the sword is stuck fast, and will take great powers of the mind to remove it. The time is now gentlemen, so are you in agreement to try your best, and carry out Lord Uther's instructions? After all, it is his last command!""

The room seemed to darken all at once, as though a black cloud had passed above the high windows, and the knights began to mutter amongst themselves. What was this all about? They'd never heard of a sword in a stone – and despite often passing the lake, no-one had ever seen it. Anyway, was that the best way to choose a new leader?' It seemed not, and two or three spoke up, and said so. The darkened room became even darker, and a bolt of lightning blinded the knights momentarily, before an angry-sounding crash of thunder silenced the men's muttering. There was no doubt as to who was the owner of the voice, but to reinforce its identity, Lord Uther Pendragon suddenly appeared in front of the high window. It was a shadowy figure, whose face was partially concealed, but the voice was clear.

He boomed. "Gentlemen, do you doubt the words of my trusted magician? For your sake, I hope this is not so. I, Uther Pendragon command obedience from all of you – it is necessary for the future of Camelot. The sword in the stone has exceptional powers, and has been protected by the Lady of the Lake, who slumbers beneath the waters. She is one of the ancient Irish Goddesses, whose own name for the sword is 'Caludbolg', first heard in far-away corner of Ireland. The sword is gifted with the power to choose who is best to rule over Briton, and not just over Camelot. If you don't wish to feel her wrath, as well as mine, I command that you obey – each to test your suitability, by removing Excalibur from the stone." And with that warning, the lightning struck once more, only this time even more ferociously, and the hall was suddenly dark as night.

Several candles flickered in the darkness, and by no man's mortal hand, they came fully alight again, and now shed a bright light, brighter than any normal candle.

Sir Lancelot raised his arm and asked for silence. A needless request, as silence was all there was, as even the knights, known for their bravery, were confused, shaken and scared all at once. He continued, "We shall carry out Uther Pendragon's wishes – he has spoken to us from beyond the grave now, and used words that leave no doubt as to his wishes. Woe betide anyone here, who decides to disobey our Lord. He has entrusted his faithful Merlin to oversee our actions and guide us through this difficult time." Lancelot held a senior role at Camelot, despite the belief that all men were equal, so his words were respected by every knight there. Those who had muttered earlier, were now silent.

In the hall, standing shoulder to shoulder beside the great fireplace, were Sir Lancelot, Sir Bedivere, Sir Gareth, Sir Tristan and Sir Kay – all five revered and respected by the other knights. A heavy silence hung in the air, whilst each man wondering how hard it could be to pull a sword from a mere stone. 'Not hard at all,' was the final consensus of opinion. No-one spoke however for at least two minutes, and then, Sir Lancelot asked Merlin, " For the sake of clarity Merlin, is it that whoever amongst us can pull the sword from the stone, will be declared the next Lord of Camelot? It seems such an easy task that any one of us could do, and not a great challenge. Are you certain there were no other conditions or challenges that we need to know? It just seems like too simple a task."

Before Merlin could answer, there was a commotion at the door, and a colourfully dressed fellow skipped into the centre of the room. He skipped, rather than walked, and he was brandishing a stick, attached to which was a bell, and several brightly-coloured ribbons. It was Dagonet – Camelot's court jester.

"Not now Sir – this isn't the time for your tom-foolery. We're trying to make an important decision about the future of Camelot. We don't need a fool to distract us." Sir Kay had no patience with the fool, and found his antics preposterous and silly - even at the best of times. But then, Sir Kay had no sense of humour, and he told the jester to leave a second time. However, Dagonet merely bowed deeply, and produced a scroll tied with tape and sealed with red wax, which he unrolled with an exaggerated flourish, and coughed before reading aloud,

" I had hoped there would be no need for me to call in the fool – but alas it seems I was wrong:

This document is written by my scribe, but the words thereon are mine own. Once I have shuffled off my mortal coil, Dagonet, our court jester will bring these words to the attention of the knights of Camelot

Heed my words Sirs, and carry out my wishes and instructions.

'Let any fine gentlemen of chivalry, travel to the lake beyond the wooded forest There to find the sword of Excalibur stuck firmly in a great stone, where it has been for many years, hidden to the eyes of man. He who can withdraw the sword and flourish it above his head in triumph will be my rightful successor – and will rule the kingdom justly and wisely in my place."

That was it! There could be no doubt, and the document was clearly signed by Lord Uther Pendragon himself. They'd heard it from Merlin, then from the ghost of Lord Uther, and now from the court jester. A strange trio of proofs – but proofs that left little doubt. The jester held out the scroll to whoever in the room wished to examine it. Sir Lancelot took the scroll and read the words again. He looked at Merlin, " We are left with no doubt Merlin, and now we are ready to obey."

The magician merely nodded his head, and said nothing. He took Arthur's arm, and led him from the hall, leaving the knights to talk amongst themselves. To end the confused chatter, Sir Kay raised his hand to silence the babble.

"At least, we now have an answer to our dilemma gentlemen, and we know the way to find our new lord. The challenge is straightforward enough, but all knights must be given an equal opportunity to prove himself. Are we all agreed on this, before we share it with the others?

"Aye! Aye! We should do that, " was the combined response, and so, the future of Camelot was decided, ironically sorted out by the strangest trio imaginable.

Before any one knight was allowed to travel to the lake, they also agreed that an assessment of the chivalry to which they all attested, should be undertaken, and only those who passed without question, would be allowed to take the challenge of Excalibur. Merlin was appointed as the assessor, being an obvious and unbiased choice.

To be chivalrous was the most important quality, required by a Knight of the Round Table, and nothing less would suffice. Merlin began the task almost immediately, and one by one, he invited each knight into a private room, where he assessed each man's character, and history. Many of the knights chose not to put their names forward for the honour of becoming the Lord of Camelot, but there was still a sufficient number, who thought they'd make a good leader. Each Knight, who was allowed to take his place at the Round Table, would already have sworn an oath, promising to live by the Code of Chivalry. The Code read:

'To never harm, deliberately hurt, nor do murder

To always treat Treason with disdain

To never be cruel, but to always grant mercy to those who seek it – even in battle

To always treat ladies, gentlewomen, and widows with respect and give help where needed

To never force or harm ladies, gentlewomen, and widows

Not to do battle in unproven quarrels, or for worldly goods – but only for God and country

To fear God and to respect his church.'

The Knights of the Round Table were therefore expected to be meticulously gentle and courteous to all, but also to willingly take up arms in the defence of king and country. This is the code to which Arthur himself, would one day swear – and he was eager for that day to arrive.

One by one, at least twenty knights visited the lake and found the stone – and sure enough, a magnificent sword was deeply embedded into it. How it had been placed there could only have been by a miracle, as no ordinary man could have done it, and no ordinary sword would have had the cutting power. Again, one by one, they tried – and one by one, they failed. The sword was stuck fast, whether placed there by brute strength or magic, no-one knew. Some knights even came back a second time, to try just once more. Even Sir Lancelot, on whom others had gambled would succeed, failed to move Excalibur even one little bit.

Sir Kay too, had tried at least twice, but with no luck, and so Camelot was still without its lord. On his second attempt, Kay even used his own sword to try to ease out the magic sword, but in doing so, his own blade had snapped in two, and he'd thrown it to the ground in disgust - right at the foot of the stone itself. Foolishly, he left the broken sword on the ground, and walked back to the castle, feeling disgruntled and angry. Good swords were expensive and hard to come by, and were always made of the best quality steel - so,

"The blacksmith could have fixed it, you chump. Why did you throw it away?," his fellow-knights were not sympathetic, and thought him a fool. Sir Kay was Arthur's cousin, and he called the boy to his room, and told him to walk to the lake and bring back a broken sword he would find on the ground. As one of the knight's page-boys, the boy couldn't refuse, and set out mournfully on the long walk. He passed under the trees which were in full leaf at the time, giving the lad good shade from the blazing sun. The lake came into sight, and the air was cooler by the water. Arthur saw the broken sword on the ground, but before picking it up, his eyes fell on Excalibur – glittering in the bright sunshine. On impulse, he reached for the giant's sword, although he already knew no-one had succeeded in pulling it out, but it was too tempting however, and his hand gripped the elaborately-carved hilt.

Like a knife sliding through warm butter, Excalibur came free of the stone, and Arthur stood there, staring at the great sword in his hand. He'd done it! He'd done what the Knights of the Round Table couldn't do. What did it mean? Why had the others found it so difficult, and he found it so easy? He gathered up Sir Kay's broken sword, and carried both swords back to Camelot. It wasn't easy – the combined weight was a challenge in itself, but he managed somehow. First, he showed Merlin what he'd done, and was surprised to see the magician merely smile and nod his head. "That is what I expected Arthur – you only had to go there, and try for yourself." He was obviously delighted, and Arthur watched in amazement, as the old man fell to his knees before him, and bowed his head. 'What was the man doing?' the boy thought.

"Lord of Camelot, soon to be King of the Celts, go forth and tell the others what has passed this day. Uther Pendragon would have been proud of you." He stayed on his knees paying homage to the boy- king.

And that was how the young, illegitimate boy became first the Lord of Camelot, and then, in due course, the saviour of Briton's Celtic nation. When the senior knights saw the evidence held firmly in the boy's hand, each one fell to his knees before him, just as Merlin had done – and no man dared question his right to be their lord and leader.

Everything fell quickly into place then, and the new lord took on his late father's role. The first task he and his knights, had to deal with, was the invading Angles, Saxons and Jutes, who were over-running the country – killing, raping and plundering innocent people, as they went. Arthur's knights attacked the invaders with great gusto, soon earning themselves the name, 'Slayers of the barbarians.' He and his knights would ride across the country, travelling over vast distances, in search of the Norsemen, and successfully driving many of them back to their long boats, and back across the cold sea, to where they belonged.

Whilst tackling this huge challenge, Arthur had also become re-united with his half-sister, Morgan le Fay, who was the legitimate daughter of Ygraine, Arthur's own mother. His father Uther had forbidden the siblings to meet when he was alive, but now Arthur was the Lord of Camelot, he decided such things for himself. Morgan le Fay was an ambitious woman, who knew that her father Galois had been murdered on the orders of Arthur's father, and because of this believed the magical castle at Camelot was rightfully hers – Queen Ygraine, who lived there now, was after all, her own mother. She believed she was in the right, and with a devious plan in mind, she seduced the innocent young man, making sure she'd fall pregnant with a son. She decided this wasn't incest, as they'd had different fathers – but even if that hadn't been so, she would still have carried out her plan.

And when her dastardly plan came to fruition, Arthur's son Mordred was born. The new mother kept the baby's birth a secret from those at Camelot, and raised him at Tintagel, well away from Arthur. Th unsuspecting father's continuous struggle with the Norsemen, kept him busy and well away from Tintagel. Morgan le Fay reared the boy Mordred on her own, teaching him all the while that he should hate Arthur, who'd stolen Camelot from him. In her twisted, greedy mind, she'd convinced herself this was so, and never missed an opportunity to denigrate the young king in her son's eyes, regularly pouring poison into his ears – she did this all the way from childhood to manhood.

She also made the solemn promise to him, that one day Camelot would be his. Even when he was very young, she would hold the child on her knee, telling him of all the evil things the Pendragons had done to his family – and stressing Arthur was the most guilty of all.

"One day, my little man, you will be a great leader, and you and your mother will live happily together at the great Camelot." The daughter of the murdered Galois was determined to punish the Pendragon family, and she was bringing up her son to think likewise.

And so, the years passed, and the boy Mordred heard numerous tales of Arthur's great deeds, of his successful battles, and of how much the Celts loved him. This made him hate 'his own father' even more. He had just heard too, that this man whom he detested, accompanied by several Knights of the Round Table, had visited the Holy Land, in an attempt to find the Holy Grail – the cup Jesus had drunk from at the Last Supper. 'What a magnificent challenge – something I could have done,' he told himself, 'and then, the people would have loved me instead of him.'

Arthur's long search in the Holy Land had come to nothing however – something Mordred was delighted to hear – and the boy's hatred of the man just grew even more intense.

The battle of Mt. Badon took place somewhere in southern Briton, and King Arthur and his knights were ready and waiting to deal with the hordes of Saxons, whose longboats had been spotted whilst still out at sea. Prior to this particular battle, there had been many others of course – sometimes just skirmishes, but often full-scale battles. Mt Badon however, was apparently a culmination of all that had gone before, and the Celts triumphed magnificently. Following this Saxon great defeat, the numbers of invaders seemed to diminish for a while. The success of this particular battle ensured more praise of the King, and Arthur's name as a hero, spread even wider amongst the Celtic people .The people told each other, their king was undefeatable!

A new arrival of long boats arrived on the shores of the country, and the beaches were swarming with hundreds of axe-wielding barbarians, intent on one thing, and one thing only – to take everything for themselves, and to kill anyone who got in their way. There had been at least a dozen long boats pulled onto the beach; there were masses of wild men, jumping from them onto the sands, and then marching across the country. Their axes swung from their belts, and their swords held ready to kill anyone who got in their way. The two armies had clashed together at the base of the high hills, both sides determined to win. The Saxons were disorientated however by the strange landscape. and were very tired from the recent sea journey, so the Celts, led by the knights of Camelot, took an early advantage. The close hand-to-hand fighting lasted for several hours, until the fields were flowing with blood and gore. Severed limbs lay strewn across the muddy fields, and Arthur was sorely aware he'd lost more than just a few men. The Celtic cavalry re-grouped, and for the third time, rode their horses straight into the core of the Saxons, who spread out in an exhausted attempt to confuse the Celts. It didn't work however, and the peasant army, led by Arthur and his knights, swooped in behind the horses, and completely destroyed the enemy.

It was a sad and bedraggled group of Saxons, who made their way back to the beaches, and to the safety of their longboats. No longer were they the swaggering, axe-wielding tyrants, who'd arrived only hours before. There weren't even enough sailors left to handle the vessels, and return to their homeland; many of the weak and wounded were left behind – some to rot in the surf. The Celts were triumphant, but as the knights' Code of Chivalry demanded, they allowed the walking men to help their wounded comrades back to the beach, and onto the ships. Some made it, and some didn't. It was a pitiful sight, but one that made the Celts rejoice.

This then, was the battle of Mount Badon, and its success certainly added to Arthur's ever-growing reputation as was to be expected, a slight exaggeration crept in when the tale was retold- it was said that Arthur, all-by-himself, had killed over 900 Saxons during the battle. An amazing feat, and one that perhaps demands a very good imagination.

Records of the Celtic success at Mt. Badon were discovered, and provided confirmation that the battle actually took place in the middle of the 500's, but unfortunately the confirming documents weren't discovered until the 9th or 10th century, when the battle was finally recorded. There was no-one left with any memory of the Celtic triumph, but at least the newly found documents confirmed a man like Arthur was around at the right place, and at the right time.

Back at Camelot, and in a break from the battles, a conversation was taking place between Lancelot and Arthur, "You're to marry, you say, and who is the unlucky lady, may I ask?" The two men had been friends for a long time, and had a mutually high regard for each other – combined with a similar sense of humour.

"I am Sir, and to a very lovely lady called Guinevere, who originally hails from Scotland, and is the daughter of a king. What have you to say to that?" Arthur was now in his mid-twenties, and was beginning to understand the importance of acquiring a male heir.

Lancelot couldn't hide his surprise, "Is that the Lady Guinevere who is living at the Priory, as their guest? I believe I have seen her, and have to agree she is very lovely," The knight had most definitely seen the lady – he'd even spoken to her, on a day they'd met whilst exercising their horses in the near-by woods. In fact, they'd recently taken to riding out at the same hour on a set day, and 'accidently' meeting on more than one occasion. He was concerned that meeting an unmarried lady without her chaperone, was not right, and certainly not something in line with the Code of Chivalry. Having said that however, he was unable to stop himself from seeing the lovely Guinevere, for whom his fondness was growing.

Lancelot shifted his feet nervously, and asked, "Has the marriage been arranged then?" Arthur told him everything had already been arranged, causing the knight to look crestfallen. But still he pursued the question, "How well do you know her, Arthur – is this not a rather hasty decision, and perhaps ill-timed, whilst the barbarians continue to attack our country?"

Arthur laughed, and told him he was talking stuff and nonsense, "Don't be ridiculous, my friend. Marriage won't stop me from doing my duty by my country. I will continue as before, to chase the damned Norsemen back to their own freezing country. I assure you that no lovely lady will stop that." He thought for a moment, before adding, "Actually, and strangely enough, Merlin feels as you do, and has tried to dissuade me from marrying the Lady Guinevere. But he is an old man, and doesn't understand the needs of the young."

"Nonetheless, I would discuss the matter more with the wise, old man – he's always had your best interests at heart, and has been a good counsellor for many years. I myself, think he may have a point – but what reason does he give for his advice? Has he explained why he doesn't favour the lady?" Lancelot wanted to hear more, but was wary of showing his hand– he knew he might appear too eager in his concerns about the lady.

"Of course, I will speak with him again – he's been more like a friend, than a mentor. In fact, I'll go straight to the apothecary now, and seek him out." And the young king swept from the room, leaving a worried friend behind. Arthur was not to know what he'd seen in Lancelot's face, was fear of being discovered, rather than concern for his friend.

"Do not marry the damsel! I tell you, she is not for you!" Arthur had rarely seen Merlin so agitated = he was quite angry, and completely unlike himself. Arthur knew he had to calm his old friend. “Why Merlin, what ails you? The lady is sweet and innocent – and of marrying age, being all of eighteen years.” He rushed to get some water for the old man , “Here, drink this.” But Merlin was too upset by Arthur’s determination to marry a lady he considered unsuitable. He ignored Arthur’s kind gesture.

Merlin wasn’t just a magician, but he was also a philosopher, an alchemist and a sooth-sayer. He was a most exceptional person, with so many talents and skills, which made most people hold him in awe. Since his childhood he’d been able to see into the future, and to predict what was about to happen. Even now, and in his mind’s eye, he could see the lady Guinevere, and the knight Sir Lancelot, entwined in each other’s arms. He’d had the vision before and had no reason to doubt his powers. He told Arthur he feared the lady’s affection was for another, and not for him, but Arthur came back with, “Nonsense old friend, she is as pure as the driven snow, and has always led a very sheltered life. Her affection cannot be elsewhere. You’re wrong this time Merlin.”

Now, Arthur was beginning to fear for the old man’s health, and knew he must quickly change the subject. It was pointless however, Merlin remained agitated, so Arthur had no option but to leave the apothecary, hoping that might have a calming effect on the magician.

Merin had made his point however, but it didn’t stop him making it again on other occasions. It was to no avail however, as Arthur didn’t want to hear it, and continued to ignore the well-meant advice. He put it down to Merlin’s advanced years.

Lady Guinevere and King Arthur Pendragon were married. The celebrations at Camelot took place right in the middle of a fresh combat between the Celts and the Saxons. The marriage preparations, and the fracas with the Saxons, had to be dealt with simultaneously. Unfortunately, this particular encounter was not successful for the Celts, and many returned home defeated and bloodied, but at least they did return, unlike many of their fallen comrades. The weary men of Camelot returned in the midst of the wedding preparations, and Arthur immediately fell in with the growing excitement. He had chosen Lancelot as his best man, although the knight seemed reluctant at first, but had no option but to accept the honour.

Despite being a new bride, Guinevere and Lancelot had agreed they would continue with their relationship – much to Merlin's annoyance. He knew exactly what was going on, but couldn't bring himself to tell Arthur, as it would upset him too much. He felt vindicated however – he'd been right after all, but as Arthur had refused to accept his advice, there was little else he could do. Arthur therefore, continued to remain in ignorance of a cheating wife, and a false friend.

The struggle with the Angles and Saxons was to continue. The invaders kept coming, although their numbers might be fewer, allowing a 'temporary respite', when Arthur could re-visit the Holy Land, and continue in his quest for the Holy Grail. This time, Lancelot decided to remain at home, which allowed his affair with Guinevere to flourish. Merlin remonstrated with the knight the knight, reminding him of the Code of Chivalry, but it was to no avail, and so the affair continued. However, the courtiers at Camelot were growing suspicious, and then angry, at the pair's disloyalty in their king's absence, and actually called Guinevere to come before a formal court, in order to defend her alleged adultery.

"Guilty! Guilty!" was the cry of the court, and the young woman was sentenced to be burned at the stake. A speedy and unsympathetic judgement perhaps – but her crime was a serious one. Lancelot escaped any judgement, as he was a single male, and obviously free to do as he pleased, but when he saw what was happening to Guinevere, he decided to leave Camelot, and to exile himself in France.

Merlin looked at the lady – straight into her eyes. He'd come to visit her in her prison cell, and when he saw how distressed she was, he felt sorry for her, against his better judgement. "Madam, how low you appear to have sunk – not only in my eyes, but in the eyes of your husband's people. What will Arthur think when he returns home – to find you in this sorry state?"

"Oh Merlin, do you think he'll forgive me? I will fall to my knees and beg his forgiveness. Lancelot has gone away and we'll never see each other again. Please will you intercede with Arthur on my behalf, and ask my jailers not to rush into my execution? To be burnt whilst still alive is my worst nightmare." She really was distraught, and held out her hands, begging him to help.

Merlin knew that, despite what she'd done, Arthur would forgive her, as he loved her dearly, so he made up his mind to plead with the judges, who'd sentenced her to death. He would do it for Arthur, as he knew how distressed the young king would be if he returned, and found her gone from his life, His pleading didn't fall on deaf ears, as the court had much respect for him, and Guinevere was finally released. She was warned however, that if she strayed once more from the sanctity of her marriage vows, the original sentence would be revived, and carried out immediately - with no need for another trial.

Mordred, Arthur's son by his half-sister, Morgan le Fay, arrived unexpectedly at Camelot. He'd heard of all that had happened there, and knowing Arthur was still in the Holy Land, he decided it was an ideal opportunity to stake his claim on Camelot. Whilst Arthur was absent, Mordred would act! After all, hadn't his mother drilled into him all his life, that he was the rightful Lord and King of Camelot?

When he arrived from Tintagel, his eyes immediately fell on Guinevere, and he quickly developed a fascination for her. She really was a lovely woman – and she belonged to his arch-enemy. This was enough of an incentive to make him chase after the lady.

"Why are you choosing to ignore me Madam?" he asked her one day, when he found her walking in the rose garden. At first, she didn't answer, but he persisted, falling onto one knee, his eyes declaring his adoration.

"Do rise Sir, this behaviour is undignified, and I am a married lady, with a living husband." She wasn't sure how to deal with this stranger, who'd just arrived at court, announcing to any who would listen, that he was the rightful king.

"The stories that abound about you Lady, would deny the existence of a husband whom you love; yet I am here, and kneeling at your feet." Mordred was not going to humour her – but he did want to take her for his own, and thwart the hated Arthur.

"Nay Sir, what you have heard is untrue. I have great love for my husband, and am eager for his return to Camelot. You must leave me now." She made to turn away, but was stopped by his hand on her shoulder – an unbelievable show of disrespect. Promiscuously, she smiled, even as she told him to leave her – whilst her wish for him to stay was apparent.

"What a shallow woman you are Madam – but then, I like shallow people, as I am equally shallow." And he bent his head and kissed her. Guinevere led the rose garden then, but Mordred continued to pursue her, believing that with her as his mistress, his claim to Arthur's throne would be even stronger.

The ever-watchful Merlin was quick to bring this new dalliance to the court's attention, and quite suddenly, Guinevere's presence in Camelot was brought to an end. The magician had tried to help her for Arthur's sake, but he knew now that his initial doubts regarding her character had been correct, and he watched her sad departure from the castle. She was being sent to a quiet nunnery at Amesbury in Wiltshire. She was to stay there as a semi-recluse for the rest of her life. Such punishment was of course far better than being burnt at the stake, but it was still the end of the young woman's life, as far as she was concerned.

Merlin believed he had failed Arthur, and because of this, decided to must leave his much-loved apothecary. He was ashamed, and knew he couldn't remain at Camelot, so he left the only home he'd ever known, and travelled deep into the woods, where he assumed the life of a hermit. Old habits die hard however, and people were unable to forget him, and he was often visited by those who sought advice and guidance, and by those seeking his skills as a soothsayer.

Arthur and his knights were now preparing to leave the Holy Land. Once again, they had failed in their quest to find Christ's last drinking cup, and therefore, there was no reason to remain so far away from home. It was time to return to Camelot – he'd been gone too long. Amongst the knights who had accompanied him on the journey, were Sirs Kay, Bedivere, and Gawaine. three of his good friends, and the best of his knights. The men were very different in nature, with Sir Kay rather sombre, Bedivere rather jolly, and Gawaine physically stronger than ten ordinary men. A formidable trio indeed!

Gawaine was younger, and was Arthur's nephew, so they'd always been closer than most. One day in the future, and unknown to either, Gawaine would do his uncle a great service, Indeed, it would be the very last favour anyone would ever do for the warrior king.

On the last night overseas, the four friends sat together around a blazing fire with tankards of ale in their hands.

"Someday, someone will find it, of that you can be sure." Kay was staring into his ale, unable hide his disappointment. "We tried so hard, and travelled so far, but we have to go home with the burden of failure." He had wanted so much to find the Holy Grail, and bring it back to Briton – but alas, it was not to be. The men chatted together, discussing how the Holy Grail was not only believed to be Christ's own cup, but also the very-same cup that Joseph of Arimathea had used to catch drops of the Messiah's blood, as he hung on the cross. A truly exceptional claim indeed, but perfectly possible. Sir kay had a dreamy-look in his eyes, as he supped his ale. He wasn't to know at the time, that Jesus's relative, Joseph of Arimathea, had already travelled from the Holy Land, bringing with him the self-same relic to leave with Briton's monastery at Glastonbury - where it's still believed to remain to this very day.

Back from their crusade, the Knights of the Round Table sat once again alongside those who had remained at home. They sat together in the circle, specially arranged so that all men would be equal; with no-one more important than the other.

The knights had returned to a much - altered Camelot. Merlin was in his hermit-hovel in the woods, Guinevere was in the nunnery at Amesbury, and Mordred and Morgan le Fay, were living in a private house only a few miles from Camelot – a hastily arranged move from the castle, when they heard Arthur and his entourage were returning. Arthur was furious when he learned of the duplicity of his half-sister and her son, especially of the man's claim that Camelot should have been his. He stood up and banged his fist on the table, "The vermin will have to be dealt with – and soon!" He was still unaware that Mordred was not merely his nephew, but rather his own son. Morgan le Fay had kept this a close-guarded secret – even from him.

"This upstart's threat means I will never be safe whilst he remains alive. His mother is no better, and has always hated me. I know that hatred stems from her belief that my father Uther murdered her own father – and for that, she now blames me. As you all know, Morgan le Fay and I share a mother, and after my birth, Lord Uther married

Galois's widow, Ygraine. And so, the story goes on – it's only right that I explain why Mordred has turned up now, claiming my throne – he sees it as his right." He looked rather sad as he spoke and added quietly, "His mother and I were quite close once, but that was when we were young." He failed to mention however, just how close they had been.

He stopped speaking and looked around the table, obviously embarrassed by how much he'd just shared. He was looking around for his friend Lancelot, but something was amiss. Where was the knight? "Something is different - where is Sir Lancelot, gentlemen? He should surely have come to this meeting. Is he perhaps ailing – and unable to come?" He asked, but sensed from the men's silence, it wasn't as simple as that.

A knife could have sliced through the silence, so heavy did it hang in the air. Several knights coughed nervously, and began to shuffle their feet. Arthur said again, "Well, is no-one going to speak? Your king had asked you a question."

The usually happy Sir Bedivere was the only one who dared answer. "Did he not leave you word, Sire? I'm sure he meant to – perhaps in his rush to leave, he forgot." Arthur told him not to be ridiculous, "Forgot! Forgot! Where is the knight?" He looked around at the silent circle, and knew something bad was coming.

Again, it was only Sir BedIvere who was brave enough to answer, "It seems Lancelot has left Sire, and gone to live in France. I fear he really must have forgotten to leave you a message. Had Merlin been here, I'm sure he would have had kept you informed." Bedivere realised his mention of Merlin was merely adding to the tension in the room, and leading to the more dangerous 'whys and wherefores' concerning Lancelot's real reasons for leaving Camelot.

The knight spoke quietly, "Sire, may I have a word with you in private?" And as Arthur agreed and made to leave the room, an audible sigh of relief could be heard around the table.

The two men stepped outside into the rose garden, where the flowers were in full bloom, and a heavy perfume filled the air. Not at all the right setting for what Bedivere had to say. From that moment onwards, Arthur would never be able to smell the perfume of a rose, without the memory of how everything went wrong in his life – and how he lost the love of his life. Bedivere had quickly learned what had happened in the king' sojourn to the Holy Land, and gently started to explain what had taken place at Camelot, He described how Guinevere had been lonely, and had turned to Lancelot for comfort, an act that eventually forced the court dignitaries to punish the married lady for her behaviour. At that time, Lancelot felt he had no option but to depart to France, – and to live there in exile. This was his self-punishment for what he'd done. There, he'd already begun to build a castle for himself, swearing he'd never return to Briton. So annoyed were the court dignitaries at what the guilty pair had done in their king's absence, that they sentenced Guinevere to be burnt at the stake.

Arthur, who'd been silent for some time, reacted to this news, by jumping up and crossing the garden to stare out of the window. His face was ashen, and he was trembling, whether with anger or with shock, Bedivere wasn't sure. He continued with his story however, and explained the lady's initial sentence was commuted to a lesser punishment, if she swore she would never act in such a vile way again.

Bedivere was looking tired and hated what he was having to do. Although, he hadn't witnessed things himself, the other knights had been quick to share the news. He went on, "It was at this point, Mordred and Morgan le Fay arrived at Camelot, claiming that King Arthur was the young man's father, and therefore, entitled to the throne in Arthur's absence. He even produced a letter, allegedly from the Holy Land, confirming Arthur had been killed there, and the throne of Camelot was empty/ It was almost certainly a forged letter, but that couldn't be proved at the time." Bedivere paused – how could he tell his friend this? It was too much! He knew his next words would upset Arthur most of all, "Guinevere turned to Mordred, and believing you to be dead, agreed to marry him, and so, she would remain as Queen of Camelot. The courtiers didn't believe Mordred's claim, believing the letter to be forged, and they chased both him and his mother from the castle. Mordred swore he would soon return, and take what was rightfully his. Judging Guinevere once again, the courtiers decided she had shamed herself anew, despite that she'd believed her husband was dead, and so, she was banished to live out her days in a nunnery at Amesbury."

There – it was all in the open now. Everything had been said! Bedivere felt relieved. He had done his best and worst together, trying to break the news gently. The king however, was reeling from one shock after the other. His dear wife was almost burnt at the stake, it was definite his half-sister's son was his own – a young man he had never liked. His friend Lancelot had committed adultery with the queen, and then deserted the country to live in France.

"By all the Saints Bedivere, how do you know all this? And how did I know none of it?" Arthur was furious.

Bedivere just shook his head sadly, and touched Arthur's shoulder. "Ah Sir, there were many eager to tell me all, when I returned home, but you were another story, as no-one wanted to be the one to tell you such things."

Arthur was clutching the hilt of Excalibur, and seemed on the point of withdrawing it, but Bedivere put his own hand over the king's, and said quietly, "Nay Sire, not yet – you must have time to digest all of this, and only then, make a decision on what to do next."

Wise words, of which Arthur knew the value. He just said, "Leave me now Sir – I must have some time alone – I have a lot of thinking to do."

After a few moments, he called for his page to go saddle his horse, 'Merlin – I must speak with Merlin,' and he rode way rom Camelot, and deep into the woods. Soon, he came upon a circle of old oak trees, where he saw smoke from a campfire curling into the sky, and there, sitting in front of a small branch-covered shed, was his old mentor. He hadn't aged at all, but then he'd always looked old.

Merlin looked at Arthur through white straggly hair - it was almost as though he'd been expecting him, and raised his hand in welcome. All he said was "Good-day young Arthur", and waved his hand as invitation to sit by the fire. He couldn't conceal his smile however, he was pleased to see his old pupil.

There was something bubbling in a pot on the fire, and Merlin used a long-handled ladle to fill two small flagons. He handed one to his friend. After a few sips of the surprisingly- tasty drink, Arthur asked, "Do you know why I've sought you out, Old Man? Yes, you probably do – you knew this day would come, didn't you? You warned me once not to do something, and I ignored you – but now I have great need of your wise counsel. "

"I know, my boy, I know. I know all that's happened – there is no need to tell me any of it." And the two men sat together, first remembering things that had once been, but then moving onto what was still to come. At last Arthur heard himself saying the words he hadn't wanted to say, "You were right about my marrying Guinevere – I should never have done it."

"Nay Arthur, you shouldn't, but you did, and that's now water under the bridge. I have been having visions of late, and because of them, I have fresh prophesies to share with you – but only if you are willing to listen this time?" The fierce warrior king took Merlin's subtle rebuke humbly, and just nodded his head.

At the end of their conversation, Arthur tried to convince the old man that he should come back to Camelot, and to his cosy apothecary, but Merlin told him that Camelot was no longer the right place for him. So, Arthur left the warmth of the fire, and mounted his horse. He now had a fixed plan in his head, and knew what he must do. Before returning to the castle however, he rode towards the small town of Amesbury – not too far away – and where Guinevere's nunnery was. He slept the night under a thick hedge, and at first light, knocked on the door, and asked for sanctuary. At first, the Mother Superior was unwilling to let him come inside, but when he told her who he was, and that he only wanted some food and water, she immediately changed her attitude, and welcomed him inside. After some bread and cheese, she took him to the herb garden, where she knew Guinevere was working.

Shocked to see her husband standing there, Guinevere quickly dropped her head in shame. She knew what she'd done, and was truly repentant, claiming she'd been weak without him by her side. She remonstrated with him, hoping to see forgiveness in his eyes, but Arthur now realised he no longer loved her, as she wasn't what he'd thought her to be. He told her this, and that he wasn't taken in by her excuses. It was harsh, but necessary. He now saw her in her true light!

He told her he'd just come to say a proper goodbye, "My wife, your weakness has been your undoing, but I wanted to tell you that although I forgive you. I'm not able to forget what you've done." He raised her hand then – her hand still covered with the soil from the herb garden, and kissed her fingers. Then he left her, a solemn figure still crying bitter tears, but he found he felt better for having given her his forgiveness. It was after all, the chivalrous thing to do. He could hear her sobs, as he left the nunnery, but he didn't look back, not even once, although he was leaving behind what had once been the great love of his life.

Now, things had to happen if Camelot was to be saved, and he must move onto his next challenge, a challenge which Merlin had begged him ***not*** to take on. The magician had told him Mordred would be his undoing, and was even now conspiring to defeat and kill him, his own father, and to take possession of Camelot. And Morgan le Fay was by his side, still pouring the same venom in her son's ears. Merlin had seen it all unfolding before him – and had left no detail untold, but Arthur told him he mustn't worry and that he knew how to deal with the upstart youth. The thought of putting Mordred in his place was a plan Arthur found he relished.

Returning to Camelot, he immediately called for several of his best knights to join him at a council of war, a war specifically against only one enemy, and that was his own son! To emphasise the importance of the meeting, he laid the great, symbolic sword Excalibur in front of him – on the mighty table of war. He fingered the sword reverently, and reminded the knights of its powers. Merlin had told him the sword had been created by the giant's blacksmith in Avalon, and had been blessed by the Goddess, the Lady of the Lake – and in its shaft, had been instilled great magical powers.

"By this sword, I will put an end to Mordred, who has now become my sworn enemy – and yet, I have never meant him any harm. He has chosen to challenge me however, and to take Camelot as his own. By my father Uther, I swear I cannot allow this to happen." And he told the knights there would soon be a battle on Salisbury Plain in Wiltshire– a great battle that could affect the future of the magical kingdom of Camelot itself – and most likely, of its king. The Saxons and the Angles had again been spotted at sea, their long boats crashing through the waves. The only difference this time was that more than a hundred long boats had been sighted, and therefore, perhaps thousands of axe-wielding Norsemen. Merlin had forewarned of this, so it came as no surprise to Arthur.

And so, the big day arrived. The year was 552 AD and the Saxon raids were imminent; the Celts had to rally themselves on, as they were exhausted by the never-ending stream of skirmishes they'd had to face – those Saxons just kept on coming! They had been concentrating more on the South recently, where the coastline made it easy for the boats to sail right into the coves and harbours. Then, then the barbarians would dash across the beaches, right into the unsuspecting towns and villages. The same towns and villages Arthur was determined to protect.

The cunning Mordred was well aware such a battle was due to take place. Didn't he have spies everywhere? The battle would be fought near an existing fortress, high on Salisbury Hill, or Salisbury Plain where the flatlands were. Mordred and his quickly-gathered group of mercenaries planned to conceal themselves on the far side of the plain, biding their time, and intending to join the fray at a suitable moment. The moment would be when Arthur was at his weakest. and Mordred would of course fight on the barbarian's side – against his father.

So bitter was Mordred's hatred of Arthur, that he'd never intended to fight on the Celtic side, despite his claims to the contrary. He intended to allow the battle to begin, and half-way through, when confusion reigned, and hopefully when the king wasn't surrounded by his knights, he and his mercenaries would quietly join the battle – but setting their sights on the Celts, and not on the Saxons. Hopefully, Arthur would be an easy target to spot.

The Saxons were already in place, awaiting the arrival of the Celts, who were being led from the front, by Arthur and his knights. Without hesitation, but in line with their agreed strategy, the Celts attacked first, using surprise itself, as a weapon. The Saxons however out-numbered their enemy, and the fighting was ferocious and bloody. Men on both sides were soon lying, crumpled amongst the long grasses of the Plain, and the smell of blood hung heavily in the air.

Cries of pain, mingled with shouts of attack were deafening – but the confusion seemed to spurt the men onwards, and Arthur and his knights were clearly to be seen in the foray. Two hours passed, and it was clear that both sides were weary, and slowing down their attacks. At first, the greater number of Saxons, seemed to be pushing further forward, and Arthur tried to rally his men, by removing his helmet to let everyone see he was still alive and fighting – he was and hell-bent on beating the enemy. He grabbed the Celtic colours from a soldier, and raised the flag high in the air.

It was at this very moment when Mordred and his men chose to join the battle, aiming straight for the middle of the Celts. The Celtic fighters didn't know what was happening, and looked to the knights for reassurance. Who were these strangers – obviously fresh Saxons to add to their problems, but they certainly didn't look like Saxons - who were they?

Mordred, on his steed, slithered like a snake across the ground, seeking out Arthur. The king was now easy to spot, as he was still holding the flag high in the air. Knights nearby were busy trying to stave off the Saxons to protect him, and failed to notice the approach of the cunning Mordred. The fighting was particularly ferocious, with the Saxons seeming even more over-whelming, when Mordred saw his chance, and first slashed at Arthur's horse's legs – he wanted the man to be standing, when he dealt the final blow; he also wanted Arthur to be looking straight into his eyes, when he felt Mordred's sword strike. The injured horse stumbled and the rider fell to the ground, dropping the flag as he went. Arthur wanted to comfort the beast, but could do nothing to help, so he raised Excalibur into the air, in an attempt to reassure his men. Mordred raised his visor to show the hatred in his own eyes, as he dealt what he thought was the fatal blow. He did manage to strike the king, and forced his sword deep into Arthur's side; he pushed it right up to the hilt. The king stumbled and gasped, as he realised what had just happened. He used his swordless hand to clutch at his side, which had been torn open, but the blood continued to gush from the wound.

He looked straight into his son's eyes – and for one moment, Mordred felt a sudden guilt – but that soon passed. However, he then made the biggest mistake of his life - he laughed into the dying man's face, the laugh turning into a sneer. With his last ounce of strength, King Arthur swung Excalibur upwards, and brought it down heavily into Mordred's chest. The man, who believed he'd just killed the leader of the Celtic nation, looked surprised at first, before falling face-down into the mud and blood of both Celts and Saxons. It was over – Mordred was dead, and Arthur was mortally wounded. The battle-cries of the Celts fell silent, as they realised they'd lost their leader. He may not have been dead, but they knew he soon would be.

The Saxons won that battle, and the Celts returned home bloodied, but not defeated. Never defeated! They would live to fight another day; sadly, most of their companions were lying in the mud alongside the Saxons – never to see their home again. Sir Bedivere and Kay, both of whom were also wounded, gathered Arthur's broken body, and the stronger of the two lifted him, and gently supported him on his horse. Arthur's own horse lay dead just a few yards away. Gawaine the Strong, followed slowly behind the knights; he was their lookout, and was determined they would all reach Camelot unscathed by any stray Saxons – or he would die in the attempt.

In Camelot, Merlin had come from his hermit's hut, and was waiting, knowing the terrible fate his protégé had met. He'd felt every blow, just as Arthur had, and now he'd returned once more to Camelot - the first time in many months, and he'd already prepared some potions and ointments, in the hope he might be able help the wounded. Bedivere placed his king in his own bed in the castle, and turned hopelessly to look at Merlin. "Can you help him Merlin? Tell me there's still hope." Merlin didn't answer the question, but he didn't have to - the knight already knew the answer.

"I can make him comfortable for a short while, but that's all I can do. I'm afraid, his wounds are beyond even my potions."

Arthur lingered for two days. Many of his knights came to see him, to say goodbye, but he wasn't able to distinguish one from the other; he just raised a frail hand in salute. What he did experience however, was a visit from those who'd gone before to the afterlife. Standing around his room were mysterious figures, most of whom he didn't recognise – but they were all men and very elderly. None of the visiting knights showed them any interest - in fact, they seemed unaware of their presence. As the visions had come to see Arthur only, this was to be expected.

The tallest figure stepped away from the others, and Arthur saw his father for the first time in many years. He whispered, "Uther Pendragon, my father – have you come like the others to say goodbye to your son?"

Uther Pendragon spoke then, "Nay my son, that's not why we've come. Your ancestors and I have come to welcome you to the Isle of Avalon. When you finally arrive there, we will be waiting." He turned to the other figures, and said, "This is your Great Grandfather Custennin, and your Great Great Grandfather Cynfawr." He swept his hand across the other old men, "and these are more of your ancestors – this is Tudwal, Morfawr, Eudaf, Cadwr, Cynan, Ceadoc, Bran and Llyr." As he said the names, each person stepped forward to identify himself, each head nodding in salutation. The men's clothes were differed from each other, belonging as they did, to several, generations - and no-one said a word. They did however, share a family resemblance, and it was easy for Arthur to see they were his own kith and kin.

"But why father – why do they come specially to see me? I am merely the next in line to carry the proud name of

Pendragon." Arthur's breathing sounded harsh in his chest, and his voice was merely a whisper; although he tried, he couldn't raise his head from the pillow.

Uther told his son, "Nay Arthur, you are not merely the next in line to carry the name Pendragon – you are the last in line to carry the name. Therefore, you will be the last Pendragon ever to enter Avalon. That's the reason my son, why so many of your forebears have joined together to welcome you." And one by one, as though on queue. the ghostly figures faded away and disappeared from the room.

To the knights around him, it seemed Arthur was having a conversation with himself, and made no sense at all. But what did that matter? He was still talking, and telling someone not to go, so Bedivere assured him no-one was going to leave him. Bedivere, Kay and Gawaine, his closest friends, remained by his side. Arthur did rally or a moment, and recognised his three friends, but then whispered, "Where is Lancelot – he should be here too? Bedivere answered through his tears, saying, "There, there Sire, Lancelot will be along soon." The words seemed to sooth the dying king,

A night and another day passed, and still they stayed, not wishing to miss any moment when he might rally, and be himself again. It was not to be however, but Arthur managed to say, "Take Excalibur through the wood to the lake, and there, throw it deep into the water, where it can rest until another day when it is needed. The Water Goddess will take care of it until that day comes. Promise me you'll do that!" And the knights nodded their heads, promising to carry out his last wishes.

"Put my body into a shallow boat, and allow it to wend its way across the water, until it reaches the island of Avalon, where I can either find eternal rest - or recover through its magical skills. I need you to do it now gentlemen, before I die. I must reach Avalon whilst I still breathe, as only then, will I be able to keep my next and final promise to you." He paused for breath, exhausted now. Bedivere asked gently. "And what is that promise, my Lord, we are listening, and will do whatever you ask of us?"

Arthur's last words then, were to be remembered for all time, , "I promise to return if ever my country needs me. In Avalon, I'll only be asleep, and if my country calls, then I will hear that call – and return." And with that, he fell into a deep sleep, and Merlin said, "He sleeps only gentlemen – do not despair, but we must make haste now, so that there is sufficient time for him to reach Avalon whilst he still lives."

Merlin didn't accompany the knights on their sad task, as they first dressed the warrior king in his suit of armour, and placed him on a carriage, which they accompanied to the lake of waters. King Artur was gently laid in a shallow boat, and on either side of the sleeping king, they placed things he might need in the after-life – sweetmeats, nuts and dried fruits, the lute he'd always loved to play, and a shield depicting his Coat of Arms. Two burning torches at the front of the boat, then saw him on his way, into the darkness of the night.

As the boat slipped through the water, beginning its journey to Avalon, the knights standing on the edge of the lake, could hear the king's familiar voice repeating, "Remember, I only sleep – and if called upon, I shall return to help my country. " It was as if the voice was actually floating across the lake, drifting through the still night air. The disappearing torch-lights were slowly disappearing into the mists of time.

And those words are why the warrior king Arthur Pendragon, the saviour of the Celts, is remembered as 'The Once and Future King'. He may return to us one day, but only if his country needs him!

Author's Note;

Even more information in support of Arthur's existence. It is reputed that the remains of the magician Merlin, lie within an ancient barrow in the grounds of Marlborough College – hence the town's name 'Marlborough', that is 'Merlin's Barrow.' Now, how did that come about, if there never was a Merlin - or an Arthur, or a Lancelot and Guinevere?

Conclusion;

There is little more to add. This is my story about Good King Arthur – King of the Britons. Whether Arthur was real or not, is up to you now. The fact that his name crops up as often aa it does in ancient manuscripts is enough for me – after all, it was a time when events were not recorded in detail for posterity. I believe no name could be mentioned so often, and so continuously throughout history, perhaps originally by word-of-mouth I grant you, if there were no foundation for his existence.

He's still a man, whose reputation is so well known, that stories about him resound around the world even today. His name alone stands for chivalry, kindness, and decency - and above all, for loyalty, truth, and bravery. All qualities the world should bear in mind, and be a better place for doing so. In the present day, there is turmoil around the globe, but with regard to Briton, we should never forget "Arthur just sleeps, until his country needs him!!

I leave you with the dilemma, 'Did a man called Arthur Pendragon ever live, and was he a great warrior king – a saviour of his people? If I haven't made it clear already – I'm in Arthur's corner, after all, there's no smoke without fire!

GUY FAWKES – WAS HE NOTHING MORE THAN A SCAPEGOAT?

All his life he'd suffered. He was aware something bad was going to happen – and to him! He had everything anyone could wish for – a crown, a loving wife, children, and courtiers who catered to his every whim. Despite all this, he lived in perpetual fear for his life – he feared ghosts, witches, goblins, and the Devil himself, especially the Devil. Who was he, and why was he so afraid? He already ruled one country, Scotland, and then another fell right into his lap – and that was England, much larger and wealthier than his native country. Overnight, his cousin had died, and he immediately became a very powerful monarch indeed, with many castles, palaces, and majestic homes, all for his personal use.

His name was King James 6th of Scotland, and 1st of England – he'd only been 13 months old, when his mother, Mary Queen of Scots, abdicated in his favour and a baby became king. He was actually born in 1566 in Edinburgh Castle, and the country was run by regents until he came of age. Unlike his mother's life-long devotion to the Catholic church, James was brought up strictly in the Protestant faith: something he was to remain all of his life. This was the reason England was quite happy to accept him as their king. The people had favoured Protestantism for quite some time, and Queen Elizabeth 1st , his predecessor, had welcomed the religion, as unlike her sister Mary, she had been strictly reared a Protestant, in line with her father, and brothers' wishes. Her wisdom however, had allowed Catholic and Protestants to live according to their want, although her style of ruling was often criticised by either side, as her official position as being Head of the Church of England meant she had no option but to shun Catholics. The Protestants criticised her for not condemning the other side out of hand. When the staunch Protestant James inherited his throne, he also was not inclined to help the Catholics. He was less flexible than Elizabeth had been , and positively hated the Catholics in his newly-acquired realm.

Four years after his birth in Edinburgh, another baby boy was born in the Tiger Bar, in the city of York's Stonegate, and he was christened Guy Fawkes by his Protestant father. The two would meet as men one day – their paths would well and truly cross. This baby was to grow up and become the very worst of King James' nightmares – worse even than the ghosts and goblins, and witches he feared. It was at the age of thirty-two years, Guy Fawkes entered the king's life in the very worst way possible.

In the year 1605, actually on the 11th November 1605, these two men would meet in the most dramatic of ways. Despite inevitable knowledge of each other, they would never actually come face to face - something for which King James was forever grateful. The two religions with their hatred for each other, was the cause of bloodshed, torture, intrigue and misery in England. (and Scotland).

I want to talk of Guy Fawkes, of his young life, his time fighting in Spain for religion, and of his involvement with fellow-conspirators - always hell-bent on removing the Protestant King James, and replacing him with his own daughter, Elizabeth, who would then be forced to rule a Catholic one, despite her up-bringing. It's important to fully appreciate the strength of the new king's personal fears of the unknown – how every day, he would have the guards check a room, before he would enter. The man lived in perpetual fear, a fear he'd brought with him from Scotland, where he'd initiated witch hunts and the burning of pathetic old crones, who'd dared suggest a simple medicine for common illnesses. They were probably sweet old dears, but not in James' eyes. It could be argued that he may have been responsible for the growing number of witch hunts, that took place at the time – not only in Britain, but overseas as well, especially in the new American colonies, where witches accusing each other was rife. Couple this with how he must have reacted, when told of a plot to assassinate himself, and murder every member of Parliament, and all to be carried out at the State Opening of Parliament, which should have been perfectly safe for everyone there. My God, his two sons would have been there by his side. By the merest of chances, some innocent man decided to warn a friend to stay away – and sent the warning at just the right time. Time to allow the Gunpowder Plot of 1605 to be thwarted. What they'd planned to do however, could easily be done again, and James had to live with this knowledge.

First however, were going to look at what made Guy Fawkes the man he was. Guy Fawkes a name that even children of today know, and know why they remember it.

'Remember, remember the fifth of November
The Gunpowder, Treason and Plot
I know of no reason
Why the Gunpowder Treason
Should never be forgot
Guy Fawkes, Guy Fawkes, t'was his intent
To blow up the King and Parliament
Threescore barrels of powder below
To prove old England's overthrow
By God's providence, he was catch'd
With a dark lantern, and a burning match
Holla boys, Holla boys, let the bells ring
Holla boys, Holla boys, God save the King!
And what should we do with him? Burn him!

****

The year is 1570, the date April 13th, and the adoring parents, Edward and Edith Fawkes (nee Jackson), are gazing upon their newly-born second child. They already have a daughter, but this baby would carry on the family name, so he was doubly precious. Edith was still in her lying-in bed, and the wet nurse was hovering near the bedroom door. She was thinking how the baby was nothing special, rather scrawny and pale in fact, but healthy enough for all that. The father still stood by the bed, staring down at his new son, whilst Edith was looking tired and drawn, so the nurse spoke up,

"I think Mistress Fawkes is in need of a sleep, Sir – shall we leave her to her well-earned rest?" She moved closer to the bed, and made to take the baby from his mother's arms, and to break Edward's besotted stare, she asked, "Have you decided on a name yet?" Neither parent answered at first, but then the father said, "We want him to be strong and straight-limbed Nurse – so his name must be chosen with care." He looked at his wife questioningly, but Edith just smiled and said nothing. Edward added, "There's a Christian name of Guy, which might be suitable. It's of Norman descent and means 'a wooded place', and it's very different to the usual names given to boys today. Apparently it stems from the Spanish name of Guido – do you think we should call him Guy my wife – Guy Fawkes sounds a good, upright name – and something he can live up to?

Edith was so very tired after the labour of giving birth, and she didn't want the pressure of thinking of names, "Of course, Husband, I'm happy with your choice, Guy is a good and original name." And so, the proud father went off to register the baby's birth, and to arrange for the baptism. Being a judicial court official, and as such, required under the Church of England's stipulations, Edward knew exactly what was expected of him. He had to swear an oath that he was an Anglican Protestant, and attended services at an Episcopalian Church. Yes, Guy would be strictly brought up as a good Protestant, but what Edward didn't know at the time, was that his wife Edith, came from a Yorkist family, where several, but secret, Catholics, were numbered. Although seemingly, to be a Protestant, as was her husband, Edith was a 'closet Catholic,' believing it to be the only true faith. In fact, her nephew had already become a Jesuit priest, and many of her relatives were refusing to attend Church of England services. These people were known as recusants, something Edith couldn't be, as she'd married the wealthy Edward Fawkes, in the knowledge she must accept his faith.

It could be argued therefore, that Guy Fawkes (sometimes spelt Faux) , had been born into a complex religious family, in an equally complex country. From *an early age, he must have had many questions, but answers wouldn't be forthcoming, as his father would brook no argument – Protestantism was the only, true faith.*

The young Guy Fawkes attended a school in York, called St. Peter's: there he received a good education, which would stand him in good stead for the rest of his life. (Such as that turned out to be!) As expected, St Peter's was an established Protestant school, but this was its legal and a public persona - secretly, it was known to be a hot-bed of Catholicism. During Guy's time at the school, the headmaster was John Pulleine, who was recognised as a practising Protestant, but he was also known by many, as having certain sympathetic tendencies towards Catholics. In fact, the school's previous headmaster had been imprisoned for twenty years as a convicted recusant, something which, as the headmaster of the school, he was not allowed to be. In the city of York, the school's nick-name was 'Little Rome', a rather embarrassing name, which spoke volumes. Educationally however, its pupils were highly rated for their studies and achievements, and this was the reason Edward Fawkes had chosen the school for his only son.

Yet again, we have evidence of the young Guy's indoctrination into a religion, other than the one in which he'd been brought up. Religion played such a large part in his life, he must have felt he was being torn in two different directions – but as with many English people, the plight of the underdog attracted more sympathy – and in sixteenth/seventeenth century England, Catholicism had certainly become the underdog. . This was inevitable following King Henry V111's Reformation, his dissolution of monasteries and religious houses, and his executions of any who disagreed with his Anglican Church of England.

Guy had reached the age of eight, when his father suddenly died. By that time, Edith had three young children and she was on her own. The future must have looked bleak indeed. Edward had only been forty-six years old when he passed, and he was buried in York Cathedral – he was after all, the Registrar and Advocate of the Consistory of the Cathedral Church of York. Quite a title! His death was entered in the registry of St. Michael-le-Belfry, although he was actually interred in York Cathedral itself, and the date was 15 January 1578. Within a relatively short time however, Edith had remarried – and this time quite openly to a Catholic recusant named Denis (Dionysus) Bainbridge. Her second husband was reputed by many, to be 'more ornamental than useful' – not the most flattering of descriptions, but then he'd been Edith's choice. Perhaps the words 'any port in a storm' may have hastened her decision. The whole family then moved from Stonegate in York to the nearby Village of Scotton, where they settled well into the community.

As they travelled along the road towards Scotton, Edith spoke to her new husband "I am most content Husband – as are my children – to be going towards village life. The city was so crowded and crammed with so many people, that disease was never very far away. I believe that's what finally took Edward – God Rest his Soul." She realised she mustn't talk of Edward, and immediately brightened, "But now, I have you – and I thank God for that every day. It's so wonderful to be free at last to talk openly of my one true own religion, although I am aware I must be careful. I am happy to share this with you." Denis just grunted his agreement, after all, what could he say? Unlike his wife, he'd never hidden how he felt about religion, and rarely mentioned how he'd never once attended a service in an Anglican church. He wasn't a deep-thinking man however, and being a recusant, actually meant he didn't have to bother going to any church, and that suited him down to the ground. He would often say, "If I'm not allowed to attend a Catholic mass, then I won't attend a Protestant one." So, all in all, it suited him very well. He had a new wife, a new family, enough money to live on, and his wife had a handsome pension left by Edward Fawkes, and it would have been handsome – hadn't he held an elevated position at York Cathedral?

The family settled down well in Scotton, and Guy continued to attend a local school, where yet again, he came under the influence of recusants who were eager for the Catholic faith to be adopted in England – this however, was something the government and King James were vehemently against. It had been Queen Elizabeth 1st, who had passed a formal act, named The Recusancy Act, which attacked those who refused to attend Church of England services. Her Act remained 'live' within the government, until the late nineteenth century, when it was officially cancelled.

Influenced by new schooling, by his family's favoured Catholicism, and by the secret number of recusants hiding within the population, it was inevitable that Guy became more and more interested in the ways of Rome – coupled with the anger growing within him, because it had been criminalised by the authorities.

It was a difficult time in England – the Protestants had suffered under Henry V111's daughter Queen 'Bloody' Mary, who was determined to bring back her own faith, and then the Catholics suffered similarly under Henry's other daughter, Queen Elizabeth. Mary had been a devoted and dedicated Catholic in a Protestant world, and Elizabeth perhaps not quite so devout, was more a pragmatic and wise Protestant, who knew exactly what was required of her. She wanted England to be a country at peace with itself, so she shunned the pesky Catholics, who just wouldn't go away. From Elizabeth onwards, the Protestant King James 1st continued the suppression of the faith he abhorred and feared. The incessant ringing of bell; the crucifixes hanging everywhere; vivid Roman colours reminiscent of the flesh and blood of Christ; the grotesque replicas of Jesus being crucified on the cross; the repetitious 'Hail Marys' spouted n every occasion – and as for a priest being able to forgive one's sins – well, it was all just too much for the life-long Protestant king. He'd been brought up with low lighting, unpretentious church services, and anyway he relished being the Head of the Church of England, with the Pope as a subordinate. King Henry V111 had been the instigator of so much turmoil within the country, and all because the Pope wouldn't grant him an annulment regarding his first marriage to the Catholic Katherine of Aragon. Although of course, that wasn't the reason Henry put forward for his request. The bible told him he should never have married his brother's wife – that was a better reason by far, and of course why Katherine had never given him a son and heir. This sounded much better, and anyway, hadn't his first minister, Thomas Cromwell convinced him that the united kingdom of Britain wasn't just a country – it was an empire, and as its king, and now Emperor, he was not answerable to any but God himself. The irony of this, was that Cromwell, as Henry's chief minister, had only found this fable in an ancient book of myths (including some tales of King Arthur and the Knights of the Round Table), and it dated

back to the Middle Ages. It was not intended to be used in the way Cromwell suggested at all, but it suited Henry's purpose at the time!

Life in Scotton had been relatively quiet for Guy's family, and with the quick passing of the years, Guy Fawkes had become a young man. A young man, who was increasingly motivated to raise funds in support of a fighting force to change the government's view regarding Catholic practices – he was particularly sympathetic about helping Spain, who had a similar fight against the spread of Protestantism. They were currently involved in 'The Eighty Years War', which was in reality a religious one. The Spaniards had long been fighting the Dutch and other parts of the Netherlands, where the new religion was spreading fast. Whilst working to raise cash to finance a planned trip to join the Spanish army in Flanders, who welcomed a great number of international mercenaries, to help in their struggle. And Guy Fawkes wanted to be one of them! He even rented out his family's land near York – land that his father had owned, but which was now his. Christopher Lomley paid for the land on a 21-year lease, and Guy immediately used the money to finance his future trip to Spain. Most of the fighting took place in the Netherlands, where the Dutch fought fiercely to defend the religion they favoured i.e. Catholicism. Many of the worst battles, took place in Flanders, which lay between Northern Belgium and the Netherlands, and much of the land was occupied by the Spanish, whom the Dutch fought to remove the foreigners from their soil. Guy watched the situation closely, and swore he would soon join his comrades in their struggle. He would go as a mercenary when the time arrived.

One day, he was having supper with his family, when he said, "Mother – Step-Papa – I have agreed to work as a footman at Lord Montague's mansion. It will give me the opportunity to see how the other half live – and you never know, I may rub shoulders with some of the elite. And of course, it will improve my finances. What do you think?" He was twenty-two years old, and felt the time was nearing when he'd have to face the reality of fighting for a cause in which he believed. Soon, he would be ready to take on the world.

As usual, only his mother had an opinion; Denis had no opinions of his own – in fact, he didn't really care what his step-son did. He was just pleased that the lad had come unscathed through his recent relationship with Pulleyn, his old Headmaster's daughter, and the fact he'd left the girl expecting a child. He hadn't married her, much to her and her father's shame, but just waited out the time until the child was born, and was not disappointed with the outcome. Baby Thomas didn't live, nor did his young mother, and Guy was able to move on to the next stage in his life – to be a footman in a grand house.

Edith cleared her throat and told her son she had no problem with his intention, "Lord Montague is a great gentleman, as well as a devout Catholic. You will learn only the right things in his household, and you never know, you may meet influential people, who will help you enhance your career." And so, that's what Guy did – he worked as a footman for almost a year, and it's believed that was when he first came across Robert Catesby – a friend of Lord Montague. Caseby was one day to become Guy's leader, when the Gunpowder Plot in 1605 was first considered; it was odd how their paths crossed – one a lowly footman, and the other a great gentleman - it was as if it was meant to be. The lowly footman would have been shocked and surprised, had he known that one day, Catesby would send him a message, requesting he return immediately to England – as the country had need of such a man.

After his time as a footman, Guy Fawkes next decision was to go to Spain, and fight alongside the Spanish, in their struggle to put down the Protestant Dutch. He actually remained in Spain for almost 10 years, during which time, there were several flattering assessments of his character and abilities, both as a soldier and a man. Near the end of his time there, a report on his skills was given to him – and it still survives in the Spanish military archives until today. The report read:

'A man of great piety, of exemplary temperance, mild and cheerful demeanour, an enemy of broils and disputes, a faithful friend, and remarkable for his punctual attendance upon religious observance.' *What words to have written about oneself? He must have been very proud! Having said that however, the description doesn't exactly fit the man who was to hold a burning torch in his hand, ready to blow up a monarchy and a whole government. Nonetheless, it was the same man!*

In fact, this mild-mannered man with an exemplary temperance, actually sought an audience with the Spanish King himself – Felipe 11, who had long been involved in the struggle to control the other parts Europe, always with the aim to subject the Protestant populations to the rules of the Holy Father in Rome. Felipe's father had disliked Queen Elizabeth 1st, the staunch Protestant ruler of England, and with the Spanish Armada, had tried to grab England from under her nose, but with God's help and a fair wind, the English weather drove the Spanish ships off course, with many of them ending up at the bottom of the sea, and the rest of the fleet limping home. The year was 1588.

Guido saw a lot of military action whilst fighting in Spain. He served under the command of their allied country of Austria, and specifically under the Archduke Albert. In the year 1595, he fought in a huge battle at Calais in France, and also in the 1600 Battle of Nieuport in Flanders, during which he was wounded when under fire. He was given an assignment to blow up a series of military wagons, and this was how he first gained a knowledge of gunpowder, and of the best way to make it most effective. His reputation as a specialist in such things grew from that moment onwards, and he was noticed, not just by his Spanish and Austrian superiors, but also by a group of English Catholics, who like himself, had volunteered their services to Spain's Catholic cause. One of these English nobles ensured that Guido was transferred under his command – not only because of his fighting prowess, but also because he judged the man to be an intelligent diplomat, who might be of more use than as a mere foot soldier and cannon fodder.

His commander was now Sir William Stanley, who gave him a very important challenge for his diplomatic skills – he was to seek an audience with King Felipe of Spain, and try his best to persuade him that the time was right for another invasion of England. Guido knew well how big this challenge was, but knew also that, if he were to succeed with the Spanish king, his name would be made within the circle of those English nobles fighting in Spain.

Guido Fawkes travelled to Madrid, where the royal court was, and stood before King Felipe, his feathered hat in hand, and bowed low in a sweeping gesture, "Your Majesty, now is the time for you to act. There is a new King on the English throne, and if anything, he is more enamoured of that faith, which both you and I detest. He is forcing it on the people of England." He started well, and felt confident, as he was aware of his sturdy, strong build, and gentleman appearance. In fact, at the time, an artist colleague of his gave a good description of him – 'A tall, powerfully-built man, with thick, reddish-brown hair, a flowing moustache in the tradition of the time, and a bushy reddish-brown beard.' Remembering this, he stood as tall as he could, and said in a calm voice, "The failure of the Armada a few years ago will not happen again Your Majesty – not with the glorious sea-faring ships and crews, of which both Spain and her allies can boast. And as I'm sure your spies have already reported, England has a great many frustrated Catholics, who are ready to throw over the Scot King James, to see their country return to the one, true faith." So impressive was he, that Felipe was inclined at first to listen to his pleas, but held back from committing his country to such a thing. In fact, what Guido didn't know, was that King Felipe had recently been looking with favour on King James' court. He had quite enough with which to contend, in dealing with the Eighty Years War. Spain was even then, already moving in the direction of a permanent peace with England. That was for the king to know however, and Guido to discover in due course! He was aware too, from his excellent spies in England, that King James (always a nervous and suspicious man) was obsessed with the dangers, presented by Catholics in his country, and had doubled his harsh treatment of them, handing out more and more heavy fines to the English recusants. To James, intrigue was all around, and he continued to be afraid of every shadow, and of who may be lurking around any corner – dagger in hand.

In the Spanish court however, King Felipe knew he must answer the man, so he said, "This great nation of Spain has been bearing the burden of the fight against the ever-increasing spread of Protestantism across Europe – how much more do you think we can do? Our Treasury is low in funds, as the war is a costly business." He looked pensive and stroked his beard, "I am afraid Sir, although I greatly admire your enthusiasm, this country is not ready to attack England with a mighty – and costly fighting force. As you know, we are already fending off such upstarts in several countries at once. An invasion by another Armada is out of the question at this time."

He was on the point of dismissing Guido, when the Englishman tried a different tactic.

"If a great Armada is not possible Sire, perhaps smaller numbers could be sent to attack from within the country – to help and persuade by the many miserable Catholics England has – and I assure you Sire, there are many."

However, Felipe's mind had already moved on, and he wanted rid of the man. He'd become bored, so he handed a pouch of gold coins to the soldier, and said, "Take this for your cause – it may help somewhat." And Guido was quickly shown the door by a man servant. He did however put the money to good use, and sent it by a trusted servant to Robert Catesby, whom he knew to be a staunch supporter of the cause – and a friend of his current commander, Sir William Stanley. Catesby would never give up the cause, as he was very bitter about the treatment his own father had received, when Elizabeth was on the throne – the old man been imprisoned for many years, and all because he'd been a recusant, who'd refused to attend the Church of England. Because of this, Catesby had fallen on hard times, gentle nobleman though he was. In fact, he'd even had to sell his family home.

Back in camp, Guido met another like-minded soldier called Tom Wintour, whom he'd known from his school days. He learned from him that back in England, Catesby was involved with several Catholic nobles, who thought as he did himself, and a plot change the country was even then, being considered.

About two years later, there was a knock on the military mess door, "Sir, there is a gentleman at the camp gate, asking if he can speak with you. What shall I tell him?" One of the guards stood there waiting for a reply.

"Did he say what he wanted, Corporal? I'm due at a meeting in ten minutes," On being told the man had said it would only take a few minutes, Guido Fawkes, as he now styled himself, told the soldier to fetch the visitor. The man was obviously from Britain, judging from his clothes, but he wasn't in uniform, so the matter couldn't be a military one.

"Well Sir, do I know you? Do you have a message for me?" Guido was already dressed to leave the mess, and stared at the stranger rather impatiently. From his pocket, the man produced a waxed sealed envelope, and handed it over. Guido took it to the window, and broke the seal. He read the message quickly, and looked up at the man, "And who are you Sir – to being me such a missive? Who has sent you here?"

The man explained that he couldn't say who had initiated the letter – he'd been paid handsomely, to ensure he placed it personally into Fawkes' hand. "All I know is that it's very important you receive it, and that you trust me to take your answer back to England. May I wait outside for your answer – I am only here in Flanders for two days, then I must return swiftly to catch the ship on the next turn of the tide."

Guido waved his hand in dismissal, and told the stranger to wait outside, until he'd had time to think about his answer. This was the most important letter he was ever to receive – and how the rest of his life would pan out, depended on his answer, He needed time to think first. There weren't any explicit details in the letter, but the words used, made it perfectly clear what was being proposed. And what was truly encouraging, was it was from Robert Catesby himself.

'I've arrived – I've been head-hunted by the people who count, who really count! I know I only met him a couple of times, but I must have made a good impression on him, although I'm sure the money I sent helped that impression. He's obviously been made aware of my knowledge of explosives and gunpowder – and since I've been absent from England for so many years, my face will not be known to people in court circles. The Earl of Salisbury, Sir Robert

Cecil wouldn't raise an eyebrow if he heard the name Guy Fawkes – and he was the head of the English Monarchy's secret police. At least that's what he thought! Oh yes, he could see why Catesby had contacted him. He couldn't control his excitement, and felt a huge rush of adrenalin coursing through his body. It was time now – and Catesby would make sure it happened. That damnable James would soon be forced to allow the Catholic community to take their rightful place in society – and to run the country as they saw fit. 'He's asking if I'd be willing to come back to England and help with the struggle against religious injustices – he doesn't have to ask, he couldn't hold me back, if he tried.'

And it was at that point Guy Fawkes' future took a colossal, and inevitable turn, and he began to plan his return home. He was friends with Tom and knew his friend thought just as he did, so together, they planned to return to England. Before this happened, an incident occurred that could have adversely affected their plans. In 1599, the English government intercepted a letter, written by Guido's cousin, Richard Cowling, to a sympathetic gentleman in Venice. Unfortunately, he headed the letter 'The Fugitives', which was the reason it caught the eye of one of Cecil's espionage team. Part of the letter's contents read:

'I pray you lette me intreate yr favoure and friendshippe for my cosen Germane Mr Guydo Fawkes, who serves Sir William Stanley: as I understand he is in greate wante and yr worde in his behalf may stand him in greate steede.......He hath lefte a prettie living here in his country, which his mother being married to an unthriftie husbande since his departure, I think hath wasted away. Yet she and the rest of our friends are in good health........lette him tell my cosin Martin Harrington that I was at his brother Henries house at the mounte........'

The letter in itself didn't specifically state what Guy was up to in Spain – it was merely a request for the gentleman in Venice to give some comfort to a soldier who'd fallen on hard times – but it was enough to add the name of Guy Fawkes to a list of fugitives fighting in Spain.

Guy had been in Spain, fighting for the cause, for almost ten years, yet still the one true faith continued to struggle for its very existence. Daily, he cursed those damned Protestants – and none more so, the King himself. He'd tried very hard to make King Felipe see the necessity of invading England, but had failed. Now, the invasion would have to come from inside the country, and he was more than willing to help make it happen.

Since Queen 'Bloody' Mary's short reign, things had gotten increasingly worse for the English Catholics. Elizabeth 1, being such a staunch Protestant, was pleased to have the honour of being called the Head of the Church of England – and there was no room for Catholic recusants

Leaving Spain wasn't easy - after all, he'd been away from England for such a long time, although most of his time had actually been spent in Flanders, fighting the Dutch. Still it was quite a wrench! Wrench or not, his mind never wavered!

That smell is the smell of England – soon to be a free England – free for all men to worship God in his own way. As he stepped from the gangplank onto the dockside, Guido breathed deeply. The salty smell of the sea, and the piercing cry of the seagulls, took him back to the day he'd left for Spain. It had been ten years since he felt this way – hopeful and certain that things were about to change for the better. Like all good military men, he carried everything he owned in a large, canvas bag, slung over his shoulder. Even the sound of his heavy, leather boots that reached over his knees, sounded reassuring – even welcoming. He was home – and about to embark on what would be the biggest adventure of his life. An adventure that would make better the lives of all free-thinking English Catholics – and the sooner he started, the sooner the world would benefit. 'This is the reason I was born,' he told himself, and he knew for certain, it was true.

Leaning against the wall of a shed, a man moved forward out of the shadows. He'd spotted the military man coming down the ship's gangplank. He stepped forward, and

It introduced himself, "I've been sent to welcome you back to England – I presume you are Mr Guy Fawkes, recently returned from Spain?" As he spoke, he reached out to relieve the traveller of his heavy bag, but Guy pulled back, suspicious of the stranger from the shadows. However, when he was told Robert Catesby had sent the man, he relaxed and gratefully handed over his burden.

He'd decided earlier that he wouldn't visit Scotton to see his mother, as his mission was too dangerous – and very, very much a secret. He didn't want it to known yet that he'd returned to England. Initially the group met in a pub at the top of the Strand, and it was there they took an oath to carry out Robert Catesby's plan: to throw England into chaos by killing its king and all of its law makers – in one enormous explosion. The plan was relatively simple, but also the most dastardly ever planned. As part of that plan, they intended to install King James' young daughter Elizabeth as Queen, and immediately arrange for her to marry a foreign Catholic prince -from somewhere in Europe. Once done, England would again be returned to a Catholic monarchy. For safety sake, Fawkes assumed the name of John Johnson, servant to one of the other conspirators. The plan was moving forward.

The Westminster streets were literally a warren of alleys and buildings, with many small businesses plying their trades, so it was easy for the plotters to set themselves up there. At first, their plan was to rent a shop with a cellar, and from there, to dig a tunnel into the one next door, the one directly under the House of Lords. Then fate stepped in, and the shop next door suddenly became vacant. and was up for rent, so they abandoned the first one and moved next door, where the cellar actually extended right under the target. It couldn't have been better, and encouraged the group to believe it was meant to be – it had God's blessing.

With sheer brute strength, they filled the cellar with 36 barrels of gunpowder – all barrels were securely hidden under straw and wood faggots, well concealed from prying eyes. It was an amazingly simple plan, and with Fawkes now the caretaker of the second shop, nothing seemed amiss to the casual onlooker. He now looked after the new shop, in particular its cellar

The date for the explosion was set for 5 November, and everyone took their place, in support of the one man who knew all there was to know about firearms and gunpowder – Mr Guy Fawkes. On the night, King James, his two sons, and both the Houses of Lords and the Commons would be together in one pace – 36 barrels of gunpowder would be more than enough to blow the lot to kingdom-cum. They would all disappear at the same time, leaving a free England, able at last, to rule the country as it saw fit. The only fly in the ointment however, was within both houses, there would inevitably be some Catholics, known to Catesby and his friends, and the plan hadn't been to hurt any of them. It was decided that nothing could be done about it, although someone with a soft heart, may have decided to tip off a friend for old time's sake – indeed, that may have been exactly what was done.

Before the night of the plot however, we have to go back to 26 October of the same year, when Lord Monteagle, a Catholic nobleman, received a letter from an anonymous source, telling him he must conjure up an excuse that stopped him from attending the State Opening of Parliament. The letter didn't say why this was necessary, but it did stress how important it was that he obeyed the warning. Monteagle immediately took the letter to Sir Robert Cecil, who told King James at once. Between them, the King and Cecil decided it was a hoax, and the plans for the State Opening continued. They also agreed it would do no harm to check – just to be on the safe side, and therefore on the night of 4 November, the cellars of the building were searched by Sir Thomas Knyvett, a Westminster Magistrate. He and his men along with his men soldiers arrived to begin their search. As they went into the shop, what they found made them suspicious – Guy Fawkes was standing there, lounging nonchalantly against a wall. He was fully clothed and still wearing his long boots. This seemed odd, as the hour was very late, and so, they arrested him. He was searched, and in his pockets, they found three slow matches, plus all the paraphernalia needed to set off an explosion. Within seconds, the barrels of gunpowder, hidden under the faggots and straw were discovered. Guy immediately gave his name as John Johnson, which he stuck to for a few days. Once introduced to the rack however, he broke down and admitted who he really was. King James had ordered that only 'gentle' torture was to be used on Fawkes, and his fellow-conspirators, but this was just to begin with, and progression to the rack was inevitable, if the culprits refused to comply. So, firstly they were hung from walls by iron manacles, with the entire weight of their bodies hanging from their wrists. For two days, Fawkes would admit nothing, and so his torture quickly progressed to the rack, where his limbs were stretched to breaking point. The rack was quite in-human and caused the very worst kind of pain. After two days, Fawkes could no longer walk, and when found guilty, had to be dragged to the scaffold, where the executioner was waiting.

It was noted by observers that Fawkes was very brave under torture, and for some time, would not give up the names of his colleagues. Two days of horrific torture son made him change his mind, and eventually he gave them the information they wanted.

All the executions were carried out over 2 days – 30/31 January1606, with Fawkes being forced to watch the deaths of the other conspirators, before it was his turn. He was left alone at the end, crippled and unable even to write his own name - he finally met his fate on 31 January. In the Westminster Archives, there are two documents, one was signed just after Fawkes' arrest – and one after his torture – the first is neat and clear, whilst the second is merely a scrawl – an illegible scribble. It took only three days for his signature to deteriorate, the rack had certainly loosened his tongue. The scrawled signature was after he'd finally provided the names of his friends. The excruciating pain of the rack was too much for mortal man to bear, and once he'd informed on his colleagues, including those who'd escaped with Catesby. They were all either shot in battle, or captured and executed. When he finally gave all the names, Sir Edward Hoby, an observer of the torture, was heard to say, ' ***Since Johnson's been in the Tower, he beginneth to speak English.*** ' Sardonic and sarcastic, but true!

In the eyes of the monarchy, treason was the most heinous and foul crime, on which to be charged. It's worth knowing however, in the 'gentler' stages of his torture – before the rack crippled him totally – he still possessed some fighting spirit. When asked by his interrogators what had he planned to do with 36 barrels of gunpowder, Guy thought for a few moments, before saying, ***"To blow you Scotch beggars back to your native mountains."*** Not perhaps the most diplomatic of answers , but one which apparently earned the admiration of King James himself. The condemned man proved he still had gumption.

Following his last day on the rack, night had come at last, and he'd been dropped onto prickly straw, which was strewn along the rat-infested floor in his cell at the Tower of London. He was in such pain that he thought he was seeing things – he must have been delirious, with a burning hot fever. Every limb was stretched and his flesh bruised and aching,. For a moment, he thought he was already dead but, '*No, I must still be alive although death would at least have been be kinder.*' He tried to move, but couldn't, then he sensed a presence – someone else was in the cell. *'Had the guards come again to rack him - please God, no!'*

The figure in the corner wasn't clear, and he tried to rub the blood from his swollen, blinded eyes, but even raising his hand was too difficult. He could see it was a woman however, and she seemed familiar. '*What on earth was a woman doing there? She couldn't be a guard!*' Then, the woman moved forward slowly out of the dark corner, and he recognised his mother, Edith. *' Maybe they'd allowed her to visit him – but no, that couldn't be. Not a condemned traitor such as he.'*

Edith looked the same as the day he'd left Scotton to go to Spain – certainly no older. She raised a hand, and made to touch his face – but he flinched, he couldn't have borne the pain. Instead, she smoothed his now-sparse locks of hair back from his forehead, and leaned forward until her face was close to his. She spoke then, and her voice sounded so comforting, and so full of pity, he would have cried, but he couldn't even do that – there were no tears.

"Oh, my Son, why do I find you like this? Why have you been treated so badly? Is it really because you choose the Catholic faith – just as I do myself?"

Guy could say nothing – what was there to say? He knew the vision wasn't real – she was just a figment of his imagination, a spirit somehow lifted from her home in Scotton – and come to say goodbye. He managed the words, "Mother – forgive me. You should not see your son like this." His voice was a croak, but at least he could still manage to speak.

"My son, I've come to tell you how proud I am – proud of the great courage you've shown, and how you've tried to help the Catholic cause. Bless you – I know God will do the same. I want you to be strong – right until the end – they may have hurt you, but you've proudly stood up for what you believe." She touched his bloodied face once more, before fading slowly back into the corner. "Goodbye, my son – God is waiting to welcome you into his arms."

Guy felt better then. He knew he was dying, but wished that might happen before he had to face the horror of the scaffold. His mother's visit had had a soothing affect, and for a few moments, he was able to close his swollen eyes – but only for a moment, before the pain awakened him again.

The date was now 31st January 1606 and Guy was 35 years old. No longer was he the tall, strong soldier he'd once been. His luxurious red-brown hair had disappeared and his scalp was covered in blood – his body had been quite literally torn apart, and he needed the guards' support, as he was taken from his cell. His eyes were bulbous and protruding, and it seemed they still carried visions of his fellow-conspirators being executed on the scaffold – conspirators whose names he'd given to the authorities. He felt shame at that – if only he'd been able to stand the excruciating pain of the rack – but shamefully, he couldn't and had to do what stopped the pain. He was a pitiful sight, and his captors whipped the crowd into a frenzy of hate, so there was little sympathy for the broken man. In the crowd however, there must have been a number of Catholics, who felt some pity for him – but they were wise enough to keep their feelings to themselves. After all, there were Protestants all around, their eyes watching for anyone who showed pity for Guy Fawkes – and so, no-one did!

The pathetic state of the man could be clearly seen, as he shuffled towards the scaffold, the crowd's jeers ringing in his ears. Physically, he looked completely different from the man who'd initially been arrested by the guards – people said to each other that his own mother would have found it difficult to recognise her son. He was no longer tall – or strong, and his thick auburn hair had almost gone – perhaps some pulled out by himself to take his mind off his agony; he tripped pitifully over his own feet, and staggered until one of the guards decided to support him. Then he stood there in full view, and for a moment, he wondered if King James was watching from some hidden window – the sort of thing the cowardly king would do. . He tried to stretch to his full height, but couldn't manage it. He opened his mouth to speak, and blood gurgled from his throat, and trickled down his front. He asked for forgiveness from the King and from the State, but it was noticed by on-lookers that he continued his Roman Catholic practices and gestures, and made the sign of the cross more than once.

As he looked down into the jeering mob, he spotted someone he'd once known. The man was standing amongst the onlookers, with a sad expression on his face. <My God, there was no doubt it was his father, Edward Fawkes - his father who'd died when Guy was only eight years old. When his eyes met with Guy's own, his expression changed and there was just a hint of a smile. Guy mouthed 'Father……' but no words came. Edward Fawkes shook his head ruefully, and pursed his lips – he was obviously upset at how he found his son, and although he'd been dead for almost thirty years, Guy knew exactly what he was thinking. He could almost hear the words, "Son, I brought you up as a good Protestant, and you should have stayed that way. You should have known this Catholic nonsense would bring you down in the end."

A tall man with broad shoulders pushed in front of Edward's ghost, and when Guy looked again, the ghost of his father had disappeared. He searched the crowd in vain, the man had truly gone.

Fawkes was well aware of what was in front of him. Hadn't he seen his colleagues suffer in the same way? For a moment, the leader Robert Catesby came unbidden into his mind, and he wondered if he'd managed to get away safely, and at least be able to fight for the cause another day. Somehow, it helped to think of Catesby, and that he was still alive! Somehow the thought helped lift his mind from where he stood on the scaffold steps.

As part of their plan, Catesby with a few fellow-conspirators had left the city already, heading for Staffordshire, where he intended to encourage an uprising in the Midlands. It was certain in that area there were many supporters of the Catholic faith, who would join together and come at King James in a two-pronged attack. Coupled with the success of the Gunpowder Plot by Fawkes, and Catesby's uprising in the Midlands – England would be saved forever. That was the plan anyway! Unfortunately for the case, the uprising failed, and Catesby and his men had to flee to the village of Dunchurch near Rugby, Warwickshire. There, the small group made a stand at Holbeche House, near the Old Lion Inn in Dunchurch, where they faced a 200 strong government company of armed men. The Inn's name was soon changed, almost immediately, to 'Guy Fawkes' House – although the man himself, never lived there. Commercialism was rife even then it seemed.

Against such odds, Catesby and his men were easily cut down and killed. Later, when his body was collected for burial, he was found clutching a picture of the Virgin Mary. He was buried where he'd lain, but later, his body was exhumed and his head cut off – it was exhibited outside the Houses of Parliament – for any hesitator to see- and fear! . What a way for him to meet his end, and he was only 33 years old? He'd been educated at Oxford and had been born in Warwickshire. A gentleman by birth, he came from a family of prominent Catholic recusants, something that had obviously set him on the anti-Protestant path. Strangely enough however, he married a Protestant in1593 (the same year as Fawkes set off to fight in Spain), and had two sons – one died as a baby, but the other lived and was baptised in a Protestant church. At some point, he must have felt torn in two directions – not a good position in which a recusant finds himself. Catesby's family home was called Ashby Manor House – one of the most historic and intriguing houses in England, and the Catesby family had lived there from 1375 to 1611; and it was there the recusant conspirators actually held their final meeting before the night of 5th November 1605.

Guy's mind returned to his present predicament and the crowd's jeers and car-calling, again broke into his thoughts. He realised he'd just asked for God – and the Kings' – forgiveness, and unfortunately he was still compos-mentis, and saw he was still standing on the dreaded scaffold. It was all still in front of him! He'd been spared the first stage of the execution of such traitors, that of being pulled upside down to the scaffold by a horse, and with his face to the ground - he was however about to face much worse. He knew he would be hanged by the beck until almost dead – but not quite – he would still be able to watch as his genitals were cut off and burned before his eyes; with luck he might just pass out before his heart and bowels were removed from his body – please God. Finally, he knew his body would be cut into four parts, with his severed head being placed on a spike on London Bridge. Each of the four body parts would then be sent to the four corners of the kingdom, where they'd be displayed for the gratification of the birds of carrion prey, and of course, so that the people would learn what happens to men, who gainsay their King.

In the case of the traitor Guy Fawkes however, 'the plans of mice and men gang aft aglay',and as the weakened man climbed the steps to the scaffold, he stumbled at the top – and either jumped or fell, crashing into the ground below. Death was instantaneous, and the sound of his neck breaking could be heard by those standing nearby. Fawkes had escaped the even more foul stages of his execution, and deprived the bloodthirsty crowd of their sport. No-one had seen it coming, and at first, there was confusion, but this soon passed, and Fawkes' dead body was mutilated as though he were still alive, and the four quarters dispensed with in the same way of all convicted traitors.

Some people will say, he had the last laugh – but a laugh at what expense? Not one he would have chosen, that's for sure. Then again, what he'd tried to do, and his subsequent execution meant his name would live forever, never to be forgotten. He had been ready to put a torch to the biggest explosion ever known – well, certainly not in the next 17th, 18th, nor 19th centuries.

****

This then, is the tale of Guy Fawkes, the man you love to remember in November. No question about his convictions – he was an ardent Catholic – but wanted it to be recognised and legalised in England. What is amazing however is, if he'd just been born a little later, he would have been a subject of King James' son, Charles, who tuned out to be a closet Catholic himself, and actually favoured that religion unconditionally, appointing only Catholics into the most prestigious positions at court. That policy however, lost him his kingdom and then his head – before another Charles (his son) came along – and despite pretending to be Protestant, he chose Catholicism on his deathbed. He hadn't really minded what a man's religion was, as long as he was allowed to enjoy himself, and just have a good time. Swings and Roundabouts – Swings and Roundabouts! What would Guy Fawkes have said, if only he could have seen into the future,

****

Before leaving this tale however, there is something I'd like to put to you, the reader. I don't want you to dismiss the story above, but I would like to give you another scenario, something to chew over before closing this book. Let's open our minds, think objectively, and consider something that might/could have been. As to whether it was, or was not, is something that to this day, continues to occupy the minds of those university academics, who study history. There is no definitive answer, as none of it can be proven, whereas history has recorded the details above, that is what happened in the life of Guy Fawkes. Having thought about it considerably, the author's findings are like pie in the sky – quite possible, not entirely unlikely - but without a shred of evidence. Still, it's not illegal to pursue an alternative scenario, so please read on.

As an open-minded and objective reader, please consider below. I hope it will provide food for thought, but I know it will not provide any clear answers. You should bear in mind that a continuous debate still goes on – and has been, since just after the failed Gunpowder Plot of 1605. It has been argued that Guy Fawkes and his leader, Robert Caseby, were not the perpetrators of the planned explosion, but rather scape goats for the monarchy and the government, who were in desperate need to blacken the name of Catholicism. They were double agents, and very much involved with the 'window-dressing' of the plot, they were in effect, merely actors, obeying the orders of their superiors. There never was an intention to blow up parliament and to kill a king and his sons – none of them were ever in any real danger. King James used his first minister, Sir Robert Cecil, as a go-between – between himself and 'the conspirators.' That is to say, the Gunpowder Plot was not planned by a group of Catholic sympathisers at all, and King James was never in fear for his life, whilst Cecil arranged everything in order to curry favour with the king, whom he hoped would reward him handsomely for his support. (He was yet to learn of James' deep pockets and short arms! Times were desperate – and the Catholics were behaving badly, intending to 'bring down the Protestant king,' and return the country to the one, true faith. It has been suggested in some debates that both Robert Catesby and Guy Fawkes were double agents – and whilst loyal to the Catholic faith, they were equally attracted to what the Crown could pay them.

The great and numerous problems caused by the English Catholic recusants, had caused King James many headaches, since coming south of the border. The stability of his throne was always in question, and all because of those damned Catholics. Similar religious troubles in Europe were bad enough, but the threat was just as big in his own country. The island of Britain had always been vulnerable from invading forces, and James knew he had to keep a close eye on the Catholics. James and his government new only too well, that the English Catholic recusant movement was their arch-enemy, and needed to be suppressed once and for all. The thought therefore, of not only disgracing those who wouldn't accept his authority, but also to be able to paint them as the braggards, who intended to hurt the people, was a very attractive prospect indeed.

Worst of all, with James' paranoid fear of something he believed was evil and dangerous, and that's what he thought of the church in Rome, which he 'knew' was controlled by the Devil Incarnate himself. He believed Catholic practices showed them to be part of medieval idolatry - and idolatry, bordering on voodoo-ism and the occult. The Scottish king had been obsessed with these things all his life. In fact, he even wrote a book about evil itself – and called it " Daemonologie.' To his way of thinking, the overblown, dramatic practices of Catholicism were akin to the unsavoury practices of witchcraft – always involving evil and cruelty towards its victims. Was this pragmatic or even logical? It really didn't matter, it was what he believed, and he was the king. He even re-wrote the bible, removing at least seven books from the original Old Testament, which had allegedly been handed down to Moses by God himself. In fact, he wrote more than one book, he actually wrote several, with one being specifically for his son, but the boy died in his teens, something James probably put down to the occult. The hunting of witches started earlier in Scotland, and slowly moved down the country to England. Many an old crone died in the fires, or were crushed to death beneath heavy boulders – and all because of James' paranoia.

This then is the background to how the new king was feeling as he sat on the throne in his new country, surrounded by ministers who saw it as their duty, to please him. One such minister being Sir Robert Cecil – a man, who also greatly disliked the English Catholics, and who possessed the right power at the right time, to arrange the Gunpowder Plot with the use of double agent. The threat posed by the Gunpowder Plot by the Catholics would be blame. on them, highlighting how bad they'd be for England. Fawkes and Caseby were two such agents..

For a moment, imagine the conversations that might have taken place between Cecil and the king – and perhaps with several others, who were included in a very secret pact. Despite the existence of the anonymous letter, warning the State Opening of Parliament should be avoided at all costs, both Cecil and the king, decided to ignore it – it was after all, a forgery, wasn't it? To ignore such a threat could have been described as rash., and certainly not a wise one. If on the other hand, you knew it would never actually happen, as it would be prevented in good time, then the decision to attend the State Opening was safe enough.

The writer of the letter was never discovered and not even investigated. Understandably, the authority's doubts were seen as reasonable, and their questioning of how genuine the letter really was acceptable. And how brave was this new king, who faced up to such a treacherous challenge? Very brave indeed – and excellent propaganda for a man, who sat on an unstable throne.!

The story of Guy Fawkes and the Gunpowder Plot of 1605 has been around for a very long time – it starts with children at school, who thoroughly enjoy burning the effigy of the man, who tried to blow up the King and his Parliament. It's fun, and gives them the excuse of going around calling out, 'Penny for the Guy Mister. Please give a penny for the Guy!' So, from a very early age, we teach our children that burning such effigies is an acceptable act.

A chilling thought, especially if Guy and his friend, Robert were actually innocent of what they were charged, and that they were only playing their part I a plan, dictated by Cecil and King James. Did we get it wrong at the time – or has history been right all along? But, that's for you to decide.

Whilst considering it, do bear in mind, that this alternative thinking may seem unlikely, that could be because we've been brainwashed by historical records of the time, written to please a reigning monarch. A monarch, although highly intelligent, was afraid of his own shadow, believing he lived under the shadow of potential foreign invasion, of assassins lurking around every corner, and of withes, warlocks, ghosts and of the Devil himself. He was also very afraid of the Catholic threat within his realm, and dealing with that was his first priority. Thus, in his mind, he had enemies both outside and inside the country, and he knew he had to deal with the Catholic threat first. As for Sir Robert Cecil, he knew on which side his bread was buttered and was only too willing to help his liege-lord rid the country of the damned Catholic threat. Anyway, he hoped James would be generous with his grateful thanks, and reward him significantly. As mentioned before, he was still to learn of James' deep pockets and short arms – the king was not a man to spent money unnecessarily, and if he could get out of a debt, he would assuredly do so.

****

So, I have presented you with a possible – not completely unlikely counter-explanation. Because of the Gunpowder Plot, and subsequent executions, the English people believed they'd been saved from an attack by their fellow-citizens, whom they knew were working under orders from the Vatican in Rome. (At least, that's what they'd been told) However, their new and courageous king had sorted them out!

The theory, an alternative to our history books, suggests that the double-agent Guy Fawkes, and his companions died horrific deaths wrongly, being completely innocent of any threat. The question has to be,' Would Cecil, and James, have been evil enough to torture and execute such innocents – when they were only acting under orders? Surely no moral man could allow this to happen – or could he? Again, that's for you to decide!

To help you with that decision however, you should perhaps read below:

One year after the Gunpowder Plot was foiled, King James ordered a national holiday and great celebrations were enjoyed throughout the country. He even passed an official Thanksging Act which thanked God for saving his life. Great bonfires, fireworks and burnings of effigies of Guy Fawkes, took place in every town and village. It was made clear however, that the celebrations were in recognition of 'God's saving of the king, and his Ministers of State'; in effect, in recognition of the stability and the superiority of the Protestant religion itself. It was made clear what those evil and misguided Catholics had been planning for the country – and King James had faced the threat and in so doing, had saved the people from great danger. Hooray for the King! Hooray for the man who saved us! That was the message sent out across the land. Even in the colonies in America, the celebrations were called 'Pope's Day', and the burning effigies were of the Pope, rather than of Guy Fawkes. The world over was told the words Catholic and evil meant the same thing. The message was clear, the Gunpowder Plot was over, and King James sat securely on the throne of the United Kingdom of Great Britain.

****

Well, that's it my friends. What are your thoughts? Was Guy Fawkes responsible for the biggest and most ambitious act of treason ever known in this country? Or was it clever planning by a scardy-cat, but smart King, and his chief minister, Cecil? Was Guy Fawkes guilty of almost succeeding in murdering so many people all at the same time – just so he could achieve his goal, and worship in a church of his own choosing? Or was the devious monarch clever in his attempt to cast blame and shame on the country's Catholics – and so manage to reach his goal? Many minds, throughout the centuries have considered this question, and now it's your turn. Are you ready to rewrite history – or are you going to let sleeping dogs lie? It's your decision!

****

Author's Notes of Interest:

1.

It's interesting to know that from the year 1215, torture was actually illegal in England – something established by the signing of the Magna Carta, and was intended to ensure the

restricting of the English kings' powers. Perhaps King James, and indeed many of his predecessors, were unaware of this restriction.

2.

To this day, and as an anti-terrorist precaution, a group of guards still search the cellars under the Houses of Parliament just before the Legislature's State Opening of Parliament. It has become a tradition, ever since that fateful night of 5th November 1605.

Arthur Pendragon - the Once and Future King

This story is either about a man who was a warrior king, or it's about a myth, and a legend. It'll be your choice in the end! Having read the story, you'll be able to form your own opinion - but before you do, here's some background to the time, when King Arthur lived, led and defended the people of post-Roman Briton, or Britannia, as the invaders had preferred.

The period is referred to as the Dark Ages, and it was especially so in Briton, the home of the Celts. Some counties believed it was acceptable to invade another land, and take whatever they wanted – killing, maiming, raping and plundering as they went along. In the fifth and sixth centuries this was an attitude, particularly held by the Germanic nations, whose own lands were not favourable to the growing of crops, nor the grazing of animals. The Norse countries were cold, often freezing-over for long periods of the year: they were also prone to regular flooding. How much better it would be if they had Briton's lush, green and fertile land. All they had to do, was to cross the sea and take it – which was exactly what they attempted to do throughout the 'Dark Ages.' The invaders who first came were called barbarians by the sophisticated Romans – the Norsemen who came, were the Norse Saxons, Angles and Jutes, and the Romans thought of them as ignorant, illiterate, uncultured and unchristian. They still worshipped their own Gods, such as Thor and Odin, completely ignorant of the one true God worshipped by the world's 'new' Christians. This Christianity was fast spreading throughout Europe, and even the Romans who, until recently, had worshipped their own Gods, now accepted Christianity.

When the Romans finally left Briton, it was to deal with growing problems developing across their vast empire, but they did leave behind many ex-soldiers, who had slowly integrated with the local people. It's long been accepted that, although they too had once been the invaders, they left the conquered countries in a more advanced condition than when they'd first arrived. By the 5th century AD however, the Romans were long gone, and Briton was left wide open to the invading Norsemen, who lost no time in sailing their long boats across the wild Atlantic Ocean.

If ever the Celtic people needed a leader and a hero, it was then – and waiting within the walls of Camelot Castle, probably in the south of the country, was a man destined to be just that, and to become the saviour of his people. That man was Arthur Pendragon, who would be remembered for the rest of time – and who, even at the point of death, loved his country and his people so much, that he promised to return if ever he was needed.

The question to be considered however is, was he one man, or was he several men? Was he the wishful thinking of a people suffering an invasion of barbarians – or was he just a much-needed figment of their imagination? Without the protection and guidance of the Romans, the Celts were at their lowest ebb, and desperately needed a strong figurehead, on whom to pin their hopes. Enter Arthur Pendragon – the man, or the myth – the decision is yours.

The various Celtic kingdoms were left fragmented because of different cultures and customs. They had of course, adopted many of the Roman ways, and learned much during the four centuries of their occupation. The Romans in their turn, had been committed to integrate with the locals, something they did in other countries, and in due course, the two did mix, and the Celts realised how much they'd benefitted from the presence of the Romans.

At the close of the 4th century however, most of the Romans had left their Britannia, in order to deal with the hordes of barbarians who'd recently crossed the Rhine, and were causing problems in the Roman-occupied parts of Europe. Their garrisons and forts were abandoned when a new Emperor was declared by the Roman military, and Constantine 3rd was duly elected. His first decision was that Britannia must now fend for herself, and he quickly transferred the military to hot-spots across Europe.

Without the protective, presence of Rome, Briton was left vulnerable, confused, and ready for the plucking – so the barbarians of Scandinavia saw this as an opportunity to attack Briton's green and pleasant land. Denmark, Jutland, and the Dutch Netherlands, pulled their battle resources together, and travelled across the ocean, their ships struggling all the way through the notoriously-high winds. Nothing could have stopped them, they were hardened against the elements, and their sea-faring skills were second to none. `they'd always had an eye on the rich pickings on offer in Briton, and although the rough seas might be challenging, the distance between the countries. And so, they came! They wanted it, and were determined to take it.

This then, was to be the beginning of a new nation of Anglo-Saxons, who in time, would over-run much of Briton, and who ironically one day in the 8th and 9th centuries, would have to defend their adopted country against a fresh horde of barbarians, called the Vikings. These were of course, their own descendants coming from the same cold countries for the same reasons as their ancestors had previously done. Both the later invading Vikings, and those being attacked, were one people, no longer referred to as Angles, Saxons and Jutes, but they came from the same northern lands that their forebears had done.

The 5th and 6th AD invasion attacks were suspiciously timely, as they first began along the English coastlines at the very time the Romans had left. The invaders' weapons were superior and efficient, as was their fighting ability, and they obviously had a very productive spying regime, as they knew for certain it was the right time to invade. Briton was ripe for the taking, and the Norse invaders wasted no time – surprise was the best attack!

Invasion, in order to better oneself, was common practice in the Dark Ages, and was taking place across the world. The morality of taking what didn't belong to you, was not a consideration, whereas a country's survival was. Other Invasions around the same time involved the Scotti from Ireland who invaded Dalriada (Scotland), the land of the Picts; they'd originally come from France before invading the Irish Isles, where they first established themselves, before moving on to attack the Picts. Soon the integrated peoples were known as Gaels – a mixture of the original Scotti, the Irish, and the Picts. The Romans had of course been aware this was happening in the North of Briton, but they'd always had trouble with the fierce Picts, and decided just to shut them out. Anyway, they were always nipping across the border to help themselves to whatever wasn't nailed down. They were nothing but a nuisance to the Romans, hence the building of Hadrian's Wall, which helped a lot, but the Picts, now reinforced by the Scotti and the Irish, proved too hard a nut to crack – and their frequent skirmishes and attacks across the border, continued.

It's easy therefore, to appreciate the desperate situation in which the Celts found themselves – they were left vulnerable and unprepared. Briton was in turmoil therefore, just when the Angles and Saxons decided to take what didn't belong to them. They had Briton in their sights, and knew of the confusion there. The time was right to steer their long boats across the sea, to plunder and attack the unsuspecting people.

And so, he came! He was an enigmatic and romantic figure who seemed to appear out of the mists of time. Suddenly he was there, just when he was needed. He rode at the head of an army of chivalrous knights, who were equally determined to chase the Norsemen out of Briton.

Eventually, Arthur Pendragon would be claimed as King of the Britons, whose name would live forever. Even today, his story and his promise can be seen inscribed on the walls inside the Houses of Parliament – a country never forgets its true heroes. Such a notabledistinction however, is awarded to very few – and in the case of King Arthur, it's even more unusual, as his very existence continues to be debated today.

It's not possible to say exactly when King Arthur led his Knights of the Round Table into battle, but it seems likely it was around the middle of the 5th Century. The Germanic barbarians (as the Romans called them) had begun their first attacks as early as the beginning of the 5th century AD, and immediately began to settle in different parts of the country. They used the template created by the Romans themselves, when they'd first arrived, one of using the iron fist at first, and then the kid one, so as to achieve a successful integration with the locals. As numbers grew in the different settlements, the names of new kingdoms slowly emerged: Wessex is a good example, as many of the western Saxons settled there: Sussex too grew in size by the arrival of more Saxons into their midst – and perhaps the most famous of all - the settlement in Northumbria, which grew enormously in size over time.

Some scholars argue that King Arthur was really a Celtic God, straight out of mythology, and not a mortal man at all; they believed his name was confused with a popular, and highly thought-of Celtic chieftain. This is of course, a consideration, but without evidence, who could ever tell? Lord, Chieftain, King, all could be one and the same. King Arthur's reputation was certainly widely-known, but it might have tended to be a little exaggerated, as folklore at the time had him killing giants, witches, and monsters – nothing was impossible as far as the locals were concerned. He was unbeatable, and his sword was ever-ready in the defence of his fellow-Celts, and that's all they needed to know about him.

Where was Camelot actually located – no-one is sure? Some believe it might even have been as far away as Scotland (Guinevere was allegedly a Scottish princess) – but then magical Camelot is claimed by so many locations – who can tell? Cornwall is a definite favourite, and shouldn't be dismissed out of hand. (The hill fortress at Cadbury is one good example.) What we do know however, is that Arthur he came from a place called Camelot - a gentle paradise where magical things often happened, and where people such as Merlin, Guinevere, Lancelot lived – names straight from the annals of time. It has also been claimed, that under Uther Pendragon's rule (King Arthur's father), there were a total of 150 knights at Camelot, all chivalrous to the core, and ever-ready to fight in the pursuit of justice. Camelot was indeed an exceptional place.

The problem of having no written records to provide evidence of Arthur's existence, is even more complicated by the fact that his story wasn't written down until the 12th century, when the scholar Geoffrey of Monmouth put pen to paper and told the tale. (With much poetic licence it has to be said.) Monmouth was an eminent scribe with a good reputation, but he was also famous for his vividly imaginative tales. As a historical scribe however, he was equally famous for his identification of ancient manuscripts – manuscripts which provided him with information about a mystical warrior king called Arthur, who'd faced the onslaught of the Angles, Saxons and Jutes. Many of such manuscripts could possibly have been based on 'word of mouth' stories', handed down from one generation to another – and it should be remembered that the spoken language of the time, had many different variations, even within the Celts themselves, let alone the additional invasion force's foreign tongues. It would have been almost impossible for details to be recorded, as whilst the country was fighting off the attackers, the scribes in the monasteries were not in a position to create new manuscripts. Religious houses were regularly sacked and robbed by the invaders, as religious valuables and holy relics were especially attractive – and so very easy to take from the simple holy men. Not a good time for the recording of events as the happened.

To defend Geoffrey of Monmouth, it is known he would have had access to resources now lost to us today: his descriptions of the Nordic raids, their consequences for the Celts, and of course the Arthurian Legend itself, cannot be easily dismissed. (As some non-believers are inclined to do) Monmouth may have had access to old manuscripts and relics from long before his own time, and with careless handling, were soon damaged or discarded. Monmouth's Arthurian legend therefore, should not be considered as mere fabrication, but rather as 'possible' bona-fide evidence, available to him in the twelfth century. Never a truer word is spoken than, 'Once it's gone, it's gone' – and that's what could have happened to Geoffrey's ancient manuscripts.

Yet another chronicler named Nennius refers to Arthur in his writings, calling him 'dux bellorum', which translates as military leader, rather than king. He claims for Arthur, twelve separate and successful battles against the Saxons; he also mentions the great battle at Mt. Badon, which is believed by many, to have been the turning point in the vast numbers of invaders. He tells in detail, how King Arthur rode at the head of his army at Mt. Badon. Other scribes throughout the centuries, have attributed many great victories to Arthur. Strangely though, the church has always been unusually silent on the subject of King Arthur. He was not a favourite of the church, who were quick to claim that our hero was notorious for relieving any of the holy houses, of their valuables and treasures. This was apparently needed in order to finance his struggle against the Anglo-Saxons. (Perhaps therefore, it wasn't only the Norse invaders who emptied religious houses of their wealth!)

For the purposes of the tale below, you should know I'm going to assume King Arthur was not a myth, but a real-live hero – a warrior king, who pulled together a broken and devastated country, giving the people hope for the future. Once ***'my'*** story of King Arthur has been fully digested, we'll return to the question 'was he or wasn't he real? As you continue reading this tale, please bear in mind that, whilst there is no actual historical evidence that the man ever lived, neither is there any historical evidence that he didn't!

****

WAS THE MAN MAD, OR JUST VERY GIFTED?

Normally, I like to build into my stories some element of fantasy or ghostly goings-on, but in the following tale, there's really no need. The central figure is himself, an out-of-this-world character, who is continuously tormented by life itself, and lives with a permanent fear of what might happen next. He suffers from hallucinations and has frequent periods of abject misery when he is occasionally beset by demons. Despite these problems, he is now one of the most gifted and popular painters in the art world, but like many a gifted genius, his talent was only recognised after his death. In his own time however, he was fated to die penniless. Luckily, he had a very generous and caring brother, who looked after him 'till the day he died.

Do you know who I'm talking about? Do you recognise his story? You might be able to guess, were I to tell you that one of his paintings recently sold at auction for just under $90,000,000. That's right – a huge sum! The artist himself however died penniless. It wasn't until 11 years after his death that his genius was finally appreciated, and his works of art began to fly off the shelves. His bright, colourful, post-impressionist works finally found their place in the world of art, and soon, his name was known throughout the entire world.

Still not sure of whom I'm talking about? Let me give you some more details of his life, starting when he was born. Bear with me, as I tell you this – I want you to get to know the man well, as this story ends with a question – a question for you - and only when you understand him, will you be able to give an answer.

****

He was born 30 March 1853 in the town of Groot-Zundert in Brabant, a region of the Netherlands, close to the Belgian border, and he was the oldest of six children. His family were upper-middle-class, and his father Theodorus, had chosen him as the oldest child, to become a parson in the Dutch Reformed Community – just as he'd done himself. The family were committed Protestants, although it seems his son wasn't quite as committed as his father. His mother was Anna Cornelia Carbentus, who'd lost her first son only one year after her marriage. Another year on, and to the exact day when she'd lost her first baby, she gave birth to another boy, who was given the same name as his dead brother. As that boy grew up. and learned about the brother with his own name, he might be forgiven for thinking he was no more than a replacement child, and was living his life for his dead brother. Could this have had an effect on his mental well-being – who can tell?

As a boy, he most likely had a happy enough upbringing, but that didn't make him a happy person, and he would often question why he was even part of the human race. When he was 27 years old, he suddenly discovered a need to paint, and after only a four-month course at a painting school in Paris, he devoted his life to the creation of works of art. He became a full-time artist, and over the following ten years, he went on to produce more than 2,100 works of art, 900 in oil on canvas, others on paper and cardboard, or on whatever material he could find at the time. Although his early works were dark and sombre, he changed both his style and use of colour, following a short time spent in Montmartre in Paris.

Throughout his last ten years, when he painted ferociously, he only ever sold one painting, and that was to a fellow-artist called Anna Boch – she paid him the princely sum of 400 Francs. He also managed to produce 43 self-portraits, but as he didn't like how he looked, he painted over many of them. His mirror-image was the cheapest model he could find, and he made good use of it. Models in Paris were so expensive, and his circle of friends so small - his own image was the cheapest subject the penniless artist could find. Even the well-known paintings he did after cutting off his ear, were obviously done using a mirror, as they all portray the bloodied bandage around the wrong ear. He'd overlooked that mirror images are in reverse. Now that is a big hint, and I should think you're beginning to have an inkling of his name now!

One thing we do know about him for certain, is that he lived with a mental illness all of his life, and regularly suffered from depression, hallucinations, and seizures – some very severe. Modern psychiatry has attempted to diagnose his condition, and have suggested schizophrenia, bipolar disorder, syphilis, hypergraphia, Geschwind syndrome or temporal lobe epilepsy – to name but a few. He may have suffered from one of these. or he may have had a combination of them, but whatever he suffered from wasn't helped by his every-day lifestyle. He lived mainly on tobacco, coffee, and bread, and of course on copious amounts of absinth; any spare money he had was used to buy precious paints and materials.

With all of the above, I'm sure you already know about whom I'm talking – it is of course, the Dutch post-impressionist artist, Vincent Willem van Gogh. (He rarely used the name Willem, and because people mis-pronounced his surname, he just signed his paintings Vincent).

However, I mustn't get ahead of myself, as I want to paint my own picture of this remarkable man's life. He may have been mentally-ill, but he was still immensely talented, something unfortunately not recognised until after he was dead. He often doubted his skill as an artist, and had a habit of painting over 'finished' canvasses – such doubts manifested themselves when he was feeling at his lowest ebb. Unfortunately, a dark depression often plagued his waking hours, as well as his nights, and he would suffer from hallucinations and fits. As an adult, he moved around a lot, probably living at over thirty addresses throughout his life, never settling for long, and never actually owning a place of his own. He was continuously on the move, never settling in one place or in one occupation – until a proverbial light bulb switched on when he reached the age of twenty-seven – and realised at last, the reason for which he'd been placed on the earth. He became a painter!

We have to start long before this however, if we're to learn what made him become the man he was, so when he was 12 years old, he was sent to a boarding school in Zevenbergen, where he remained for two years, before moving on to the King Willem 11 school in Tilburg

for a further two years. Soon it was 1868, and the 15-year-old Vincent moved to stay with a cousin in The Hague - Anton Mauve, who was already established as a talented painter. He spent a year at his home, but wasn't inspired to take up painting as a career – it seemed that art was not his subject!

After a few months, he left education completely, never to return, and travelled home to visit his family. Most of the time there he spent lazing about the house, and the rest sleeping and going for long walks. He liked nature, flora and fauna in particular, and he'd once told a tutor that the two things he enjoyed most at school was sleeping and wandering in the countryside. As the tutor taught history, he gave Vincent a deserved three whacks of the cane.

"Vincent, this isn't good enough, you're not setting a good example for your brothers and sisters. What are you planning to do with your life?" His father, Theodorus the Protestant pastor, had called the young Vincent to his study. "I thought the time at boarding school would have given you direction, but it seems not. And what about your time with your cousin Anton – he has written to me, and said he tried his best with you, and taught you all he could, but apparently, you were indifferent to his attempts. Come on boy, what do you have to say for yourself? I'm waiting!" For a moment, Vincent thought he was back at school, and waiting for the cane. He was standing stiffly in front of the fireplace, knowing he mustn't sit down until he was invited to do so. He was wondering why his father had always been so strict with him, much more than with his brothers and sisters – but then, he was the oldest.

Soon, he had the answer, "You are my eldest child, and I still have great expectations of you. At one time, you were to become a pastor like myself, but you tell me now, that no longer interests you. I don't know what I'm going to do with you." Theodorus looked how he felt. His hair was standing on end, where he'd roughed it in exasperation, and he was slumped behind his desk, holding his head in his hands, which didn't help the hair situation.

Vincent knew he had to think quickly and an idea suddenly popped into his head. "I'll tell you what Papa, perhaps I could give short sermons about nature, and how important it is to all of us, and how we should respect it. Sometimes, people need to be reminded of this."

It wasn't really a solution, as it didn't help the boy shape his future life, but at least it was something, so Theodorus agreed his son could come along at the end of the next church service, and speak to the people for 10 minutes. And that was Vincent van Gogh's first job – only one of many still to come. His short sermons became quite popular and after a year or so, he moved to Borinage in Belgium, and worked as a lay preacher there. He preached to the hard-working miners, but it wasn't to last, and he began to look around for a bigger challenge, and one with more money – or at least some money. Truth to tell, he was actually forced to look for another challenge, as he'd been sacked from the preaching job in Belgium, the reason given being. 'that the young man failed to do his best and to work hard.' Vincent was smart enough to look for alternative employment, before the mining company threw him out on his ear.

So, in 1883, he moved back to live with his parents for a short while, primarily because he had nowhere else to go. His parents noticed a change in their son - he'd become more sombre, really rather morose – a sadness would come over him in waves, and they soon learned it was best to keep away from him when these moods struck. His very best friend, was, and always would be, his brother Theo, who was as cheerful and positive thinking, as Vincent was not. Their friendship was to remain strong for the rest of their lives however, and often when Vincent was between jobs, and had no money, he would write to Theo asking for a loan, or a gift, and his brother never let him down. He wrote to Theo often, telling what he was up to, and luckily, Theo's wife Johanna, had the foresight to gather and save these descriptive missives, to safeguard them for a future date, although at the time she knew not why. The reason would one day reveal itself however, and she would bind them together and have them published. Did she have a premonition perhaps? How could she have known that one day, her brother-in-law would emerge as one of the world's greatest painters? Whatever drove her to do this is the reason we have the artist's life story – and perhaps that story would add to his fame as an artist – who knows? During his short life, he would write more than 800 very long and detailed letters, mostly to Theo, but also some to the rest of his family, to his fellow-artists and friends, such as Paul Gauguin and Emile Bernard, the friends in Paris.

Things were difficult just then, and he knew not to ask his father for money whilst he was 'between' jobs; the answer would have been, 'Well, find another job then.' His brother was a much easier touch however, and for whatever reason, Theo had always adored his older brother, and sure enough, the return letter would contain the required 'loan'. Theo would always remain his good friend, and luckily, he'd also left his Dutch home, and become a successful art dealer in Paris, and was able to support his needy brother.

Vincent tried his hand as an art dealer himself, whilst living in The Hague, where he'd once attended boarding school. He was employed by the art dealers Goupil & Cie , and was employed as an upper-class salesman. Unfortunately, he was unable to hold his tongue, and was often critical of the paintings he was selling. He would often point out flaws in the works – flaws that he'd decided were there – s a result, he sold very few works of art. In fact, he was a pretty useless salesman, and in the end, Goupil & Cie couldn't afford him, and had to let him go. The position had been found for him by his uncle, who was a partner there, but even he couldn't deny his nephew's lack of success as a salesman. The company however were very decent, and instead of sacking him, they offered him a transfer to their London office. (This kindness could have been because his uncle's influence of course!)

Arriving by train at Ramsgate in England on Sunday 16 April 1876, the twenty-three-year old Vincent stepped onto the platform with a spring in his step. He was feeling reasonably happy at the prospect of a new life in a new country. The unusual feeling of such positivity was alien to the young man, but he was pleasantly surprised by the new experience. As was his habit, he immediately put pen to paper, and wrote to Theo, describing the unusual happiness he felt; ***'……….These are really happy days, the ones I'm spending here……..'*** he wrote.

In fact, in the short time he lived in Brixton, he wrote at least ten letters to relatives at home, praising the area of that town, where he'd found digs almost immediately. He again moved house however, and found even better digs in the Oval in London, where he formed the habit of taking regular walks around the streets every chance he got. He was genuinely interested in what the new country had to offer, and he soon adopted a regular route over Westminster

Bridge, enjoying the busy roads and the frequent pedestrians and carriages – London was fascinating even then, and was at least twenty times bigger than anywhere he'd lived before.

It was as though he couldn't settle however, and he drifted from one set of digs to another, soon finding himself at Number 87 Hackford Road in Stockwell, where his widowed landlady was one Mrs Ursula Loyer. The house was a pleasant Georgian terrace, and Mrs Loyer's daughter Eugenie also lived there, along with a fellow-lodger, Samuel Polowman. Needless to say, he soon fell in love with the young Eugenie, and the inevitable proposal of marriage took place.

"But why my sweet Eugenie – you know you like me, just as I like you. Please reconsider, and say you'll become my wife. I have an income and can provide for you, if that's what's worrying you – and I intend to get promoted in time, so one day you'll be even more comfortable." He was pleading with the young woman, whom he believed he knew very well, although he'd only been living at Hackford Road for 3 months.

"I'm truly sorry Mr van Gogh, and I am deeply touched by the honour you do me, but I'm unable to accept your proposal. I'm afraid I can't marry you." Eugenie had absolutely no intention of doing what he asked – she didn't even like the foreign fellow, who always seemed to smell of garlic – and who was happy one minute, and deep in the doldrums the next. On one occasion, she'd even seen him lose his temper over a most trivial thing, and it scared her. "I'm going now Sir – please let's say no more about this, just accept I have no love for you."

She rushed past him, and closed the door behind her. She hoped out of sight was out of mind, at least where he was concerned. Alas, it was not to be so, and Vincent proposed twice more, before finally giving up. He'd tried his best – and failed. As he stared out of the window, he could feel the familiar dark cloud invading his mind, and he felt an acute dejection at the girl's words. They added to his sense of failure, which was never very far away!

It wasn't the first time, he'd had his proposal of marriage rejected however – and it probably wouldn't be his last. Before he'd left to come to England, when he'd been working in The Hague, he'd also asked Caroline Haanebeek for her hand in marriage, but she'd just laughed, and told him not to be so silly. Not a very nice way to be turned down. This second refusal therefore, was the straw that broke the camel's back, and he swore he'd ask no other woman to marry him. (Which didn't turn out to be true, as 1881, whilst temporarily living back in his home-village, he asked another young lady – Kee Vos-Stricker if she would do him the honour – but she too refused.)

"Oh Sir, I shall miss having you around the house – you've been like a son to me." Mrs Loyer was prone to exaggeration, although she was disappointed he was leaving as he always paid his rent on time. That might have soon changed however, as the London branch of Goupil & Cie had also 'let Vincent go' – as he really wasn't a good salesman, in fact he was a very bad one. Uneven paint textures, unrealistic shapes, mis-matched colours – you name it, and Vincent was always willing to point them out to potential buyers.

"Madam, I too shall miss you – and your charming daughter, but alas, I must go where the work is." And he was off, leaving the suitably- sad-looking widow, who was going to miss his weekly rent money. Having said that however, she'd often told her other lodger that she was worried about Mr van Gogh, as his moods were apt to change from moment to the next for no apparent reason. He would sometimes shut himself in his room, and speak to no-one, claiming he had a bad headache - and on those days, the landlady knew to keep out of his way.

He was again changing his occupation, and heading for Isleworth, where he'd been offered the position of language teacher at a boys' school. The prospects were good, and the money was better than at the art dealers – but then, as he'd worked there on commission, he'd rarely managed to make much money. For whatever reason he found it difficult to settle at one job, but he was luckily good at languages, and had no difficulty in speaking French, English and of course, Dutch – this new job might just be the one!

"Speak slower please Sir – I don't understand." The boys enjoyed claiming his guttural accent was difficult to understand, whilst the truth was really that they enjoyed teasing the foreign chap. Now in his mid-twenties, his outward appearance was changing a little, and he was becoming more bohemian in style. His long hair hung over his collar, giving him a shabby-chic look, he'd grown a beard and had taken up smoking a pipe – in fact, he was rarely seen without a pipe in his hand. He'd been in England for almost 3 years, and had easily picked up the language, although it was true he still did have a strong Dutch accent

He told the schoolboy, "Do not pretend – you understand me perfectly well. Is that not so?" He was holding his head as he spoke, and the boys realised they should stop their teasing, as the master looked as if he was going to have 'one of his headaches' – and when that happened, each boy knew to keep silent. In fact, more than once, he'd completely lost control, and shouted like a madman at the stunned class – such erratic behaviour didn't bode well for a schoolmaster.

"Yes Sir, now I understand," the boy hoped he looked suitably contrite, " You want me to conjugate the verb to have, is that right?" Vincent didn't bother to answer him, but just nodded his aching head. He knew he had to return to his room quickly, before his head exploded – soothing absinthe would soon sort it out - a drink of which he'd become very fond lately. He allowed the boy to stumble through the conjugation, before he made a swift escape from the classroom.

" You must all study quietly until I get back." He called over his shoulder, as he left the room. As with his reputation as an art salesman, his reputation as a school master was also not a good one, and he was aware his fellow-masters were whispering behind his back. "Those fits will be the death of him, if he's not careful," was the gossip in the staff-room. Another teacher responded with, "Well, it'll certainly be the death of his position at this school."

And inevitably, he was soon called to the Headmaster's study. He knew the reason, but didn't want to hear the words. "You must leave Mr van Gogh – this school is not for you. Your behaviour is too erratic, and I have a duty to protect the pupils. I have discussed it with the Board of Governors, and we have all agreed that you must leave. You will receive one month's severance pay, but I will not be able to give you a reference, as it would have to be a truthful one, and I don't believe what I would write, would help you obtain your next position."

Vincent couldn't find the energy to either plead for his job, or to vent his anger on the Headmaster, so he just swore his worst Dutch expletive, and left the room. He knew he was heading for one of his seizures, which scared himself as much, as they did others. Where was he to go now? He'd failed at everything he'd touched so far, and feared he would achieve nothing. What future was there for him? Next day he packed his bags, and set off for Holland – it was time to go home and see his parents – or maybe to lick his wounds. The year was 1881, and he was almost 23 years of age. He had no prospects, but he knew at least he'd be welcome at his parents' house. He stayed at home for almost a year, and in the last months, began lay-preaching again – and even added some Protestant missionary work to his efforts. Finally, his father could be proud of his morose son.

It was at this point that Vincent made his third – and last proposal to a local woman, Kee von Stricken, who treated his question as a joke at first, after all she hardly knew the man. When she realised he was serious, she left him in no doubt that she wasn't interested. Vincent's delicate disposition had suffered yet another blow!

One day in the van Gogh's comfortable home, Vincent was having afternoon tea with his sister Willemien (known as Wil). "Paris? You're going to Paris? Why would you want to do that?" Wil, although much younger than he was, had always assumed the role of big sister, as though their ages were reversed. He smiled at her outburst, knowing it was a sign of how much she cared for him.

"Why not Paris?" was his rejoinder, "I just know there's something out there for me – I've just got to find it, and I've already tried so many things. I don't seem able to find what I'm really looking for. Paris is an exciting city, with all kinds of people, doing all kinds of things – surely there'll be a place for me there. Anyway, Theo has said I can stay with him in his apartment, until I find something, and he's settled well in the city."

"Ah, so that's the real reason – free accommodation, with food thrown in to boot." She was smiling ruefully – she knew him so well. "Is Theo's apartment big enough? Will there be room for both of you? You've been comfortable here, haven't you – helping Father in his work?" Wil was genuinely worried about her big brother, who hadn't been looking his best

recently – it really looked as if the Bohemian look was here to stay.

He explained he'd been happy enough at home, but lately something had been driving him to reach out and discover the purpose of his life. Of course, Wil didn't understand what he was talking about, but he didn't mind – he knew what he meant! Anyway, both his sisters – Anna and Wil, – had once lived abroad themselves. They'd visited England, Anna as an assistant school teacher, and Wil as a pupil at the school. So, why was his deciding on Paris so unusual? The two sisters had stayed in the village of Welwyn near London for nine months - the trip was intended to broaden their minds, and was something society demanded of well-brought-up young ladies.

"You've been around quite a bit yourself Wil – what about the time you lived in London? That must have been exciting – and that's what I'm looking for. I know I must be good at something – but what? Whatever, I've decided to go to Paris, and that's that. Now, before we fall out, let's go for a stroll down by the river – the meadow flowers will be in full bloom." And they strolled off arm in arm, admiring the flowers, and the leaf-laden trees along the way. 'If only my mind would let me feel like this more often – at peace with the world!" Vincent thought dreamily, and was glad Wil had finally accepted his plan, as he was really very fond of her. The two shared a love of walking, and of admiring nature's gifts, which were all around at that time of the year. He thought how nice it was to walk in the open air with the sister, who was rarely seen without a book in her hands.

Before he left home, Vincent made her pose as his model, and he drew a very detailed portrait of her – she was delighted with the results, and said she'd keep it forever - something she actually did. Six years later, her love of literature would manifest itself in a short novel she'd written about 'plants and the rain'. She sent it to Vincent, obviously wanting his approval - Vincent's typically under-stated response, was ***"many a flower is trampled.'*** But then, she'd probably have understood his words – they were strangely alike.

Although, this story is primarily about the artist van Gogh, it wouldn't be right not to mention all of his siblings, and not just Wil. After all, they must all have had some effect on him as they grew up. Anna the eldest sister, ended up by being the most normal of the children – she married, had three children and even looked after the interests of her sister Wil, when she fell into hard times. Theo too, appeared to lead a pretty normal life. He'd settled in Paris, married, and also had three children – so on the face of it, nothing drastic happened to him. Nothing drastic that is, until he heard of Vincent's death, at which time, he went into an immediate decline and in a short time was admitted into a hospice to die. Knowing he no longer had Vincent, Theo suffered one epileptic fit after another, probably symptomatic to his encroaching dementia. In the end, he was to die a cruel and painful death, mainly due to an advanced case of syphilis. Following his last epileptic fit, he never regained consciousness and died only four months after Vincent's death - perhaps not so normal a life after all.

When he'd gone, Johnna was left to raise the three children on her own. She was however, a very competent lady, a multilingual Dutch editor no less, who took it upon herself to accumulate and eventually to publish all the letters that had passed between her husband and Vincent. Added to this, she also collected the other letters Vincent had written to his family and friends, and some of those he'd received in return. There were a great number of them in total, and it was Johanna von Gogh Bangor therefore , that we have to thank for her diligence and foresight in gathering everything together – you see, she believed that one day, her brother-in-law's paintings would be appreciated, and his fame as an artist would grow. In fact, it was through her efforts following Theo's death, that Vincent's 'still-ignored' works of art, were finally brought successfully to the public's attention, and they began to sell, and sell, and sell. The sad part of this achievement was that Vincent never knew how popular his post-impressionist style would become. Without Johanna's perseverance, and without her ready-acceptance of the intense relationship between Theo and his brother, the world may never have known the wonderful works of art left behind by Vincent van Gogh. Works of art such as his glorious Sun Flowers, quaint buildings and interesting people – or of course, the sensational Starry Night. Her brother-in-law may have created the masterpieces, but it was Johanna who gave them to the world.

Theo had called his son Willem after the brother he'd loved most. The boy was born in 1890, the same year as Vincent's death. When he heard Vincent was dying, Theo rushed off to Auvers to be with his brother, leaving behind his wife and 6-month old baby. After the birth of his third child, he left behind a second son, who was called Vincent. Sadly, this Vincent died at the young age of thirty-three - leaving behind his own son, whom he called Theo. However, continuing in the van Gogh's family misfortunes, this Theo was executed by the Nazis for his participation in the resistance movement. A brave young man, but one who followed suit in the van Gogh family curse.

Vincent's favourite sibling, Willemien, (Wil) was to lead a life of mixed consequences. In her youth, and just like Vincent, she tried to find a job that suited her, but also like her brother, she found it difficult at first. She tried being a governess, a florist, a nurse, and a scripture reader – but nothing seemed to be right. She even became involved in the early Dutch feminist movement, initially as a member of a women's library in The Hague. Her interest in academic matters pushed her into further worthwhile causes, and she joined the organising committee of the1898 National Exhibition of Women's Labour. She became very involved in encouraging the promotion of female workers into more senior working roles – she was quite ahead of her times in this, and was active in what was becoming an important time for women. She became known as being one of the female fighters in the development of women's rights in the Netherlands. Definitely an accolade!

Unfortunately, she burned herself out – and only a few months after this peak of activity, she had severe episodes of mad tantrums, and ended by being committed to the Veldwijk Asylum in Ermelo, east of Amsterdam, where she was sadly to become institutionalised. She would remain there for the rest of her life, suffering from acute depression. Shortly after her admission, her doctor wrote about her;

'She is always angry and acts wild.....she screams, bites and scratches and throws punches.....she refuses to eat and hallucinates.' He also recorded that she often spoke of suicide, and mentioned specific occasions when she actually tried to kill herself. The sad woman, who'd played such an important role in changing the world's attitude towards women, was to spend the next 38 long years in an institution for the insane. (It seemed she and Vincent had been close in more ways than one!)

Life treated Vincent's middle sister Elisabeth (known as Lies) no better. Lies went to work as a nurse, looking after a lady who was dying of cancer. She was happy in her duties, and her tasks were light. Her patient's husband was called Jean du Quesne – he was a lawyer, and a very personable gentleman. Lies and Jean fell in love and in 1889 they had an affair, which unsurprisingly ended with Lies becoming pregnant. What could she do – she would certainly not be able live this down in Holland? The sick lady was ill and bed-bound – what would people say when they heard of the liaison? Indeed, what would Lies' own family say – especially her father, the pastor? To have a child out of wedlock was bad enough, but to steal a dying woman's husband was beyond the pale. Lies told everyone she was travelling to England for a holiday along with a female friend - but of course, the female friend was Jean du Quesne. Arriving in Normandy, they never even managed to cross the English Channel before the baby arrived – a little girl was born in a Normandy Hotel, and the couple named her Hubertine. What could Leis do then? She couldn't go home from her holiday with a baby, could she? No, she'd never live it down – so, she abandoned the child in Normandy, and left her with a young widow, who lived locally. Jean du Quesne gave the widow some money, which helped her to continue running her shop in a village; and so, Hubertine grew up in France, the daughter of a widowed store-keeper.

In 1922, Lies actually returned to Normandy in an attempt to reunite with her daughter,

but the loyal, 35-year-old Hubertine refused to leave the only mother she'd ever known – and Lies was forced to return home alone. She was never to marry, and died 'childless' in 1936. Her daughter Hubertine fared no better, and ended her life as a penniless hawker, selling sweets and small gifts in the streets of Marseille. She was however, 'eventually discovered' there by a journalist, who knew all about her famous uncle Vincent van Gogh – but the young woman was not to benefit from her uncle's new-found fame, and three years after this, she was dead – still penniless, just like her Uncle Vincent.

Other than Theo, Vincent had one more brother, called Cor (Cornelius). He was a brave young chap who went to South Arica to do his bit in the Boer War. Unfortunately, it seemed he wasn't as brave as he thought, and to get away from the fighting, he committed suicide. A sad end for someone who'd gone there to support his country, and to prove his loyalty.

This very much potted history of the van Gogh family shows how significantly a strain of mental health issues ran through several van Goghs. Vincent therefore had little chance of a totally normal life – it seems he was cursed from the very beginning.

****

Now we must return to the artist's own story - just at the point where he'd decided to join Theo in Paris. On arriving in that city, he found he found he easily fitted in with the community of artists around Montmartre, and he even enrolled himself on a short painting course at a local college. That was it – he was hooked! His new friends and that short training course completely turned his life around. He'd always been interested in art – but in art produced by others, but now, he experienced an urgent need to produce his own works. He quickly picked up the rudiments of painting and sketching, although he was always being told off by the college teacher, because of his erratic style of painting. Theo knew many of the artists in Montmartre, and it was he who introduced them to Vincent, who immediately formed a rapport with them. He very quickly became an integral part of the community.

It really was a turning point in his life, and after the very few months at the art school, Vincent van Gogh the painter, emerged. He naturally favoured a post-impression style of painting, and took to wandering around Paris searching for free subjects and models. At this time, he painted mostly flowers, fields, trees, and quaint old buildings – all costing him nothing. He loved bright colours, especially the bright yellows and oranges, which he believed were life-giving. As he had no money to pay for real models, he made a great number of self-portraits, as all that required was the use of a mirror.

Theo supported his brother throughout his whole time in Paris, (and also throughout his entire life) and seemed never to let him down. He'd always been proud of his older brother, and he loved him as a kindred spirit. His Paris apartment was just about adequate enough to accommodate both himself and his brother, so whilst Vincent was in Paris, Theo had a permanent lodger. The address was in Montmartre, at Number 54 Rue Lepic – and it was there that Vincent's new, special style of painting continued to develop. At the beginning, he tended to prefer a very dark palette, but that didn't last long, and he quickly moved on to the bright, vibrant style he would adopt throughout the next 10 years. His share of Theo's apartment on the third floor was small and cramped, untidy and messy, but it was home, and it was free.

Of an evening, the painters would gather in the Montmartre taverns, and one particular night three friends were sitting at their usual table. It was easy to see they were painters, as much of their material was splattered across their untidy clothes, but they wore those splodges as a badge of honour. Their glasses were half-empty and a fresh bottle of absinth was inviting them to remove its top. Since arriving in Paris, Vincent was eager to learn as much as he could, and his fellow-artists were eager to teach him – they were discussing the need to paint the feel of a shape, rather than the actual shape, and the recently-arrived Vincent was holding forth on the subject, whilst at the same time, opening a new bottle of absinth. His new friends were Paul Gauguin and Emile Bernard, who were also aspiring post-impressionists like himself.

"No. my friends, I don't agree – impressionism is dead, we represent the new, post-impressionism style, and it's our job to show the world that idealism, rather than duplication, can be shown on the canvas – idealism about the way we feel, and see everything around us. It's the mind, don't you see, and how a vision can be portrayed as a suggestion? " Vincent was on his high horse, and thoroughly enjoying the conversation. He didn't let his newness to the subject affect his opinion, and that night he was on a high, with his head full of alcohol and his lungs full of nicotine – just the way he liked it. The agony of misery and black thoughts were forgotten for the moment.

"Yes, yes old man, we hear you – and you're preaching to the converted, you know. Both Emile and I also like to paint as you do, using the wild, short brush-strokes to show emotion and pathos, much clearer than realism – but the finished work must always be viewed from a short distance – the perspective is best that way." Gauguin was equally intense when discussing his art, but Emile just sat there, listening and quietly, sipping his drink – a man of few words perhaps, but usually a few wise words. Neither of the other two realised they were making the same point, and were actually in agreement with each other, but they enjoyed the discussion, particularly the sound of their own voices.

Gauguin was perhaps not quite as extreme as Vincent – sometimes he even thought the other's work was rather nebulous, but he certainly never voiced his opinion. The new friends had quickly learned it was wiser to avoid upsetting the new arrival, in case one of his sudden dark moods erupted, and he indulged in one of his outbursts.

The usually quiet Emile broke into the discussion, as he was beginning to feel bored with the repetition" I think it's simple really – we are not trying to paint an exact reflection of real objects or of what we see in front of us, but rather an impression of what the subject says to us – more what we feel, rather than what we see." He looked around the table, feeling quite smug, as he believed he had summed it up neatly. " Is that fair, gentlemen?" he asked.

The others grunted their agreement, and reached again for the absinth – it wasn't the first time they'd had this conversation anyway, and it was unlikely to be the last. It was odd, but absinth always seemed to make everything clearer, at least that's how they felt, so they drank, and debated, debated and drank, all the while condemning the philistines of the world, who didn't appreciate excellent art when they saw it. (The constant cry of the artist yet to be appreciated) After that, all three would usually leave the tavern, and wend their shaky ways to where they knew the ladies of the night were to be found. And so, ended a typical night for the artists of Montmartre. They would paint as long as there was daylight, and carouse well into the night – well, as much as their meagre money would allow.

These discussions were part of the artists' charm, and anyone local, who overheard their conversations, chose to ignore them, as they couldn't understand one word. At the time, Montmartre was an artist's paradise - not a paradise in the sense of beauty and tranquillity, but in a mad, wild freedom of expression and ideas. Gaugin and van Gogh actually exhibited paintings at a joint venture in 1887, and called it 'The Impressionists of the Petit Boulevard', where they showed their post-impressionism to the world – well, to the world of Montmartre anyway. Unfortunately, most of the viewers didn't appreciate what they were looking at, and the muttered words 'daubs' and 'splodges' hung in the air. It was probably at this exhibition that Vincent sold the one and only painting whilst he was alive. He sold it to a fellow-artist - it was called 'The Red Vineyard', and was bought by a lady called Anna Boch. (For 400 Francs – not bad for his one and only sale, and it would buy a lot of paint and absinth.)

It was a period in his life Vincent would never forget, a time when he produced so many of his famous paintings and sketches. The fly in the ointment was that, other than Anna Boch, no-one wanted to buy what he produced, and his finances continued as poor. Just to survive therefore, he needed Theo's continued support more than ever. He needed money for his absinth, tobacco, and bread, as that's what kept him going – and of course, buying his precious, but expensive paints.

In 1889, after 2 years in Paris, Vincent experienced a sudden deterioration in his mental health; he was suffering from a deep depression, and began to question what his place in the world really was. Some days he was so demented, and couldn't even hold a brush in his shaking hands. Those who knew him, feared for his sanity.

He moved on then, from the busy, over-whelming city to a place called Arles, where he rented a house – a bright yellow house that he came to love. In fact, 'The Yellow House' would become one of his most famous works – the painting is sought after, and hangs in pride of place in a gallery. The actual Arles yellow house in the painting is unfortunately long gone. He rented four rooms in the building, and stayed at No 2 Place Lamartine, and it was in this relatively short period in Arles, he was at his most prolific, producing 187 works of art. Unfortunately, he still couldn't sell any of them, despite Theo's best efforts in Paris.

In first coming to Arles, Vincent had originally intended to start a community of artists, which in itself, was proof that he was still capable of positive thoughts – and had the community been successful, it would have meant he could stop leaning on his long-suffering brother for handouts. Unfortunately, his plans never came to fruition, so the artist just painted and painted, smoked his pipe, drank his absinth, and visited a local prostitute called Rachel.

Whilst he'd been in Paris, and probably influenced by his artist friends, Vincent's style of painting had undergone a change, and he now used such bright colours, they positively shone from the canvas. Indeed, it was here that he produced some of his most famous works – the Sunflower series. He also painted incredible scenes of the countryside, as well as many still-lifes – all subjects cheaper than those offered by the models in Paris.

Paul Gauguin came to stay with his friend in Arles, and for two months, they worked together in harmony – until it all suddenly changed one day. A tension had been growing between them for a while, and one day, after a particularly heavy bout of drinking, an argument ensued. It was close to Christmas, the 23 December to be exact, which would turn out to be a day Vincent would never forget. In a sudden outburst of his drunken depression, he threatened his friend with a razor, before turning it on himself, and doing the unbelievable.

We have to remember, that although having Gauguin with him had been pleasant, Vincent was still going through periodic black clouds of depression, and sometimes suffered from hallucinations and outbursts of anger, much of which would sometimes fill his waking hours. He was often sleep-deprived, hungry except for the occasional loaf of bread, and desperate for the pipe tobacco he craved. His life could turn into a nightmare on the flip of a coin. He was known to paint more at night than during the day, as he far preferred the darkness. It could be so dark, he would have to wear a hat to hold lighted candles around the brim. He seemed to be increasingly in a bad mood, and even his cronies at the local inn, started to avoid his company. His neighbours had even begun to collect signatures for a petition to have him removed from his home, and hopefully from the village - something the local Gendarmes were quite willing to do. The neighbours had taken to calling him ***Le Fou Roux*** (the Red-headed Madman), and avoided him at every opportunity.

On the day of question, Paul Gauguin had obviously been pushed to the limit by Le Fou Roux, and knew the man was in the very deepest of depressions, so he wisely began his preparations to return to Paris . Just that morning, Vincent had poured out his feelings into a letter to Theo, telling him he'd only had six hot meals in a year, and all his teeth were loose and painful. He was obviously feeling very sorry for himself, and at his darkest, when he wrote:

..........................' I do know there is a release, a belated release. A justly or unjustly ruined reputation, poverty, disastrous circumstances, misfortune, they all turn you into a prisoner. You cannot always tell what keeps you confined, what immures you, what seems to bury you, and yet you can feel those elusive bars, railings,

walls. Is all this illusion imagination? I don't think so. And then one asks; my God, will it be for long, will it be forever, will it be for eternity?

Do you know what makes the prison disappear? Every deep genuine affection. Being friends, being brothers, loving, that is what opens the prison, with supreme power, by some magic force. Without these, one stays dead. But whenever affection is revived, there life revives. Moreover, the prison is sometimes called prejudice, misunderstanding, fatal ignorance of one thing or another, suspicion, false modesty.

But to change the subject, if I have come down in the world, you have in a different way, come up in it. And if I have forfeited sympathy , you have gained it………………………...'

And he ended the letter with:

…………………'And for now, I shake your hand, thanking you once again for having been so good to me. If one of these days, you feel like writing, my address is chez Ch. Decrucq, Rue du Payillon 8, Cuesmes, near Mons, and know that it will do me good to hear from you.

Yours Vincent'……………..

I make no apology for offering this snapshot of how the artist was feeling at the time – it clearly shows how damaged he was. The letter was a small part, a very small part of a very long letter – and it suggested abject misery, coupled with a confused mind, and a very sad feeling of failure. This then was the background to the scene that was taking place in the kitchen in Arles on 23 December, when Vincent had drawn the razor on his friend.

After having many more than one Christmas absinths, Vincent's fury suddenly flared up, in fact it was obvious he didn't know what he was doing, and instead of stabbing Gauguin, he turned the razor on himself, and sliced the lobe of his ear clean off.

"My God man, what have you done?" Paul rushed to get a towel. "I. told you not to drink that mixture of turps and paint – you really are your own worst enemy." He wrapped the towel around Vincent's head, wondering what on earth he was supposed to do.

On top of the absinths at the inn, this last concoction was just too much – and it sent Vincent off into one of his seizures. Darkness, depression, confusion, made him almost blind, and he just sat staring at the floor, with blood gushing from the open wound. The towel was already saturated, and a puddle of blood was forming on the floor, but he was so steeped in both absinth and misery, that he felt no pain. In fact, he looked puzzled, as though he thought someone else had done the deed.

Staggering into the street, he pushed past Paul, and came upon a young boy, whom he sent back to the town brothel, carrying the severed ear-lobe wrapped in a paint-smeared cloth. The boy was told to give the small parcel to the lady who lived there, and say it was from Vincent van Gogh. The irony was, the boy actually gave the ear to the house cleaner, telling her who had sent it. One can imagine the woman's shock when she opened the blood-stained present - probably not the nicest gift she'd ever been given.

Why he hurt himself in this way, no-one knows, and even to this day, no-one has come up with a feasible suggestion – how could there possibly be one? The boy told the local doctor about the bleeding madman , and luckily for Vincent, the doctor arrived quickly and immediately hospitalised him before he could do any more damage to himself. This was when, Paul Gauguin beat a hasty retreat back to the safety of Paris – and who could blame him?.

Except for – and you might find this interesting:- There is an alternative theory to the mad ear-cutting. Paul Gauguin was known to regard himself as a great swordsman, and liked to show off to anyone who would watch. It's been subsequently suggested that the two men had returned from the Inn, much the worse for wear, and in the middle of an argument, Paul grabbed his sword (which he just happened to have brought with him from Paris), and in a moment of anger, sliced his friend's ear clean off. Vincent himself, was innocent of the deed. The rush of blood had an immediate sobering effect on both of them, and they agreed a story to tell the doctor. They realised they had to come up with a story to keep the Gendarmes at bay, or Paul could be arrested for assault- even attempted murder. And the best they could think of was, that in a moment of frustrated anger, Vincent carelessly used his shaving razor in a mock sword-fight and sliced off part of his own ear. Not a great story, but a possible one! They never had to admit to the truth as everyone accepted the mad painter was perfectly capable of doing such a thing to himself.

On hearing of his brother's hospitalisation, Theo left his busy practice in Paris, and rushed to Vincent's bedside, leaving behind his wife and a newly-born baby. Following the ear-cutting incident, it's easy to imagine the relief he felt on hearing of Vincent's plan to volunteer as a patient at the Saint-Remy asylum. For a while at least, someone else would be responsible for him, and Theo wouldn't have to worry. Theo himself, had never been a well-man, and even as a boy, he'd suffered from a weak constitution – therefore to, hear what Vincent was intending, must have been as if a great weight had been lifted from his sickly shoulders. Recently, he'd been feeling rather bad, as he thought he'd been neglecting Vincent. He'd not long ago married a young lady – Johanna Bonger, and when he told Vincent of this, the news seemed to push his brother over an invisible edge, and he became morose and petulant. Was it jealousy or fear - Theo had always looked after him, and now this woman had stolen his affections? As far as Theo was concerned, it seemed he couldn't do right, for doing wrong!

After a short time in the local hospital, the wound was bandaged, and the artist returned home. Whilst in hospital, he'd also confided to a chaplain who was there to support the Protestant patients, that he wanted to commit himself into an asylum, and it was the chaplain who'd actually suggested Saint-Remy, which had a very good reputation. Unfortunately, it wasn't free, and only after some persuasion, Theo agreed to meet the asylum's costs – and this on top of having a new baby too! It was something he could ill afford, and for obvious reasons, he insisted on the cheapest, third-class accommodation that was available.

In early May 1889 therefore, Vincent was voluntarily admitted into the Saint Remy-de-Provence Asylum, just 18 miles outside Paris. Before he went however, he did another self-portrait, only this time, showing his bloodstained, bandaged ear. In the finished painting however, the bandaged ear is on the wrong side – he'd forgotten, or didn't care, that a mirror-image is not a true reflection – and so the finished painting was in reverse. It was to remind him of the terrible thing he'd done (or his friend had done) and at least at the asylum, he could do less harm.

The asylum had accepted him however, and for the first time in his life, he felt safe. He was always free to leave the institution of course, but he saw it as a sanctuary, and didn't wander far at first. As a voluntary patient, he was allowed to leave the building each day, and eventually he began to walk further, and visit the surrounding fields and woodlands, always on the lookout for fresh subjects to paint. In fact, it was in the year he spent in the asylum that he produced some of his most respected works – Starry Night being one of the best.

At the beginning of his time at Saint-Remy, some of the staff found his style of painting intriguing, and had questioned him about what he was trying to achieve. These conversations were always in his more lucid moments, and on the good days, he would try to explain to them, "It's a style of painting that my friends and I are pursuing – the centre for such work is in Paris. The style is not strictly impressionism in the exact sense, but it's a post-impressionism, where the canvas is intended to reflect how the artist is feelings, and how he sees the subject, both in his mind and in his heart. It's bold and bright and full of innuendo." He was enjoying himself and was reminded of the many discussions in the tavern at Montmartre. The staff however, heard the explanation as gobble-de-gook and smiled behind their hands. But then, Vincent already knew they were Philistines, all of them, but he did persevere, "Look at this one I'm doing just now – see the small, visible brushstrokes that offer a vague impression of shape and form, the colours are pure and unblended – the finished work is cushioned by natural light." He was well aware of what they were thinking, and in a way, he was playing a part for them. He didn't care whether they understood or not - they weren't artists after all.

In the eyes of the unconvinced, the painting looked like mere daubs of paint – brightly coloured daubs of paint of course but still just daubs. They had to be seen from a short distance for the full affect – and they thought what an odd concept this was. He turned back to his work, thinking, 'Morons', and never tried again to explain his work. But then they were wise enough never to ask him again.

Throughout the year at Saint-Remy, Vincent van Gogh suffered a great deal – he had repeated seizures and fits, sometimes having to be placed in a straight-jacket for his own protection. He often complained of seeing demons in his room; he was morose and wouldn't eat; sometimes he was aggressive, believing the whole world was against him, and it depressed him to think his friends in Paris had deserted him, although he'd made them swear they wouldn't visit the asylum. He'd forgotten he'd made them promise this, and in any case, he preferred to wallow in the sadness of their cruel neglect.

Despite all of this happening, he continued to paint, buying materials with the money Theo still sent. He wrote copious letters whilst at the asylum, mostly to Theo, but also to other relatives. His letters were some of the longest letters anyone has ever written – page after page, full of references to how low he'd sunk, how little he was worth, and how much he was unappreciated. Sometimes, but only on a good day, he would mention the beauty of the countryside and the wonderful, clear air of the area – but not often. The letters were so long, it's doubtful Theo ever read them all – they would depress even the most positive of people. Having said that, Theo could sometimes give as good as he got, as his replies to Vincent, could be just as lengthy – but not so morose. One time, Vincent sent him a set of six sketches and asked for his brother's opinion, and as he'd always done, Theo praised them highly, and went on to say he was arranging a new exhibition of some of his other works in Paris. He obviously hoped the news would raise his brother's spirits, but sad to say, there just weren't enough enlightened people around, and none of the paintings sold at the exhibition. Theo did send him a new of brushes however – the ones Vincent was always asking him for– plus he put 50 Francs in the package!

The months passed, and Vincent continued to paint, producing one of his most highly-regarded works – the beautiful and dream-like Starry Night. This painting is considered to be one of his best, but Vincent told others he was never happy with it – but then, he also said that about several other works he'd produced whilst in the asylum. He couldn't have been more wrong about Starry Night however – it inspires pathos, beauty and promise to the eyes of the beholder. Vincent's own emotions are laid bare in that night sky when he painted the haunting beauty of the stars from his small, barred window in the psychiatric unit. It's easy to picture him in the middle of the night, wearing his hat with the brim that held the circle of lighted candles to help him see. Did the sky through that asylum window really look like his 'Starry Night', or was it how he imagined it in his mind, and felt it in his heart? The answer to that is easy – he always painted from the heart!

Whilst working on a painting, he was fine, but soon he realised the time he'd spent in the asylum hadn't really helped him much. If anything, he felt worse than when he'd first arrived there. Whilst immersed in a work, especially a new one, his mental health was stable, but at the beginning of the year 1890, when he painted what has been called his saddest work, his depression shone clearly through the brushstrokes, and the end-results were brim-full of sentiment and pathos. It showed a deep insight into the feelings of an old man sitting on a chair crying – crying for the life he knew was soon going to be taken from him. He was close to the end of his life, and he knew it - as did the sympathetic artist who captured in his short, quaint brushstrokes, the precise moment when the old man saw the Grim Reaper coming towards him. Little did the artist know, as he worked on this painting, that the end of his own life was not very far away.

He was still experiencing the deep-routed unhappiness which often caused him to lose control, and to become unaware of his actions. It had been almost a year, and as he felt no better for his time in the asylum, he decided it was time to face the world again. He wrote to Theo, saying he felt he couldn't breathe these days, and needed the fresh air of freedom – away from the asylum. He also told his friends, Mr and Mrs Ginoux how his health had actually deteriorated whilst at Saint Remy:

'........... ***Latterly, I had contracted the other patient's disease to such an extent that I could not be cured of my own. The other patient's society had a bad influence on me, and in the end I was absolutely unable to understand it. Then, I felt I had better try a change, and for that matter, the pleasure of seeing my brother, his family and my painter friends again has done me a lot of good, and I am feeling completely calm and normal............'***

It was evident that he was now ready to come out of hiding, and immediately the thought became the deed. He gathered up his many, many paintings, and had them shipped to Theo's new house in Paris. His brother had written that he'd recently moved house, as he needed a bigger place, if he was going to continue housing all of Vincent's works. Theo's wife was obviously a very long-suffering woman, and she willingly seemed to accept the strong bond that existed between the brothers. Vincent travelled the 18 miles to Paris, and to the couple's new home, where he stayed for three days only. His last few weeks in the asylum had not been great, and as a consequence, he'd suffered a serious relapse – a relapse from which he recovered once, only to have another a few weeks later. It was not a good time! The second relapse happened after a short visit back to Arles, where he'd gone to deliver a completed painting to his friend Madame Ginoux. On his return, things seemed worse than ever, but he still managed to complete one of his greatest works, the now highly-acclaimed old man waiting 'At Eternity's Gate'. He'd actually started it several years before, but found he couldn't finish it then – he managed however to do it justice before leaving the asylum.

After staying with Theo and Johnna for the three days, he arrived at the village of Auvers-sur-Oise, 20 miles from Paris, and booked into the Auberge Ravoux there. (An Inn)

It was a community popular with artists, and so he immediately felt at home. He had an attic room on the third floor – a very modest home, but it suited him well enough. At first, he felt invigorated and eager to wander the fields and the by-ways, always searching for that new something he could conserve for posterity. He'd come well equipped with brushes and paint – Theo had seen to that – and now he wanted to paint better than ever before. His positive thinking was a good sign, and was reflected in the repeated use of bright yellow dominating many of his creations - but then, so did bright blues, pinks and greens – his works were more vivid than ever before, with no more of the earlier, foreboding greys and blacks. A popular theory behind the shift from his sombre early works, and for his choice of so much yellow paint, was that he might have developed and been suffering from Xanthopsia – better known as Yellow Vision. Xanthopsia is a colour vision deficiency where there is a predominance of yellow in a sufferer's vision. This is apparently due to a yellowing of the optical media of the eye itself, and might explain his repeated use of the colour yellow, or it may just have been that he liked yellow!

At the Auberge Ravoux he had a table of his own, where he always had breakfast. (probably only bread and coffee) One morning, there were a few local lads in the Inn, who'd met early for a drink, and because they had nothing better to do. Vincent ignored their loud, raucous laughter, and finished his breakfast in silence. He knew they were laughing at him, and he wanted to get outside and begin his work. It was still quite early, and the air was pure and crisp, although the hot month of August was fast approaching. It was a wonderful day for painting, so he gathered up his easel, and bits and pieces, and set off into the countryside. The young men's laughter followed him down the path, but he ignored it.

'Ah, this will do nicely,' he told himself and began setting up his easel. He'd already made a sketch of some ancient, twisted tree roots he'd found there – they'd made him think how like life itself they were - roots twisted around each other, affecting each other's paths, intermingling and criss-crossing, but always reaching out for someplace new to go. He was soon engrossed in painting his impression of what the tree roots were saying to him, and he'd already named the picture "Tree Roots' – unsurprisingly enough. What he didn't know was that this was to be the last painting he would ever do!

To share his newly-discovered enthusiasm, he'd written to Theo just two days before, stressing his much-improved attitude:

' ....I am giving my canvases my undivided attention. I am trying to do as well as certain painters whom I have greatly loved and admired...........Perhaps you will take a look at this sketch of Daubigny's garden – it is one of my most carefully thought-out canvases. I am adding a sketch of some old thatched roofs, and the sketches of two size 30 canvases representing vast fields of wheat after the rain...............'

A few days earlier, he'd also written to his mother and sister:

'.............I myself am quite absorbed in that immense plain with wheat field up as far as the hills, boundless as the ocean, delicate yellow, delicate soft green, the delicate purple of a tilled and weeded piece of ground, with the regular speckled of the green of flowering potato plants, everything under a sky of delicate tones of blue, white, pink and violet. I am in a mood of almost too much calm, just the mood needed for painting this...........'

He was obviously feeling far more positive than he'd felt for some time, which is why the following words will be difficult to believe. Back at the Inn, the owner Monsieur Ravoux, was talking to his thirteen-year-old daughter Adeline, remarking that dusk had fallen, and it wasn't like van Gogh to stay away so long – he always liked to keep regular habits. They were worried about him, but what could they do? Around 9 pm, and stumbling inside out of the darkness, Vincent suddenly fell through the door, but without his painting materials. It wasn't like him to abandon such valuable possessions. He was clutching his stomach, and he seemed bent to one side. Madam Ravoux asked if there was a problem, and could she help, but he started to climb the stairs up to his room, and although he tried to answer her, he couldn't quite manage it. All he blurted out was ***' No, but I have..........'***

before disappearing inside his room.

The inn-keeper could hear groans coming from the bedroom, and so he went upstairs – only to find van Gogh already stretched along his bed. "Monsieur van Gogh, what ails you – are you ill?" Then he saw the bleeding wound near the injured man's heart. Between groans, van Gogh explained how he'd set out for the wheat field to work on his painting, and then added, ***" I tried to commit suicide by shooting myself."*** No explanation , no reason given for such a drastic act – just a simple confession of attempted suicide.

Monsieur Ravoux ran to the artist's friend Gachet, who was a physician, and told him what had happened. Gachet dressed Vincent's wound, but then left the Inn quickly, because as he explained later, he'd considered it a hopeless case. Another Dutch artist called Hirschig, who was also staying at the Inn, sat by the wounded man's bedside alongside the inn-keeper. As the time passed, van Gogh asked for his pipe and tobacco, and although reluctant at first in case it hurt him, they eventually gave in, as it seemed to reassure him. He groaned repeatedly, dozed off, and slept in fits and starts, remaining silent for most of the night. The next morning, the Gendarmes arrived and questioned him about his suicide attempt, to which van Gogh replied, ***"My body is mine and I am free to do what I want with it.***

Do not accuse anybody, it is I that wished to commit suicide."

He lingered for almost 30 hours more, and throughout all this time the recently-arrived Theo sat by his bedside, feeling frustrated that he couldn't ease his brother's discomfort. He was holding Vincent's' hand, when the dying man spoke his last words, ***" The sadness will last forever."*** There couldn't have been a bleaker prophecy from the sad man, whose name would one day be known to the whole world.

When the bullet entered his body, it had missed all the vital organs as well as his spine, but the doctor was unable to remove it, so deeply was it resting in the wound. The result was that van Gogh actually died from this infected wound. Theo wrote to his wife Johanna…………' ***He was glad that I came and we are together all the time. Poor fellow, very little happiness fell to his share, and no illusions are left to him. The burden grows too heavy at times, he feels so alone……..*** Then, after Vincent had passes, he again wrote to Johanna, ***'…………some of his last words were 'I wish I could pass away like this' and his wish was fulfilled. A few moments and all was over. He had found the rest he could not find on earth………***'

On 30 July a few of Vincent's fellow-artists came from Paris - Emile Bernard arrived in Auvers, but was too late to say goodbye to his old friend. He did however take the time to speak with the locals, and to listen to what they had to say about the tragedy. In a record he made of Vincent's passing, he repeated that the artist had gone into the countryside on the Sunday evening, and went on, ***'……..he left his easel against a haystack and went behind the chateaux, and fired a revolver shot at himself. Vincent had carried out these acts deliberately and with absolute lucidity……….when Dr Gachet had told his patient that he still hoped to save his life, Vincent said, ' Then I'll have to do it over again………..'***

And this appears to be the accepted version of events at the time, and the reason given on the Death Certificate was simply 'Suicide.' It was completely accepted by Emile Bernard, despite the fact that he'd been in Paris at the time of the shooting – but then he'd heard it straight from the locals' mouths, and had been told how Vincent himself had confessed to the deed.

Having said all of this however, it brings me to an alternative, suggested explanation as to how Vincent van Gogh met his end at the young age of 37. Once you've read both versions, you'll be well-placed to decide which scenario you favour. It's worth considering both accounts, although of course, only one can be the truth – but that the decision can only be yours.

****

Firstly, you should know that Vincent van Gogh had once declared in private correspondence to his friends, that he considered suicide to be sinful and immoral. Strange that he could change his mind about such a basic and fundamental belief, but then influences in life can sometimes do that. It's also worth remembering that the incident occurred very close in time to recently-written letters to Theo, to his mother and sister, and to several friends – all displaying a very positive attitude to his life and work. Strange that feeling so positive, he found he just couldn't go on.

Then, there are the two kilometres from the wheat field back to the Inn – two kilometres which he managed to cover, whilst suffering from what turned out to be a fatal wound. A strange determination for someone who'd just shot himself. As well as that, he also climbed the stairs to the comfort of his bedroom, turning away help that was offered. Great feats for a man who'd wanted to end his life only a short time before. (The question is "Did he really manage that walk, or could he have been carried back by 'some people unknown' and dumped outside the Inn)

Also, with his mental health problems known to everyone, the question has to be asked, where and how could he possibly have gotten a gun - a point that was glossed over and ignored at the time by the authorities? Also, why did the Gendarmes fail to find, either the gun, or the painter's easel and materials? Unanswered – but relevant - questions that were allowed to go unanswered at the time. A strange over-sight indeed!

A post-mortem examination carried out by a physician, found that the bullet had actually entered the deceased's body at an oblique angle, rather than at a straight one, which would be how a self-inflicted gun-shot wound would have looked. Suddenly a new thought arises, 'Is there a different scenario of the crime? Could the defenceless painter have been murdered by someone unknown?

Very recently, a modern expert confirmed the entry of the bullet into the wound was such that the man couldn't have shot himself. He also added that, even if by some quirk, he had managed it, there would have been traces of black powder burns on his hands and on the skin around the wound itself. None of these tell-tale signs were mentioned at the time, and the same expert concluded, '…………….***It is my opinion that in all medical probability, the wound incurred by van Gogh was not self-inflicted. In other words, he did not shoot himself………..'*** Yet another intriguing part of the mystery!

Now - do you remember the young men in the Inn? The ones who'd just called in for an early drink, and who were loud and raucous, irritating the quiet artist, whilst he was having breakfast? There were three of them, all worse for their early morning drinking. One of them was known for his eccentric mode of dress – he was in the habit of wearing a cowboy suit. He also carried what he claimed was a replica gun, although he liked to pretend it was a real one. These drunks may have followed the scruffy, unshaven artist just for the fun of it, and for something to pass another boring day. To them he was a pitiful human being, and ripe for their jokes and jibes, and they'd all disliked him on sight. After all, he'd looked down his nose at them – who did he think he was - the scruffy, smelly tramp? Drunken young teenagers, one who liked to act as a cowboy, and who had a 'suspicious replica' of a gun – and who were all intent on amusing themselves - and so they followed the artists to the wheat field, near the chateau.

When they caught up with him, they taunted him, and he told them to get lost . They gathered around him, poking fun at the tree roots he was painting. "He's not even a good painter!" they insulted his work, and perhaps only intending to scare him, the cowboy drew his gun and aimed it at him. To everyone's surprise, the gun turned out not to be a replica after all. Too late, the trigger was pulled, and the target fell down immediately, and lay in a crumpled heap on the ground. Frantic at what they'd just done, they ran away, taking the painter's bits and pieces with them – as to why they did this, who knows? They were probably not thinking straight, and in the panic, thought it might confuse whoever found the wounded man. This would explain the missing gun and the painting materials – and did they decide to carry the man back to the Inn, and leave him where he'd be found? After all, they hadn't actually meant to shoot him – and it might just be a flesh-would, that could be repaired. None of it is out of the question!

If Vincent van Gogh had taken his own life, surely he'd have dropped the gun where he fell – and the Gendarmes would have found it there – but they didn't. If he'd carried it back to the Inn, it would have been found there, but it wasn't! How did the gun disappear so mysteriously – and why did the authorities not seem to care? The cowboy could have taken it home with him, after all it was his, and he was proud of it. But he was never asked? Why would he be asked, as Vincent had admitted to suicide? The cowboy was in the clear! Did the teenagers run off home, after dumping the artists body outside the Inn, did they keep a low profile, and stay well away from the Inn, where it was all happening?

However, that still leaves us with the question as to why Vincent didn't just tell the gendarmes that the teenagers had done it? Why did he cover up for them? Why claim suicide rather than attempted-murder? It makes little sense until we put ourselves in van Gogh's place, and recollect the misery and confusion he'd lived with all his adult life, his victim mentality and his inability to accept there was a place for him in the world. Happiness was merely an illusion as far as he was concerned – misery was so much more familiar. Poor chap didn't really stand a chance, where his family's inherited instabilities are considered.

But let's go back to the wheat field where the injured painter had now gained consciousness again. He'd passed out for some moments, when the bullet had entered his body – but his mind was beginning to clear, and he was experiencing a strangely comforting feeling of safety - it was as if the angels themselves were singing to him. A gentle peace was slowly enveloping him as he lay under the warm July sunshine. Even the pain he felt didn't really bother him – somehow it seemed remote, as though it belonged to someone else. The vivid blue of the sky, and the gentle, white clouds hovering over his head like a silk umbrella, reminded him life was God-given. It was a beautiful sky – such as only an artist could appreciate. The smell of the swaying stalks of ripe wheat filled his nostrils, and he breathed deeply, filling his now-shattered lungs. For the first time in many years, Vincent van Gogh wallowed in the gentle caress of peace and tranquillity - something that had always been missing from his life. This was what he'd always wanted – it was how he'd wanted to feel many times before, but somehow it had always alluded him. Suddenly, everything fell into place, and he knew why he felt like this – he was dying and wrapped around him were God's welcoming arms – come to take him home. Now he knew the cowboy had done him a favour! This was how being alive should feel!

Despite feeling so wonderful, his natural instinct told him he must get to his feet, and make his way back to the Inn – there he could rest and wallow in this wonderful feeling of bliss and tranquillity – something he'd always searched for, but always failed to find.

Now, none of this is impossible, and would help explain his words to the Gendarmes, ***.......'Do not accuse anyone...........it is I who wanted to kill himself.........'***Did he actually feel gratitude to the teenagers for easing his life-time of torment, and so, he made up his mind to protect them from the punishment they would surely receive for what they'd done. And he never did tell anyone! He protected them to the end!

****

And there you are - two possible scenarios – one accepted, according to those who lived through the incident at the time – and one that wasn't allowed to see the light of day. After all, how much easier it was just to accept a dying man's assertion that he'd taken his own life. As the writer, and following my research, I know what I believe happened – but I'm afraid you must decide for yourselves. Before I end however, I should tell you of the last day that the body of Vincent van Gogh was still above ground. His funeral was yet to come.

It was the afternoon of 30 July 1890, and Vincent van Gogh's body was laid out in 'the artist's room', where his friends had gathered. Around the room were the final canvases he'd produced over the previous months, and as had become 'the norm', they were vividly bright, and beautiful. Around the coffin were masses of flowers – nearly all yellow - all kinds of blooms, but predominantly Sunflowers and Dahlias. An easel, with his folding stool and brushes had been placed amongst the flowers. The villagers who'd known him, stood pressed closely together, as were some of his fellow-artists. Lucien Possarro and Auguste Lauzet numbered amongst the painters he'd known from his days in Paris. Of course, Emile Bernard was there, but not Paul Gauguin! Emile remarked on the beauty of the flowers, reminding the mourners yellow had been Vincent's favourite colour, and added, ***"He believed Yellow was the symbol of the light that he dreamed of , as being in people's hearts, as well as in works of art……."***

Sitting in the middle of the room, the coffin was covered with a white sheet, and the sunshine dappled the walls with the bright colours of the flowers. The little cemetery outside Auvers was filling up slowly with new graves, and the procession moved up the hill towards it. The day was hot with blazing sunshine, and Vincent van Gogh was laid to rest there, his grave looking down over the wheat fields he'd admired so much. The air was full of the heady smell of the now-ripe wheat, which was ready for harvesting. Theo and others didn't attempt to hide their tears, and cried bitterly at the loss of a brother and a friend – and at the loss in such a cruel way. Vincent's friend, Dr Gachet tried to speak through his tears, but his words were indistinct. However, they were sincere, "***He was an admirable man, an honest man and a great artist, who had only two aims in life – art and humanity……..'***

As the mourners slowly left Auvers, Theo gave each person, one of his brother's paintings to remember him by, and he took as many as he could carry back to Paris, where they stayed in the family for many years, eventually to be donated to the Lòuvre in Paris. Monsieur Ravoux was given two paintings he'd especially admired, and he too, kept them for some years, selling them in 1905 for just $10. He'd worried that because of their age, they would deteriorate over time, and become worthless. Perhaps it was the biggest mistake of his life, as 11 years after the painter's death, his paintings were beginning to grow in popularity, and handsome prices were finally being paid. Too late for Monsieur Ravoux and alas, also for Vincent!

One final touch of love and devotion – and evidence of how much Johanna understood the close bond that had always existed between her husband and Vincent – she arranged for Theo's body to be exhumed and buried alongside his dear brother's body in the small cemetery in Auvers. A sign of love and devotion, if ever there was one!

And so, we're at the end of this tale – a tale about a brilliant painter, but alas, not about a happy one. In his short 37 years of life, he'd done many things, gone many places, and experienced a multitude of emotions. He was haunted by his own demons, but managed to fight through them, to produce some of the most soul-searching works of art the world has ever seen.

He may have died a pauper, but he left behind a rich legacy!

www.ingramcontent.com/pod-product-compliance
Lightning Source LLC
LaVergne TN
LVHW010055170826
845678LV00012B/2152